Educating Angels

Insisting on changing the tone and focus of the debates over public education, this courageous and lucid book is an indispensable manual for those who want to change the present in order to promote a better future. | **Raphael Sassower**, Professor of philosophy, University of Colorado/Colorado Springs, author of *A Sanctuary of Their Own*

Imagine an educational system designed to foster mindfulness and self-actualization leading to individual happiness. In his book, Tony Armstrong does just that and explains how to build it for our children. | **Tim Couch**, Texas teacher in his 21st year

Educating Angels *is a much-needed work of scholarship dealing with the fundamental purpose of education. Dr. Armstrong provides a comprehensive guide and resource to exploring the teaching of happiness. After providing an excellent justification for altering the nature of education, he provides concrete examples of how this "new" pedagogy of happiness could be implemented in classrooms from pre-K to college.* | **Joseph Yuichi Howard**, Professor of political science, University of Central Arkansas

Amid the charlatans and profiteers who aim to make education more efficient, this book challenges the assumptions of a broken system and calls for us to reimagine the education of our children as if they matter to us. | **Jeffrey Mask**, Professor of philosophy and religion, Wesley College, author of *At Liberty Under God*

Educating Angels *is a must read for those who worry about the state of education and our children.* | **Joann Prewitt**, former teacher and retired Education Associate, Delaware Department of Education

Educating Angels

Teaching For
The Pursuit of Happiness

Parkhurst Brothers Publishers

Marion, Michigan

www.parkhurstbrothers.com

Parkhurst Brothers books are distributed to the trade through the Chicago Distribution Center, and may be ordered through Ingram Book Company, Baker & Taylor, Follett Library Resources and other book industry wholesalers. To order from Chicago Distribution Center, phone 1-800-621-2736 or send a fax to 800-621-8476. Copies of this and other Parkhurst Brothers Inc., Publishers titles are available to organizations and corporations for purchase in quantity by contacting Special Sales Department at our home office location, listed on our website. Manuscript submission guidelines for this publishing company are available at our website.

Printed in the United States of America
First Edition, 2013
2013 2014 2015 2016 2017 2018   16 15 14 13 12 11 10 9 8 7 6 5 4 3 2 1

Library of Congress Cataloging-in-Publication Data

Armstrong, Anthony, 1951-
Educating angels: teaching for the pursuit of happiness / Anthony Armstrong. — First edition.
pages cm. — (Our national conversation; volume 15)
ISBN 978-1-62491-013-5 (pbk.) — ISBN 978-1-62491-014-2 (ebook)
1. Education — Aims and objectives. 2. Education, Humanistic. 3. Educational change. 4. Happiness. I. Title.
LB41.A745 2013
370.11 — dc23

2013019782

ISBN: Trade Paperback   978162491-013-5, first retail suggested $20.00
ISBN: e-book   978162491-014-2

Cover and interior design by Mary Jo Meade | Edited by Mary Jo Meade
Front cover photograph by Susan Hall

Acquired for Parkhurst Brothers Inc., Publishers by Ted Parkhurst

112013

EDUCATING ANGELS | CONTENTS

OUR NATIONAL CONVERSATION
VOLUME FIFTEEN

1

An Education Worthy of Angels

*What the best and wisest parent wants
for his own child, that must the community
want for all its children. Any other ideal for our
schools is narrow and unlovely; acted upon, it
destroys our democracy.* | John Dewey

My students might be angels, though they do not particularly look or act like angels. If the light of angelic souls shines through their eyes, I am blind to it. Yet each of them embodies the unfathomed depths of a human mind and perhaps the transcendent attributes of an eternal soul, so whether or not they are angels, I see the *worth* of angels in them. I ask what difference I and educators in general should strive to make in the lives of these miracles of the universe. What education is worthy of them?

If we thought our children had the divine worth of angels, would we insist our schools treat each of them as an end in himself, aiming for his highest *personal* good and the fulfillment of his deepest aspiration? Or would we continue to aim first and foremost at turning each child into a contributor to what we think society needs — a worker, an engineer, a soldier, a taxpayer, a consumer, a partisan for a social cause?

When we treat children as ends in themselves, we acknowledge their innate worth and the possibility that their lives have a purpose beyond our ken and determination — a higher purpose. When we use them as means to social ends, we demean their worth and assign them a purely instrumental purpose. Whether we should treat them as ends or continue to treat them as means is a vital moral question, but it is also an immensely important *practical* question. How we answer the question of the difference we *ought* to make in children's lives will determine the difference we *do* make. If we neglect the inner resources children need to achieve their deepest aspiration, we will not only impoverish their lives, we will impoverish the societies they will inherit.

But do children share a common aspiration that we can help them achieve through education? I agree with the great philosophers that the primary subjective purpose of a human being is happiness, that happiness is our highest personal good. William James echoes the wisdom of ages when he says,

> *If we were to ask the question: "What is life's chief concern?" one of the answers we should receive would be: "It is happiness." How to gain, how to keep, how to recover happiness is in fact for most men at all times the secret motive of all they do, and of all they are willing to endure.*[1]

Daisaku Ikeda infers the purpose of education from this insight: "The goal of education must be one with the goal of life. And this means that it must enable students to attain a life of happiness."[2] This goal of education accords with the purpose of democracy. If education offers knowledge and hones skills that empower students to pursue their personal goals, it follows that the purpose of public education in a democracy, where the state is obliged to serve the interests of its citizens, is to empower each child's lifelong pursuit of happiness.

You won't see this acknowledged in mainstream debates about education policy. Politicians, policy-makers, educators, business leaders, and pundits debate our failure to prepare students for jobs in the 21st century global economy and to ensure our national economic competitiveness. They grapple over the content and use of accountability tests, which stress basic job skills. They argue about the poor job schools are doing teaching civics and values. Some issue dire warnings about the future of democracy and moral order, while most brush off such warnings as less pressing than economic needs. Partisans exchange salvos over sex education, teaching evolution, the content of American history texts, and the public funding of private schools.

Politicians and educators contend over funding, job security, pay, class size, technology, and administrative costs. Teachers advocate and dispute methodologies while largely ignoring the question of the aims of education.

With the exception of a few oases in the desert of public debate, the happiness of our children is not an explicit concern. The word *happiness* is seldom used in these discussions. Few participants point to education's contribution to personal happiness as the main point of the enterprise. The question of what education can and should contribute to students' pursuit of happiness is seldom asked, and even less often answered.

The question is *implicitly* answered in these debates, though. No doubt advocates of educational causes at least vaguely assume that what they advocate would serve students' happiness. But little of what they call for is directly aimed at their happiness. It's more directly aimed at the good of society as these partisans see it, while their assumptions about what their causes would contribute to students' happiness are unspoken and unexamined.

Does this matter? Yes. Profoundly. Allowing our schoolchildren to be treated mainly as instruments to achieve social ends will teach them that using people is normal, expected, and ethical. This is a weak foundation for the ethical values we hope to impart. And if the happiness of the majority of citizens is best promoted by empowering their individual pursuit, then the good of society is best served by this as well. After all, the good of society consists of the good of the individuals that comprise it. As John Dewey says, "Only by being true to the full growth of all the individuals who make it up, can society by any chance be true to itself."[3]

Dedicating our children's education to empowering their personal pursuit of happiness would benefit society far more than current practice. Putting society first comes at the expense of students' personal empowerment through relative neglect, which is abundantly evident in current practice. But the reverse is not true. Teaching students the awareness, knowledge, and skills that will help them choose a more discerning path to happiness would not detract from worthy social goals. It promises happier societies with fewer social problems.

Our children's prospects for happiness, the health of our societies, and our success in imparting core moral values depend on how focused our schools are on empowering students' pursuit of happiness. This is a big claim that begs explanation and support, so let me summarize the argument developed in the rest of the book.

Changing the current focus calls for explicitly embracing empowerment of the pursuit of happiness as the primary purpose of education. This is necessary to get the subject of happiness — its nature, sources, and means — taken seriously in our schools. This does not mean agreeing on what happiness is, what causes it, and the best way to achieve it and then teaching our collective wisdom to students. The practical meaning of freedom is the right to pursue happiness *as one sees it*. Rather we ask schools to do what they are already designed to do: provide the knowledge, understanding, and skills that empower students to achieve what they want in life no matter what that may be. The difference is that schools would give considered attention to providing the knowledge, insight, and skills directly related to the pursuit of happiness per se.

Happiness should be presented as a puzzle that each student must solve for herself over the course of her formal education. In the early years students would be taught inner awareness, observing their feelings and paying attention to which feelings they like most — and least. They would be brought to see the connection between feelings and thoughts. They would learn that feelings are not directly caused by what is happening in the world around them, but by their *judgments* of what is happening. Students would be shown how to influence what they feel by managing thoughts and judgments. And they would learn techniques to improve their outlook and develop resilience in the emotional turbulence of life.

This would balance schools' almost exclusive focus on external experience with a focus on internal experience — which is long overdue.

Most educators no doubt assume they are serving the happiness of their students by imparting knowledge and skills important to achieving worldly goals. Students want jobs, careers, status, esteem, money, social efficacy, etc., because they were taught to believe these things are the keys to happiness. Whether or not an educator agrees that the keys to worldly achievement are the keys to a person's heart, the prescribed content of the subjects she was hired to teach implies it.

Counsels of the wise throughout the centuries as well as modern research caution that the keys to the heart lie not without but within. The importance of attitude, beliefs, and mental practices to your ability to feel as you choose is broadly recognized and easily demonstrated. Thousands of studies show that being aware of what is going on in your mind through disciplined observation delivers a cornucopia of what psychologists call *affective* benefits. Affect is simply another word for feeling. The ability to tap these inner resources requires skills that must be taught and developed through practice. Though there is growing interest in teaching such skills in schools, it has yet to appear on the radar screen of mainstream discussions about the ends and means of education.

In addition to learning the skills of inner awareness, early-year students would explore beliefs about happiness by means of stories used as windows on how people pursue happiness. They would try to figure out what characters in a story seem to think happiness is and how to get it. As kids progress to higher grades, they would be given more pieces of the puzzle of happiness to examine: the findings of science, philosophical and religious perspectives, reports of personal experiences, and realizations drawn from their own experiments with feelings. Teachers would lead students in communal investigation of perspectives, assumptions, and evidence. This involves open class discussion and questioning. Reading, writing, and speaking would all focus on finding a personal answer to a common question. As I explain later, research shows that framing the subject of a course in terms of a quest for answers to a question is one of the most effective ways to teach.

Communal investigation brings all the skills of critical thinking to bear. Open discussion and inquiry hone communication skills. The methods of inquiry I recommend constantly exercise reading, writing, and group problem-solving skills. The difference is that a happiness pedagogy would center on a common quest with direct personal relevance to each child. Students could reap the fruits of these efforts in terms of their ability to influence what they feel in the short term rather than waiting for the benefits we adults tell them will be theirs far in the future. Personal relevance and immediate benefits feed *the motive to learn*, which gets far too little attention in current educational practice. This alone commends the happiness pedagogy I advocate.

Another compelling reason to embrace this pedagogy is that teaching inner awareness is the key to getting students to internalize the values we want them to embrace. Through directed inner awareness, we can better ground the virtues of benevolence in our children's hearts. What we think about others determines how we feel about them and therefore treat them. This determines how a person feels, period. If a person is angry with someone, anger is what he feels. If he appreciates someone, he feels appreciation.

We unavoidably reap what we sow in terms of feelings with our thoughts and behavior toward others. Inner awareness brings feelings into clearer focus and allows us to more objectively weigh them in the scales of pleasure and pain. What such awareness eventually reveals is that negative judgments of other people and unkind treatment cause unpleasant feelings. On the other hand, "it feels good to do good." And it feels good to *think well* of others. The tenor of your thoughts determines the tenor of your feelings.

A happiness pedagogy would aim to make students consciously aware of this connection. Through inner awareness, they would be led to repeatedly experience it. This would nurture the self-reinforcing motive to regard and treat others well that is sorely missing in the token efforts to teach values in our schools at present.

Some schools incorporate "well-being" courses into their curricula, and interest in making happiness a central concern of education seems to be growing, but so far I have not discovered a fully developed curriculum built around empowering the pursuit of happiness. I present plausible elements of such a curriculum to show its enormous potential to make a positive difference in kids' lives.

The chapters ahead provide the rationale and a more detailed description of the approaches I just outlined. Here is an overview of the progression I foresee:

Grades K-3
Inner Awareness, Social Awareness, and Affective Skills

In the early years, teachers trained in the art would lead students in inner-awareness exercises and discussions about feelings and what causes them. Children would be taught awareness of the connection between thoughts and feelings as well as between acts and feelings. They would be made aware that how they treat and regard others affects how they feel. They would learn a vocabulary of feelings and frequently discuss feelings, which not only helps a child develop awareness and understanding of her own feelings, but also gives her deeper insight into what others feel. Empathy grows from such insight.

They would learn techniques for causing feelings as well as taking the edge off of unpleasant emotions such as fear, anger, frustration, and envy.

K-3 students would also begin their exploration of the larger question of happiness through films, discussions, creative activities, and readings as their reading skills progress.

The practices of awareness would continue through all levels of education.

Grades 4-6
Broadening and Deepening the Exploration of Views on Happiness

As reading and critical thinking skills advance, students would more directly explore the question of happiness through literature, history, the arts, science, civics, economics, etc. They would begin to consider a range of philosophical and religious perspectives on happiness. Guided class discussion on these perspectives would be a regular part of the curriculum.

Grades 7-12
Structured Analysis of Perspectives on the Big Questions of Life

Students would engage in more structured and systematic analyses of perspectives on the Big Questions of life — reality, human nature, the nature and sources of knowledge, the good life, and the social good. The Big Questions are those a person at least implicitly answers with every important choice he makes. Exploring alternative answers to these questions makes a student aware of his own "operating assumptions" and allows him to consciously choose what to believe in light of awareness and reason. The choice of belief is important, for such beliefs inform a person's understanding of happiness and how to pursue it.

Expectations for reading, writing, and critical thinking would progressively rise through the grades. Students would also work on a written personal philosophy of life, revising it throughout the latter years of K-12 education.

Higher Education
Integrated Core Curriculum Based on Inquiry into Big Questions

I plug in to the current trend toward a "first-year experience" and cross-disciplinary, "integrated" courses in the core curriculum of colleges and universities. Exploring the Big Questions of life by means of analyzing alternative perspectives is a natural and effective way to integrate the disciplines because it invites perspectives that cannot be claimed by any particular subject area. The continuing aim of empowering students' pursuit of happiness would also provide the integrating principle necessary to devise a coherent, meaningful core curriculum. The inquiry that began in the latter half of the K-12 years would continue with an exploration of the farther frontiers of human thought and scientific investigation while employing the more exacting methods of scholarship.

Consider the potential social benefits of a happiness-empowering curriculum. How would it affect society if the majority of students began their adult life significantly happier and more likely to remain happier than is currently the case? Robust findings of research make the case that happier people are far less prone to self-destructive and antisocial behavior. They are far less likely to abuse drugs, commit crimes, and be cruel to other people. A mountain of evidence backs the claim that happier people are kinder, more compassionate people. They are also more creative and productive. They are more cooperative and socially engaged. They are more likely to lend a hand in times of need. And their happiness is contagious. Others are uplifted by their happiness.

What would we as a society gain if we succeeded in making students more aware that thinking well of others and treating them kindly makes them feel better while the reverse makes them feel worse? How we treat other people is the heart of morality, so we could expect a kinder, more moral society and healthier relationships in families and communities.

Such virtues as caring, kindness, cooperation, civility, honesty, responsibility, and generosity — all of which move people to treat others well — determine the quality of the social environment. They are the glue of society, the buttresses of democracy, and they act as regulators to inhibit the harm and amplify the benefit of economic activities. They also contribute to individual happiness. Much depends on the benevolence of citizens, but little is consciously done in our schools to promote it.

Objections and Obstacles

But what about jobs and the economy? Wouldn't this touchy-feely happiness stuff detract from the basics of what students need to know to get a job and grow the economy? On the contrary. The changes I advocate would directly impact only a fourth to a sixth of current curricula, so I am not advocating completely tearing down and reconstructing education as we know it. The approaches I recommend would not divert from teaching the basics of reading, writing, communicating, and critical thinking. They would constantly exercise these skills and greatly improve students' motivation to learn them. We can also reasonably expect that students would be better at group problem-solving, since that is what communal inquiry into the puzzle of happiness essentially is.

More than this, the introduction of both inner awareness and philosophical and religious perspectives that are ignored in contemporary education would deepen kids' understanding of themselves and others. Students would be more aware of the heritage of human thought and gain insight into the human condition. In addition to the inestimable personal value of such awareness and understanding, it translates into more productive relations between colleagues and is a considerable advantage in dealings with customers. People of all cultures and nationalities share the same core aspirations. A person with insight into these aspirations is a valuable employee in the global economy.

Even if all this were not true, though, economic ends do not justify ignoring the larger question of our children's happiness. This is a moral issue of great consequence. Good jobs and a healthy economy may ease the pursuit of happiness, but the great weight of evidence shows they are not the *keys* to personal happiness. To sacrifice the personally transformative promise of a happiness pedagogy to purely economic ends is a crass betrayal of our children.

I am not naïve about the difficulty of persuading enough people to make a difference that this is so. On the surface, it seems reasonable to assume most people would agree that education should aim to improve our children's chances for happiness. I am convinced that the fact that this purpose is not explicitly enunciated in prominent education reform movements is not due to the uncaring hearts of those concerned. I've encountered more plausible reasons through my research and the lessons I've learned trying to promote the cause.

A lot of people assume that the job of schools is to educate minds, not hearts. Some even say that feelings have no place in the classroom. My reply is that we need to be clear about the stakes.

My argument is founded on the theory that the ultimate value of any experience lies in what we feel about it or what it contributes to a future feeling. In the word "feeling" I include both types, emotions and non-emotive feelings. Emotions are feelings that spur us to seek experiences that move us away from fear, anger, hatred, lust, boredom, and all other forms of dissatisfaction. Non-emotive feelings are those that we at least temporarily want to keep experiencing — happiness, fulfillment, joy, peace of mind, love, etc. Remove feelings from an experience and we are left with a robotic awareness of what our senses are reporting without caring about the experience. Caring is feeling, and without feeling we would not prefer any one experience over another.

The senses deliver usable information, but its value depends on what it contributes to what we want to feel. If what we're really looking for in all we pursue is a desired feeling, then the value of our perceptions is determined by what they contribute to our ability to feel as we wish. The same is true of thoughts; if they were completely divorced from feelings, thoughts would have no more experiential value than a computer calculation, with no interest in the process or result.

We value what we desire, appreciate or find useful, things that we hold in positive regard. So it follows that we value those feelings that are *preferable* to our current feelings. They are the treasures we seek through our experiences. The focus of our desire may be people, possessions, comfort, entertainment, love, esteem, understanding, truth, aesthetic surroundings, and all else that glitters in the eyes of our minds. But the value, the reward, for getting what we want, lies in the feeling associated with experiencing it. No feeling, no experiential value.

It is the heart that bestows value on human experience, not the feelings-barren reasoning of the mind. Jesus said, "For where your treasure is, there will your heart be also." This must be so if what we treasure in our minds is really an expected feeling in our hearts. The implications of this realization are profound, and they are troubling given how we as a society educate our children.

If value is bestowed by the heart, the value of education ultimately lies in what it contributes to the aspirations of students' hearts. We need not look too closely to see what is apparent: very little of what is taught in schools is directly aimed at their hearts. They are taught knowledge and understanding of the external world and skills useful in achieving external goals. All this undoubtedly has *some* relevance to students' individual pursuit of happiness, but *how much* relevance it has is seldom a conscious concern. If we do not consciously aim at a target, we are unlikely to hit it.

Some argue that it isn't the government's job to *make* people happy. They're right that government shouldn't try to make people happy. This would violate people's freedom and is far beyond the capacity of government. Considering the typical politician, it would be at best a case of the blind leading the blind. But America's Founding Fathers explicitly embraced the Enlightenment proposition that protecting and promoting citizens' free pursuit of happiness is the purpose of government. In modern times, public education is the least controversial means for governments to serve this purpose. I devote the next chapter to presenting the case that empowering the pursuit of happiness is the most democratic — as well as most moral — purpose of education.

A number of people I've talked to are morally opposed to making happiness the overriding concern in schools. Their main objection is that moral duty is a higher aim than the "selfish" desire for happiness. As I said earlier, altruism and happiness are linked. Treating others well is the heart of morality, so morality is better served by a happiness pedagogy than the anemic attempts to teach values in today's schools.

One of the most frustrating obstacles I've encountered is the difficulty of having a coherent, meaningful discussion about happiness. Happiness is an all-purpose word whose meaning can change with context, and people don't generally share the same core understanding of it. Almost everyone seems to think of happiness in terms of sources — circumstances, relationships, accomplishments, virtues, beliefs, etc. — rather than the nature of happiness — what it *feels like*. Perhaps they assume that the feeling of happiness differs from person to person, though I suspect it has more to do with not having given the matter much thought.

Without a common understanding of at least the basic attributes of happiness, I might as well be speaking in tongues when trying to explain why and how schools should empower its pursuit. I therefore present a practical understanding of happiness and its pursuit in the next three chapters. These chapters lay the conceptual foundation for the happiness pedagogy I suggest.

All movements of serious educational reform face another huge obstacle: inertia. Much of it is due to vested interests in the status quo and fear of change. The best way to overcome such inertia is to persuade the people with vested interests — parents, educators, employers, fellow citizens — that they stand to gain rather than lose by embracing the proposed change.

I make the case that all involved will find empowering students' pursuit of happiness more rewarding than the current state of affairs. Parents' hope that their children will be happy has a better chance of coming true. Teachers' desire to make a greater difference in the lives of their students is more likely to be satisfied. I am also convinced most teachers would find that exchanging their role as purveyor of authoritative facts for the role of expedition guide in search of personal treasure is a more interesting, effective, and meaningful way to teach. Employers would find graduating students better prepared with critical thinking, communication and people skills. Having for many years thoroughly considered where their passion lies, graduates would be more motivated and clear about their direction. All citizens could anticipate a society with less antisocial behavior.

You cannot see the larger failure of contemporary education until you see it in light of this promise. Contemporary education is characterized by ambiguity of purpose, by inattention to feelings and the inner sources of experience, and by ineffectiveness in encouraging benevolence. We are failing our children's hearts — and our own as well. Whatever the obstacles, we can and should change this.

A well-constructed happiness pedagogy would make students more aware of choices and their consequences. It would reveal the inner sources of feelings and how to tap them. The children of the future would consciously experience the affective benefits of benevolence. They would gain the wherewithal to make wiser choices and a greater ability to realize them. Thus we would better serve the higher good of each of the possible angels in our schools as well as the greater good of the society they will inhabit as adults.

2

The Purpose
Of Liberal Education

What then is the purpose of national education?
Rather than devise complex theoretical interpretations, it
is better to start by looking to the lovely child who sits on
your knee and ask yourself: What can I do
to assure this child will be able to lead the happiest life
possible? | Tsunesaburo Makiguchi

Education is universal and mandated in almost all modern societies. Providing for the education of all citizens is a function of the modern state in keeping with the purpose of government. In democracies, the purpose of government is to serve the common purpose of the citizens. The luminaries of America's founding were clear about the purpose of both citizens and government. John Adams advised:

> We ought to consider what is the end of government, before we determine which is the best form. Upon this point all speculative politicians will agree, that the happiness of society is the end of government, as all divines and moral philosophers will agree that the happiness of the individual is the end of man.[1]

Thomas Jefferson agreed:

> The only orthodox object of the institution of government is to secure the greatest degree of happiness possible to the general mass of those associated under it.[2]

Adams and Jefferson were products of the Enlightenment, sharing the belief that societies can be improved for the benefit of all with the aid of informed reason. They expressed an ancient wisdom in saying that happiness is the "end of man." Aristotle named happiness the only self-sufficient end.

> *If, then, there is some end of the things we do, which we desire for its own sake (everything else being desired for the sake of this) ... clearly this must be the good and the chief good. ... Happiness ... is something complete and self-sufficient, and is the end of action.*[3]

Prominent Enlightenment philosophers insisted that governments exist to serve the people, that they should be accountable to the people, and that the people are best served when they are free to pursue happiness as each sees fit. This last belief is the core argument for freedom. John Locke put it this way:

> *There is only one [way] which is the true way to eternal happiness. But in this great variety of ways that men follow, it is still doubted which is this right one. Now neither the care of the commonwealth, nor the right of enacting laws, does discover this way that leads to heaven more certainly to the magistrate, than every private man's search and study discovers it unto himself.*[4]

This is the premise of the democratic revolution Jefferson and Adams championed. It founds the logic of liberty: The happiness of society is the end of government. The happiness of society consists of the happiness of the individuals who comprise it. The greatest prospect of happiness for each and all is found in allowing citizens to pursue happiness as each sees it. Thus the purpose of government is to provide the best conditions for the free pursuit of happiness.

At a minimum, governments are expected to provide order, security, infrastructure, and a currency of exchange to fulfill this purpose. Democratic governments are also obliged to allow and protect individual freedom. These are considered favorable conditions. But modern governments are obviously expected to do far more. They aim not only to provide conditions conducive to the free pursuit of happiness; they also aim to enable the individual pursuit to some extent. In modern times, providing an education is the least controversial way to do this. Enabling individuals to pursue personal goals with knowledge and skills is therefore among the main purposes of education in modern democratic societies.

Traditionally, schools taught virtues for the sake of society and the salvation of souls, using the rod to reinforce the lessons. Schools were also meant to serve the needs of democracy. Jefferson warned that democracy would not long endure unless children were educated to embrace and adequately fulfill the duties of democratic citizenship. The need for workers who could read, write, and cipher was a prime driver of the push to provide universal public education. It is no accident that public education grew with industrialization in America and abroad. Preparation for the job market remains the top purpose of education in the minds of most people.

These functions of education are meant to meet the needs of *social reproduction*. Succeeding generations must be taught the norms and know-how required to keep a civilization going. Education helps meet social needs that must be met regardless of what individual students want. Yet what they want in the fullness of their rights as adult citizens is the *point* of free societies. This point is often obscured, but never completely lost, in the discourse about what schools are for. The knowledge, skills, awareness, and understanding taught in our schools serve social needs, but they are also thought to empower individuals to pursue their personal goals.

Education has always been considered the ticket to a better life. In modern times, education is society's main means to provide at least a pretense of equal opportunity to achieve personal goals. Our schools teach more than job skills to enable students to pursue these opportunities. They also try to pass on the cultural heritage of humanity, broaden students' awareness of their society and the world, deepen their understanding of the human condition, introduce students to pleasures of mind and social interaction, and encourage them to think critically and creatively for their own sakes. All this belongs to a *liberal* education that serves society at large, but is also thought to benefit each student personally. The subjects of the liberal arts at least implicitly aim to *liberate* the minds of students and provide the mental wherewithal for a more discerning pursuit of happiness.

If happiness is the common end of all human striving, and public education is the main means for governments to empower each citizen to pursue his own ends, it follows that empowering the pursuit of happiness is the main purpose of public education. It is not so clear, though, that this is a *practical* purpose. Many people who agree that happiness is what we are all after in a philosophical sense see no practical gain in making happiness the guide to shared enterprise. The desire for happiness may move us, but the diverse pursuits of human beings seem to make it impossible to discover a guiding principle in the concept. A motive that moves people in many different directions is too ambiguous to guide us in any particular direction.

But liberal education is designed with such ambiguity in mind. The knowledge and skills taught in our schools are intended to serve a variety of goals, both social and personal, as such learning is thought useful to virtually all pursuits in life. What would change with a happiness pedagogy is the inclusion of the sort of knowledge and skills more directly related to students' ability to *feel* as they choose. I delve more deeply into this in the chapters ahead, but I first need to explain what I mean by the "ability to *feel* as they choose" and why I think it is essential to empowering the pursuit of happiness.

A Practical Understanding of 'Happiness'

Most people use the word happiness to mean a highly desirable feeling. Some disagree, seeing it more in terms of a worthy life, but happiness as a desirable feeling is a broadly shared understanding of the word. Words are used to communicate, and popular meanings are best suited to this purpose. We can draw some important conclusions for education from the twin premises that happiness is a desirable feeling and happiness is the real goal of all our striving. It would cheapen the meaning of happiness to apply it to any and all desired feelings of the moment, but whatever you do to feel better than you do at present can be reasonably considered a step in the *pursuit* of happiness. Seeing the pursuit in terms of steps makes the subject of happiness more accessible.

Aristotle set the bar high in saying happiness is "something complete and self-sufficient," something beyond further desire. Some agree that happiness is a "peak" experience, something akin to ultimate fulfillment or bliss without end. Others set the bar lower and are willing to accept general contentment or even a relative absence of pain as meeting the requirements. These are concepts of a destination, though, and each student will decide this for herself. A happiness pedagogy can and should inform students' long-range choices, but empowering their pursuit includes teaching the skills necessary to feel as each chooses *in the present*. Progress toward a deeper and more lasting happiness is made or delayed in the moment-to-moment steps one takes, by which I mean both the inner steps of the mind and the outer steps of the body.

Experience is exclusively in the present. This is the only *experienced* dimension of time. Even when we recall a memory or think of the future, the experience of what we are recalling or projecting is in the present moment. No matter how grand the prospect of a future feeling, its experiential value is in what it contributes to what we feel *now*, whether the present now or a now yet to come. Put simply, this means that a feeling must actually be consciously *felt* rather than merely *expected* to have value. This simple realization suggests something of considerable practical importance: our ability to improve what we feel from moment to moment is the ability to enhance the value of any and all experiences.

The pursuit of happiness need not be seen as a journey across a barren and punishing desert to reach a distant, imagined paradise. It is more fruitfully seen as a journey where the oases of relative joy and satisfaction grow increasingly frequent as the moments of anxiety, dissatisfaction, and pain grow ever less frequent the further one progresses toward lasting happiness. If the joy of enjoyed moments grows deeper and the moments longer as the barbs of unpleasant feelings become less sharp and painful, each step of progress is its own reward. "Every step of the journey *is* the journey" according to a Zen saying. This is a highly practical way to look at the journey to happiness.

Even if feeling better means no more than slightly reducing the pangs of worry, the pressure of stress, or the depth of depression, it is worth your while to learn how to do it. Not only does it promise some relief, but knowing you are not defenseless in the face of pain gives comfort in itself. And what you do to lessen today's pain can be developed into an increasingly effective means to move from pain toward some measure of joy.

For the most part, we are guided by present and prospective feelings. To move toward what you vaguely hope to feel gives you at least some sense of direction: "I will feel better when I get my promotion, finish this project, or make it to the weekend." We imagine conditions we presume will make us feel better than we do: the love and regard of others, a better job, more money and possessions, less stress and more fun, and so forth. If or when I experience *x*, I will feel better than I do now, is the common mantra of the human mind. Such expectations are often unrealistic and unrealized, but disappointments teach lessons about how to improve your choices and chances.

Most of us are prone to blind urges at times. Many have a tendency to feel an itch and choose the temporary relief of scratching it at the cost of greater itching afterward. Yet the cumulative lessons of experience can teach a person to overlook the itch of the moment in favor of something more deeply satisfying, more stable and sustained, and less costly. Thus experience can make our choices more discerning and our pursuit less blind and aimless.

The *concept* of happiness guides few in any consistent way, though some pursue notions of happiness with great dedication. Those who see happiness as living according to the will of God, or discovering the inner self, or being wealthy, for example, can be quite focused and consistent in how they live. But even without such clarity, trial and error can lead us closer to what we unconsciously seek. The human race may not be as rational as we pretend, but we are not bad at learning what experience repeatedly teaches. We can eventually find our way by groping in the dark. Naturally, it would help if we could shine some light on our surroundings.

In a sense, that is what education is for. It is supposed to improve on trial-and-error learning. The awareness, understanding, and knowledge our schools teach offer a clearer view of the world and brighten the light of reason. They greatly improve students' ability to see and negotiate the wider social terrain. Combined with relevant skills, they could do the same for students' ability to see and negotiate the inner terrain of mind and heart.

From the earliest years of schooling, children should be taught awareness of feelings. Among other benefits, this would make them more aware of what they prefer to feel, of the relative desirability of feelings. Educators could extend this awareness to the *causes* of feelings, to the relationship between what a student feels and what he is thinking, doing, or perceiving at the time. Children should then be taught well-proven techniques and habits of mind to influence what they feel. These attainments would enable students to take more discerning and successful moment-to-moment steps toward feeling better. And they would start to enjoy the rewards of their progress in their first year of school. This would introduce a rare self-reinforcing *intrinsic* motive to learn.

Awareness of feelings is the first step to choice. We often find ourselves in the grip of a feeling that unconsciously rules our thoughts and behaviors. Simply observing feelings such as fear, anger, jealousy, loneliness, and boredom brings them to conscious awareness. Such awareness is obviously a requirement of conscious choice. It can also loosen the grip of an unpleasant feeling by shining light on it. On the other hand, conscious acknowledgement of joy, peace, appreciation, and fun enhances these pleasant feelings. It can remind us to "smell the roses" and focus our minds on the enjoyment of the moment. Observing feelings also makes it easier to judge their relative desirability, which is key to discerning choice.

The ability to influence feelings requires some awareness and understanding of what is causing them. Recognizing the source of feelings is useful even if they are automatic reactions to our environment, because we can do something to change our circumstances. It is more profoundly useful, though, if our feelings are reactions to our interpretations, thoughts, and beliefs. The contents of our minds are easier to change than circumstances, at least when you learn *how* to change them. Robust evidence shows that children can be taught how to influence what they think and therefore feel, and that they greatly benefit from learning these skills.

Taking the edge off of the unpleasant feelings and amplifying the pleasant feelings of the moment is rewarding whether or not these steps lead to a sustained peak feeling worthy to be called happiness. They enhance your enjoyment of your experiences. If happiness is ultimately a skill of mind, such steps may be the necessary means to develop this skill. Even if happiness is more an involuntary response to favorable circumstances, as many people seem to believe, awareness of feelings and their relationship to circumstances offers crucial guidance in choosing which circumstances to seek.

Many will object to devoting precious school time to teaching students how to feel better in the present rather than focusing exclusively on preparing them for the rigors of the emotionally bruising, stressful, competitive world of adults. Some will call teaching students how to feel better "therapy," and some already insist emotions have no place in the classroom. I obviously disagree with their understanding of value, both in general and in regard to education. Others say young people are already *too* in touch with their feelings, pointing to their self-absorption and preference for instant gratification. I argue that such tendencies are due more to a *lack* of awareness of feelings, their sources, and consequences than to being "too in touch." Consciously observing feelings helps avoid being unconsciously absorbed by them.

Besides, short-term steps to feeling better would not be the only aim of a happiness pedagogy. From start to finish, our children and youth would investigate notions of happiness, presumed sources of happiness, and ad-vocated means to achieve happiness. Their education would inform their long-range choices as well as their short-term steps. As it turns out, it will not be difficult to harness the subjects already taught to this aim of educa-tion, though a more philosophical core curriculum is needed. I outline a way to do this in chapters ahead.

But I need to more fully address the objection that concern for your own feelings is selfish. This is a serious objection because it questions the assumption that happiness *should* be the primary purpose of hu-man beings.

Many have argued that happiness is morally unacceptable as the primary human end, that there are higher ends to which happiness *should be* sacrificed if it conflicts with these ends.[5] In this view, the pursuit of happiness is essen-tially self-centered and therefore insufficiently other-directed. What is usu-ally meant by this is that the pursuit of personal satisfaction either comes at the expense of others' desires or without regard for their feelings and needs.

The assumption that the pursuit of happiness is inherently selfish springs from a narrow understanding of happiness. Love is counted among the most desirable of feelings and service to others is commonly thought to make a per-son feel better. I argue — and provide evidence — that the deeper satisfactions of serving others are far more likely to guide the pursuit toward their benefit and away from harming them. It is entirely plausible when Nel Noddings sug-gests that "Happy people are rarely mean, violent, or cruel."[6] One of the more robust findings of research is that people who score high on happiness ques-tionnaires tend to be more altruistic than those with low scores.[7]

Selfish behavior is not inherent to the pursuit of happiness, nor is it a promising means. Behavior considered morally desirable is more likely to result from a discerning pursuit of happiness than from the pursuit of mo-rality without prospect of happiness.

Some argue that the fulfillment of moral obligation or duty, whether prescribed by the will of God or reason, should not be motivated by, and is even negated by, prospect of reward. Prospect of reward taints the pure moral motive they say. Immanuel Kant argued that a moral law could not be cat-egorical and universal if it springs from the motive to experience pleasure or satisfaction in the fulfillment of duty rather than derived from pure reason.[8]

He admitted, though, that pure reason does not supply its own motive. And there is a perverse logic to the assertion that sacrificing one's happiness for the sake of others is a requirement of morality. It implies that in a perfectly moral world everyone would sacrifice their happiness for the sake of others and no one would be happy.

I doubt that those who claim they are willing to sacrifice their happiness for a higher cause actually have an alternative motive. The desire to feel worthy by doing what you believe is good and right is a powerful motivator. Acting in accordance with your normative beliefs yields affective rewards while acting contrary to them causes the discomfort of guilt and "cognitive dissonance." People go to great lengths to avoid guilt. I believe the "sacrifices" people make are at least partly offerings made to avoid or appease the gnawing pangs of the emotion. The affective price one pays to avoid an even greater cost is still the pursuit of a preferred feeling.

Jeremy Bentham, who defined utility in terms of happiness, said "When a man attempts to combat the principle of utility, it is with reasons drawn, without his being aware of it, from that very principle itself."[9] Kant himself observed,

> We are pleased to flatter ourselves with the false claim to a nobler motive, but in fact we can never, even by the most strenuous self-examination, get to the bottom of our secret impulses; for when moral value is in question, we are concerned, not with the actions which we see, but with their inner principles, which we cannot see.[10]

The path of righteousness is as much a path to a person's understanding of happiness as any other. The wellspring of motive is in the heart. We can divert and delay our heart's desire due to the cautions of the mind, but even in this the heart moves us. No feeling, no volition.

If education *can* contribute more to our children's happiness, it *ought* to. Serving their highest interest is the meaning of treating them as ends. Too many of the current aims of education treat them as means. This is not only morally questionable; it also has troubling practical consequences.

Of Ends and Means

What began as a luxury of the elite, the education of all citizens has become a crucial means to both social and individual ends. Education helps socialize children to complex and rapidly changing conditions. Schools reinforce norms and guide the acquisition of knowledge and skills that serve the needs and interests of society — the function of social reproduction. Beyond this, education offers the mental wherewithal to pursue personal goals — the function of empowerment. The same knowledge and skills serve both purposes to some extent, but we should not pretend that both purposes are equally served with the current emphasis on social purposes. They are not.

When social goals determine what and how educators teach, they treat students as means rather than as ends in themselves. This may not seem morally dubious if you assume that social and personal interests are essentially the same and that serving the former best serves the latter. If, however, the focus on social aims in our schools impoverishes our children's prospects for happiness through relative neglect of that which empowers their personal pursuit, our priorities are morally dubious. And slighting the core aspirations of our children does not bode well for the betterment of society either.

The needs of society must be met, of course. As Dewey says, "what nutrition and reproduction are to physiological life, education is to social life."[11] The values, attitudes, knowledge, and skills that make a particular society possible must be passed on and "as societies become more complex in structure and resources, the need of formal or intentional teaching and learning increases."[12] Will Durant calls this the "transmission of civilization." Gilbert Chesterton describes it as passing the "soul of society" to succeeding generations.

Democracies offer the many advantages of freedom, but reproducing them is more difficult. They require a higher order of attitudes and skills than those required by authoritarian forms of government. As John Stuart Mill said:

> He who lets the world, or his own portion of it, choose his plan of life for him has no need of any other faculty than the ape-like one of imitation. He who chooses his plan for himself, employs all his faculties. He must use observation to see, reasoning and judgment to foresee, activity to gather materials for decision, discrimination to decide, and when he has decided, firmness and self-control to hold to his deliberate decision.[13]

The exercise of civic responsibility relies more on the moral underpinnings of voluntary compliance in democracies. The discerning exercise of freedom requires more awareness, understanding, and skill than obedience to the dictates of authority. Such virtues as respect for human dignity, acceptance of equality, tolerance, commitment to the rule of law, and vigilance against abuse of authority are more important in societies where people are relatively free to live as they choose. Responsibility relies more on intrinsic motivation in a democracy than in authoritarian states where the extrinsic motivation of threat is more pronounced.

We should bear in mind just how important the role of education is in reproducing democracy. In fact we should take this vital function of liberal education far more seriously than we do. The health of democracy flows from the commitment and empowerment of the people, not structures of government. Constitutions live by virtue of the vigilance of the citizens and their willingness to resist the willful violation and abuse of the rule of law. We must plant the seeds of freedom and cultivate the plants if we would enjoy its fruits. But we should also recognize that this purpose of education, however vital, treats students as means rather than ends in themselves.

This has practical as well as moral implications. The health and protections of democracy suffer when we allow our government to treat citizens as means. We weaken the fences on the violation of human dignity, betray the moral heart of our ideals, and cheapen our own worth by allowing our fellows to be reduced to instruments used for a purpose not their own. These ill effects are compounded when students internalize them. We are teaching the next generation of citizens that it is morally acceptable, even desirable, to treat people as instruments by systematically treating students as instruments during the years of compulsory education.

Using people to serve our own purposes means diverting them from their interests for the sake of ours; our gain comes at their cost. The dictum to treat others as ends is not necessarily violated when we persuade them to contribute to a mutually beneficial end, such as pitching in at times of need and meeting civic responsibilities. We human beings usually have mixed motives and ambiguous aims, so our true intent is not always clear. Ambiguity does not excuse willful disregard of the moral implications of our intent, though. And our concern here is not the many ways people unconsciously manipulate others, but rather the systematic manipulation of young people compelled to submit to it by the state.

We criticize totalitarian and authoritarian governments for using schools to produce loyal, obedient citizens for the good of the state — which translates to the good of the rulers. Such states also give top priority to producing workers and technicians. Democracies are not *quite* so crass in their patriotic indoctrination, but they are not so different from authoritarian states when it comes to the priority they give the economic purposes of education.

Economic concerns dominate public discussion about education in all the democracies with which I am familiar.[14] In the dominant script, national economic welfare is determined in the arena of global economic competition. National success in a global market of fluid capital, instantaneous communication, highly mobile resources, and internationally organized enterprise increasingly depends on the competitive advantages offered by the national workforce, advantages largely achieved through education.[15]

The skills, knowledge, and attitudes of workers, managers, entrepreneurs, and "symbolic analysts" are considered critical to a nation's ability to create and attract capital and jobs and thus contribute to the general welfare. Scientists and engineers are needed to accelerate technological innovation. Businesses need workers with technology-related "21st century skills," which are the main focus of much of the current debate about education reform.[16] Pushing "STEM" disciplines (science, technology, engineering, and math) is the current rage. Some propose we start moving kids in this direction in pre-kindergarten.

Most people seem to accept the assumption that harnessing education to economic ends is vital to national well-being.[17] National economic purpose thus easily translates to the primary purpose of education, which is pretty much taken as a given in public discussion and debate.[18] According to the prevailing rhetoric, job training is hands down the main point of schooling. Individual interest takes a back seat to national interest, but this purpose does not necessarily deny happiness as a general end. Rather it presumes the main path. As Nic Marks points out, "We have organized our modern societies around a particular model of how to pursue happiness. We have assumed that increasing economic output would lead straightforwardly to increases in the standard of living and thereby human happiness."[19]

It would be foolish to discount the importance of national economic concerns or decry the blindness of students who believe happiness flows from financial success. Material well-being is a necessary condition to pursuing non-material aspirations in the minds of most people. And insisting that jobs and money do not yield happiness is not very consistent with the principle of empowering students to pursue happiness as they see it. They may well have been brainwashed by the incessant propaganda of commercial interests reinforced by a materialistic culture, but this will not be undone by opposing propaganda. If they are to learn the attitudes and arts of freedom, the decision of what happiness is and how to pursue it must be left to them.

But privileging and reinforcing the economic notion of happiness is not consistent with the principle either. Freedom to choose does not mean much if one is unaware of alternative choices. To leave the economic notion of happiness effectively unchallenged by awareness of alternative notions is a serious, glaring omission if empowering the pursuit of happiness is the primary purpose of education. To consider the issue essentially decided by prevailing opinion blatantly contradicts this purpose.

It is rather apparent, though, that better preparing students for the demands of the global economy does not really aim at their individual happiness. It is primarily meant to serve the interests of businesses and politicians posing as national interests. Seriously consider the claim that giving priority to STEM disciplines in our schools is the best way to enhance students' prospects for happiness. You are unlikely to see it put so crassly, but this claim is logically implied if STEM advocates wish to avoid the onus of treating students as means rather than ends. It would be more honest to admit the obvious: the economic ends of education are not really about the higher good of the students as individuals.

The purpose of national security usually includes a strong economic dimension as well, though it has a broader scope to include components of national power that are not directly economic. The educational level and qualities of a citizenry are considered an important aspect of national power. Since it involves many dimensions of influence, those who see education as an important means of national security are interested in many types of ability, but those involved in the creation and use of technology are probably of greatest interest in those countries capable of realistically competing for power.

The potential impact of national security interests on education in America was dramatically illustrated by the profound effects of the launching of the satellite Sputnik by the Soviet Union in 1957. Fear of Soviet technological superiority led to large and sustained measures to harness education to the creation and production of sophisticated technology. Either directly or indirectly, the American government never ceased to use public education as a means to support the purposes of national security. Defense-related resources given to institutions of higher education also saw a bump after 9/11, when government funding increased interest in Homeland Security-related degrees. These resources necessarily divert the missions of the receiving institutions to some extent.

Security is essential to all aspects of both social and personal well-being, so it cannot be simply disregarded as detrimental to the purpose of liberal education. Wariness of the extent of the intrusion of national security interests into the education of the young, however, is more than wise considering the cautions of history.[20] Security concerns strongly favor the power interests of those with state authority and feed their predilection to justify the sacrifices they impose on citizens by exaggerating threats and what is required to counter them.

Other than the preference given to math and science and the funding of defense-related research in higher education, there is not a wholesale diversion of education to the ends of national security per se. But some insist this is a mistake we must remedy. An editorial in my local paper bemoaned the failure of almost a quarter of American high school graduates applying to enlist in the armed forces to achieve the minimum score for admittance. The editor claimed the data "reinforce the urgency to make military service readiness an education priority."[21] If we followed the editor's advice, we would have one more priority that treats students as means rather than ends.

A variant of the civic purpose of education is the desire to make students agents of social change. Calls for harnessing education to the cause of social progress began to sprout as early as the Enlightenment. Freeing minds from the fetters of stultifying beliefs and traditions has since grown into insistence on using education to address poverty, prejudice, inequality, oppression and all other forms of social injustice. This purpose has some merit: education played a role in the impressive social progress of the past century. But we thereby treat students as means to social ends. This is not without cost to our children's prospects for happiness or to the causes we would promote.

Truth is one of the most hallowed purposes of education. Education is considered a means to impart truth to our young and to prepare them to help advance the cause of truth in higher education. Admittedly, imparting truth to children is not so hallowed, because children are initially taught by means of metaphor-laden stories. Plato's advice to use "medicinal lies" to instill morality and character has been well-heeded through the centuries, though we moderns might choose to regard them as age-appropriate *simplifications* rather than lies. Battle lines are formed under banners of truth when students progress to higher levels of science and history, though. Truth is more a political football than a shining purpose in primary and secondary education.

But for many in higher education, true knowledge is the revered end of post-secondary scholarship. The quest for man-revealed truth has animated higher learning since at least the Enlightenment, and the members of modern academe still proudly don the robes of this tradition and pay obeisance to the cause of truth even when they are deconstructing it.

The quest for truth as an end in itself is not as hallowed as it once was. The progressive optimism of earlier eras is now considered naïve. Postmodernists spotlight the usual manipulations of power and partisan advantage below the noble veneer of authoritative verities. And philosophical doubts about the existence, attainability, and even utility of truth in an absolute sense continue to puncture the certainties and pretenses of those who worship at the altar of science. But truth still resonates in the ivory towers of higher education as the exalted purpose of scholarship and, to those who cling to Enlightenment academic tradition, the highest aim of human endeavor.

Truth as end is the core justification for academic freedom; the cause of truth requires that one be free to follow wherever the trail leads. We should never forget how important the quest for truth has been to the cause of freedom. Its appeal has helped force the retreat of the claims of religious and civil authority to our beliefs and has helped remove many chains of dogma, superstition, and prejudice from our minds. It has also led to a great abundance of socially useful knowledge, especially that which aids the development of technology. Some therefore argue it is not so much truth as end that is questioned, but rather particular notions of truth and the motives of the partisans of these notions.

However conceived, though, the pursuit of truth as end comes with a cost to other ends of education. It has freed scholarly research from limiting expectations of social utility to a considerable extent. It has justified the priority of research and scholarship over the teaching mission in many institutions of higher education. And giving truth the highest priority greatly influences what is taught and how. Any end held primary logically renders all other ends either means or diversions. To some extent, truth as end necessarily comes at the expense of empowering the pursuit of happiness as end. This reduces the humanistic value of the pursuit of truth. Daisaku Ikeda explained the view of Tsunesaburo Makiguchi, Japan's influential philosopher of education:

> *Makiguchi removed "truth" from his list of values, seeing truth as essentially a matter of identification and correspondence; value, in contrast, is a measure of the subjective impact a thing or event has on our lives. While truth identifies an object's essential qualities or properties, value may be considered the measure of the relevance or impact an object or event bears on the individual.*[22]

The effects of giving priority to truth over personal "impact" are especially evident in how the liberal arts are taught. Liberal arts disciplines, in particular the humanities, seem uniquely suited to empowering the personal pursuit of happiness. They reveal dimensions of human experience and alternative paths expressly related to that pursuit. The liberal arts offer perspectives on both external and internal human experience. They offer vistas that reveal not only otherwise unnoticed terrains of social conditions and relationships, but also the varied landscapes of human minds and hearts. They expand dimensions of awareness and imagination far beyond those readily apparent in the mundane experiences of life.

The world in which we subjectively live is the world of which we are aware, and the liberal arts expand students' awareness of the world as well as themselves and illuminate the connection between the two. Parker Palmer contends, "The single most important thing teachers can do is explicitly connect the 'big story' of the subject with the 'little story' of the student's life."[23]

The purpose of liberal education has been described as providing knowledge and understanding to help students better achieve a "meaningful and satisfying life," "human flourishing," the "immortality of wisdom," the "art of living a good life," "self realization," "joy in creative expression and knowledge," understanding the "significance of what [one] does," "consummatory appreciations," and the enhanced ability to change "the meaning of experience." "If a person's life is to be sufficient and satisfying," Philip Phenix contends, "he needs above all to enjoy intrinsically worthwhile experiences and not only instrumental preparatory ones."[24]

The liberal arts, and the humanities in particular, explore the aesthetic dimension of experience. They can enhance what Alfred North Whitehead called "aesthetic apprehension."[25] Dewey said that "aesthetic formulation reveals and enhances the meaning of experience."[26] The appreciation of profound and clever ideas and formulations, the satisfactions of intellectual problem-solving, the wonder of new vistas of beauty, the fascination of the human drama, the grip of poignant moments, all the varied fruits of mind that sweeten our affective experiences and inform our pursuit of happiness are native to liberal arts subjects.

But the affective value of the liberal arts and their contribution to informing the pursuit of happiness is eclipsed by other purposes. Affective value is rarely acknowledged as a concern. In primary and secondary education, the liberal arts and the humanities in particular are de-emphasized to the detriment of any purpose they might serve. And the priority given to reasoning skills over creative and affective expression starts early and becomes progressively dominating. Ken Robinson has a point when he says, "I think you'd have to conclude the whole purpose of public education throughout the world is to produce university professors."[27]

This is most true of higher education, of course. Aside from the professional disciplines, the modern university is devoted to scholarship and the training of scholars as an end in itself even though only a small percentage of undergraduates are destined — or desire — to become scholars.[28] Professors consider themselves scholars; their degrees require scholarship and many are rewarded more for scholarship than any other aspect of their profession, including teaching. Most emphasize scholarship and its skills in their courses, passing on the values of their profession in the conviction that this is what higher education is for. Truth and the expansion of knowledge for their own sakes are preeminent aims even within liberal arts disciplines.

These aims determine not only what is taught, but how. Palmer intimates the problem:

> As is true of any subject, how we teach the humanities is as important as that we teach them, and the humanities are no freer from the cult of expertise than the sciences are. Too many students learn about Socrates' dialogical method by hearing someone lecture about it instead of participating in it. Too many students study a great poem or novel through the lens of critical opinion instead of a personal engagement with the text. And too

*many students learn about the arts by studying famous artifacts instead of
making art.*[29]

The personal interests of educators — teachers and administrators —
are usually not explicit among the acknowledged ends of education, but these
interests sometimes overshadow all other ends put together. Considerations
of career, money, job security, prerogative, work load, power, and convenience
are sometimes given priority over the interests of students. Of course, deni-
als and rationalizations are ready to hand, as they always are when perceived
personal interests are at stake. But anyone familiar with what actually goes
on in our schools knows of what I speak. My point is that educators have
jobs because communities pay them to educate their children. When educators serve themselves at the expense of the children entrusted to their care,
educators are using kids rather than serving them.

All the foregoing purposes of education are causes championed by interest groups. Partisan wrangling over curricula, method, books, and media
are part of the landscape of democratic education. Matthew Lipman observes, "The school is a battleground because it, more than any other social
institution, is the manufacturer of the society of the future, and virtually
every social group or faction therefore aspires to control the school for its
own ends."[30] The personal interests of the students are obscured by these
ends, and they suffer for lack of priority.

Happiness is the universal primary end of citizens; therefore the democratic state is obliged to serve this end first and foremost. Both the moral
principle of intrinsic human worth and the democratic principle that the
state exists to serve the people demand this. No public institution should be
exempt from this expectation, least of all the institution entrusted with the
education of our children.

If we are concerned about the lessons of morality we impart to our children, we should remember what we do has greater impact than what we say.
To assume children are not sophisticated enough to know when they are being used for the sake of something other than their own is risky. In all likeli-
hood, they absorb the lesson that it is okay to treat people as means during
the thousands of hours they are treated as means in our schools. By word
and deed, we as educators and we as participating citizens unwittingly lay a
morally weak foundation for the superstructure of values we mean to teach.

More than this, when we allow schools to treat our children as means in our name and with our blessing and participation, we lose our own moral bearing, fail to respect the precepts and ideals of liberal democracy, establish a precedent for the wielders of state authority to extend the practice to a widening circle of citizens, and fall short of the promise of liberal education to liberate the full potential of our children.

Mill said, "Human nature is not a machine to be built after a model, and set to do exactly the work prescribed for it, but a tree, which requires to grow and develop itself on all sides, according to the tendency of the inward forces which make a living thing."[31] One does not promote the health of a forest by stunting the growth of the individual trees that comprise it. We do not promote the health of society by neglecting the "inward forces" that drive our children's pursuit of happiness. We not only betray the most vital interest of our children's hearts when we slight their personal empowerment in favor of molding them to be instruments of interest groups; we also betray the higher interests of society.

On the other hand, if we dedicated education to empowering students' personal pursuit of happiness, we would teach them that serving others is common and desirable for its own sake. This is a much firmer foundation for interesting students in the welfare of others. I believe it would benefit hosts of possible angels for generations to come.

I might bring the argument closer to home to parents of children in school and argue that their children are among those whose personal interests are slighted to benefit the social and private agendas of others. To sell their happiness short is to fail the deep obligation most of us feel to the dependent beings we introduced to this world.

We also have a personal stake in this beyond the benefit of our children. How we see and treat others affects not only how we feel about ourselves, but how we feel, period. We pay an affective price when we use others for our own ends. We reap an affective reward when we serve the happiness of others. If we work to ensure that the education of our society's youth is dedicated to the central, enduring pursuit of their lives, we will not have to wait for such rewards, for they are the natural effects of our intent.

I am inclined to believe most educators care deeply about the fate of their charges, but they are diverted and distracted by confusion of purpose. The hearts of those involved in educating the possible angels in our schools are not the problem; the problem is the devaluation of their hearts through the external focus of the contemporary aims and methods of education. Parker Palmer puts it this way:

> How can we who teach reclaim our hearts, for the sake of our students, ourselves, and educational reform? That simple question challenges the assumption that drives most reform — that meaningful change comes not from the human heart but from factors external to ourselves, from budgets, methodologies, curricula, and institutional restructuring. Deeper still, it challenges the assumptions about reality and power that drive Western culture.[32]

If we sincerely care about the difference we make in our children's lives, we must embrace a purpose of education aligned with the purpose of their hearts. I believe we would discover that in so doing we would better serve our own hearts as well.

Clarity of Purpose

This book exists due to my deep conviction that empowering the pursuit of happiness in schools would profoundly benefit students throughout their lives and would prove socially transformative. I am also convinced that a well-developed pedagogy of happiness would invigorate teaching and learning in general to the benefit of all worthy aims of education.

Clarity of purpose promises considerable advantages in itself. Clear purpose focuses, coordinates, and informs shared enterprise. Purpose defines the meaning and nature of the enterprise and helps all participants understand their role in it. Purpose provides the end by which to judge the rational choice of means, and establishes the measure of progress. Since we assign value — one sense of meaning — to aspects of experience according to how well they align with what we want, clarity of purpose brings greater clarity of meaning. A clear purpose of education aligned with students' highest interest would make their education more transparently and richly meaningful to them.

In an age of bewildering complexity, clarity of purpose offers a guiding light through the thicket of clamoring, competing agendas. And a purpose that aims at the highest good of each and all would inspire the energy and commitment of a higher calling. People are willing to forego personal gain for the sake of a greater good they believe in. This is no small advantage in confronting the many agendas that diminish the education of our children.

One might assume that with all the concern, effort, and resources that go into education, we would have long ago put forth the effort to reach general agreement about the main point of the undertaking. Whatever effort was made has so far failed. Partisans of various agendas fiercely contend to influence what is taught in our schools. But I am not sure this is the main problem. The muddled confusion due to embracing many ends with little or shifting priority among them that prevails in most schools may have more to do with human nature than the pressure to find compromise between contending agendas.

I say this because the desired outcomes of education are constantly deliberated in schools, by boards, and in departments of education. But almost invariably the result is a bulleted list of goals presented as ends in themselves. It takes only a little reflection to realize the skills and subject knowledge that populate these lists are not really ends. The value of these attainments lies in what they contribute to the satisfaction of human desires summarized in the concept of happiness. The bulleted goals are means to this end. This pervasive confusion of ends and means has serious consequences. One cannot rationally choose means and determine their relative priority without reference to a final purpose. Yet this is what routinely occurs. This is not a problem of conflicting agendas; this is a basic failure of human rationality. I call it a *philosophical* failure.

The fact that we are constantly striving to define and improve the outcomes of education shows people are not satisfied with the status quo. Educators, parents, and politicians mostly agree we can and should do better. But if all the effort to improve education is worth it, then achieving greater clarity and consensus about the meaning of "better" is worth it as well. As Diane Ravitch points out, "If we want to improve education, we must first of all have a vision of what good education is."[33]

Is the purpose of empowering students' pursuit of happiness clear enough to guide our efforts, practical enough to make a meaningful difference, and appealing enough to achieve the near-consensus necessary to adopt it as a guiding principle of public education? The chapters ahead make the case for answering yes to the first two questions. As for consensus, empowering the pursuit of happiness is at the heart of the aims and ideals of liberal democracy. The vast majority of Americans and citizens of other democracies embrace these aims and ideals. I also believe that the argument that empowering students' happiness is the only purpose of education that expressly treats our children as ends in themselves will resonate with many people, especially with parents.

A change in purpose brings a change in perspective. What was deemed important may become less so; what was valued less or ignored may loom larger. But to gain the benefit of a new perspective, one must climb above the obscuring clouds of multiple primary purposes. One must forego seeing school missions in terms of bulleted lists of discrete means masquerading as aims with no particular priority. Empowering the pursuit of happiness can simply be added as the bottom line to existing mission statements and provide as little guidance as the other vague generalities and platitudes that inhabit such statements.

To avoid this, educators must recognize that empowering the pursuit of happiness calls for major, concrete changes. It establishes happiness — the ability to feel as one chooses — as the end and therefore the guide to choosing the means of education. It defines the most desirable outcome and requires adjusting the measures of students' progress. Students should be clear about happiness as the end and should be invited to ponder and explore happiness and develop the relevant skills throughout the years of formal education. Since the right and ability to pursue happiness as one understands it is the practical meaning of freedom, educators should strive to broaden students' awareness of different perspectives, of different answers to the questions of happiness.

Education can impart the knowledge, develop the skills, and deepen the understanding best suited to choosing a path to happiness and progressing along it. Social needs must be addressed, but the means should be as consistent as possible with the end of empowering the pursuit of happiness.

A clearer, more meaningful purpose of education will serve the higher interests of students and society. It will also make the job of educators more meaningful and rewarding. We all stand to gain when schools embrace the true democratic and moral purpose of liberal education.

3

The Nature
Of Happiness

*Happiness is the feeling you're feeling when you
want to keep feeling it.* | Anonymous

My students readily accept Aristotle's observation that happiness is the only human end sufficient unto itself. They agree with the Enlightenment postulate that the happiness of citizens is the end of government. They seem to enjoy debating answers to the question "What is happiness?" Only rarely does a student directly answer the question, though. Rather they talk about sources of happiness: relationships, achievements, careers, money, sunny locales, lifestyles, etc. Some throw in ideals like freedom and justice because I ask the question in political philosophy courses. But then I ask "What does happiness *feel* like?" Perplexity.

I don't blame them. They had never been asked the question before. At first blush, it might seem like a trick question with no particular answer. People prefer different feelings at different times, and preferences differ from person to person. Many people likely agree with the response to a *New York Times* column on the subject of happiness: "The assumption that any one way of being, feeling or living is a path to happiness or fulfillment for us all is beyond ridiculous."[1]

Feelings are also difficult to describe. We have to use words for other feelings to try to describe a particular feeling. What does love feel like? Joy, longing, appreciation, fondness, expansion, completion, and neediness are some words we might use, but each comes with the same definitional problem. We do not directly experience anyone else's feelings. We can only draw the meaning of a word for a feeling from the well of our own experiences. We cannot be sure anyone else experiences what we consider sadness and joy the way we do. Facial expressions and behavior are clues, but a frown or a smile is an *expression* of a feeling, not the experience itself. For these reasons and more, there may not seem to be much point in asking what happiness feels like.

But there is. Each of us implies an answer with each step we take in our pursuit of a desired feeling. The answer may be unconscious, ambiguous, contradictory, and unwise, but you must have at least a vague idea of what you prefer to feel in order to choose a direction and a path. The question of what happiness feels like may not have a general answer, but asking it can shine the light of awareness and bring considered reflection to bear on the central pursuit of your life. It begs consideration of the attributes of different feelings, which allows you to compare their merits. Clarity about what you prefer to feel makes your pursuit of happiness less blind and increases your chances for success.

Educators do not have to be experts on the attributes of feelings to engage students in an investigation of them. Teachers will have to organize and guide the investigation, of course. They will need a basic background in the psychology, biology, and philosophy of feelings. And at least some educators will have to know how to guide students in the art of inner observation. Learning how to pay attention to feelings is essential to recognizing and comparing their merits. It is also essential to getting a handle on what causes particular feelings.

Talk about the attributes of feelings no doubt seems nebulous, but this chapter will make it clearer. I explain what I mean by the *nature* of happiness in this chapter, which involves an exploration of the basic attributes of feelings commonly associated with happiness. I present a model of a philosophical exploration of the nature of happiness and identify some candidates for "most desirable" feelings that point the way to the higher reaches of happiness.

Basic Psychology and Biology of Feelings

The belief that feelings are for the most part beyond our conscious control is based on the assumption that our feelings are automatic responses to external circumstances and events. This is not the case. Feelings in the sense of emotions — feelings that *move* us to feel differently — are responses to our judgments, whether conscious or unconscious. Perception involves the filtering, sorting, and interpretation of the information delivered by our senses. Perception also includes awareness of internal states that are subject to filtering, sorting, and interpretation. The judgments embedded in our thoughts give rise to emotions.

Sigmund Freud had it the other way around, contending that emotion causes thought. Modern cognitive psychology recognizes that thought gives rise to emotion, but what we feel colors what we think, so there is a feedback loop of reinforcing cause and effect between thought and emotion.[2] Jonathan Haidt explains it this way: "Thoughts can cause emotions ... but emotions can also cause thoughts, primarily by raising mental filters that bias subsequent information processing."[3] The matter of causality is important because it is easier to consciously change what you think than simply will yourself to feel differently.

Perception is very selective when it comes to information allowed to reach our conscious awareness. According to the noted research psychologist Mihaly Csikszentmihalyi, "While everything we feel, smell, hear, or remember is potentially a candidate for entering consciousness, the experiences that actually do become part of it are far fewer than those left out. Thus, while consciousness is a mirror that reflects what our senses tell us about what happens both outside our bodies and within the nervous system, it reflects those changes selectively, actively shaping events, imposing on them a reality of its own."[4] In a sense, says Robert Holden, "perception is projection."[5] Kant observed that "We see things not as they are, but as we are."[6]

To repeat, the interpretation or judgment of what we perceive largely determines what we feel. Thus changing beliefs, thoughts, and attitudes that shape our judgments is a means to influence what we feel. We also have some control over the information that reaches our consciousness through the focus of *attention*. Attention determines, amplifies, and orders the information we consider currently important. *Intention*, or will, is the standard by which we judge perceptions: what we feel about an aspect of a current experience is based on whether we think it enhances, hinders, or threatens our prospects of realizing what we intend. Seeing it start to rain when you intend to go for a walk colors your feelings about the rain. Intention, of course, is basically synonymous with purpose.

The unattended, and therefore subconscious, memories and patterns of response that reside in our minds influence our feelings as well. To the degree that we can bring such influences into the light of consciousness and "reprogram" patterns of response, we can reduce their unwelcome effects on our feelings. It helps to pay attention to the physical sensations of the body, because the presence or lack of tension in the body is a more reliable barometer of the relative desirability of feelings than mental judgments. Tension in the torso or neck indicates something is bothering you whether or not you are aware of feeling bothered.

Strong emotional responses like sudden fear and anger trigger biochemical responses that course through the body for about ninety seconds.[7] Such responses are stored as "patterns" that are automatically triggered in similar circumstances, patterns that are difficult to override unless they are superseded by subsequent experiences or consciously examined and neutralized.[8] A neurotransmitter called dopamine is associated with pleasant feelings. Perceptions and thoughts interpreted as highly positive trigger the release of dopamine.[9] Repeated experiences of pleasant feelings build virtuous patterns, literally in the form of neuronal circuits. What we think can engage a particular circuit, which triggers an associated emotional response.

Jill Bolte Taylor, a respected brain scientist at Harvard, says: "The more conscious attention we pay to any particular circuit, or the more time we spend thinking specific thoughts, the more impetus those circuits or thought patterns have to run again with minimal external stimulation."[10] These circuits tend to dominate the "cellular gossip" that informs our experience of self.[11] They can therefore largely determine the quality of our feelings.

All but a fraction of the processes of the brain are unconscious and at least semi-independent of conscious control.[12] Haidt uses the metaphor of the rider of an elephant: the rider is the more rational, controlled aspect of consciousness we might call the will, while the elephant "includes the gut feelings, visceral reactions, emotions, and intuitions that comprise much of the automatic system."[13] The elephant is not easily controlled, and often ignores or rebels against the decisions of the will. "The rider can't just decide to change and then order the elephant to go along with the program. Lasting change can come only by retraining the elephant, and that's hard to do."[14]

A body of evidence based on the study of identical twins suggests that happiness is in large part — 50 percent according to one summary of studies — determined by inherited personality traits, by the "cortical (from cortex) lottery" of genetic endowment.[15] In other words, one is born with a basically unchangeable "affective style" or "set-point" of happiness. This genetic determinism was once broadly acknowledged in the relatively recent field of positive psychology, though it is now subject to reasonable doubt.[16]

The theory says a person with a low baseline of happiness can become generally happier; they just can't aspire to the level of happiness someone with a much higher baseline can achieve. Sonja Lyubomirsky, a veteran researcher in the field of positive psychology, contends that about 40 percent of our level of happiness, which comprises our "potential for increased lasting happiness," lies within our power to change.[17] Like most researchers and practitioners in the field, she holds that conscious changes in how we view and think about things can change the embedded patterns of thought that suppress our experience of happiness.

The focused attention of meditation and prayer can change the very structure of the brain.[18] Yongey Mingyur explains that "through retraining, the brain can develop new neuronal connections, through which it becomes possible not only to transform existing perceptions but also to move beyond ordinary mental conditions of anxiety, helplessness, and pain and toward a lasting experience of happiness and peace."[19]

In the materialist perspective of reality, which holds that only uncreated matter and energy exist — no God or spirit — the capacities, limits, and processes of the brain set the rules for what we can and cannot hope to achieve in our pursuit of happiness. Csikszentmihalyi maintains, "the primary reason it is so difficult to achieve happiness centers on the fact that, contrary to the myths mankind has developed to reassure itself, the universe was not created to answer our needs."[20] Yet he also notes that "over the endless dark centuries of its evolution, the human nervous system has become so complex that it is now able to affect its own states, making it to a certain extent functionally independent of its genetic blueprint and of the objective environment."[21]

The materialist perspective does not deny hope of attaining a higher level of happiness, but it insists our consciousness is chained to the limits and vulnerabilities of our bodies. This dims the prospect of sustaining happiness and sets a certain end to it. Religious beliefs mostly deny these limitations. Ultimate happiness has a divine source unencumbered by physical limitations in most religious perspectives.

Perhaps lasting happiness awaits us in heaven, but here on earth most of us spend far more time pursuing than experiencing a feeling beyond further desire, the motive force that seems to propel our lives. Clarity about the basic attributes of happiness begins with clarity about the attributes of desire and its satisfactions.

Desire and Satisfaction

Desire is essentially synonymous with *want*. Both words imply dissatisfaction with what we are currently experiencing. As I said earlier, whatever the immediate object of our desire, it is the feeling we expect from fulfilling the desire — what we generally call the *satisfaction* of desire — that we seek. The subjective value of any object of desire lies in its presumed power to cause the satisfaction we hope to experience.

We can identify different types of desires and satisfactions. Though a desire does not have the compulsory nature implied in the word "need," Abraham Maslow's hierarchy of needs offers a rough categorization of desires: those associated with meeting biological and physiological needs, those associated with security needs and preferences, our longings for bonding and belonging, the related desire for the esteem of others, and the yearning for "self-actualization" — the achievement of one's full potential.[22] An adaptation of Maslow's hierarchy includes cognitive and aesthetic needs as well as a "transcendence-of-self" need that moves us to help others achieve self-actualization.[23]

Maslow's hierarchy suggests that emotional needs are not equal; those near the top are qualitatively different from those at the base in terms of depth, degree, and duration of their satisfactions. The achievement of one's full potential is thought to be more deeply and lastingly satisfying than the sating of lust and hunger, for example. Types of emotional needs imply types of perceived *lack*. Seeing desire in terms of perceived lack invites the question of whether desires have an irreducible variety of causes or have a common source.

The answer to this question is crucial to understanding the nature of happiness. It would, for example, shed light on the relative desirability of different types of feelings. Are the satisfactions of different types of desire more or less equal in terms of the quality of experience? Or are some deeper and more lasting because they more effectively address the core perception of lack at the heart of all desires? The answer would help resolve the issue of whether happiness is mostly a function of quantity — the relative frequency of pleasures or the "ratio of satisfied desires to desire"[24] — or of quality — the relative desirability of satisfactions.

Desire, as was said, implies a lack of some sort, a dissatisfaction with current experience. In this sense, desire is a kind of discomfort, a tension that calls for resolution, which logically places it in the pain section of the pleasure-pain spectrum. The satisfaction of a desire has a symbiotic relationship with the preceding "pain" of desire. For example, the satisfaction of hunger requires hunger, the satisfaction of lust requires lust, the satisfaction of acquiring a possession requires a preceding dissatisfaction with the lack of possession, the satisfaction of comfort requires discomfort to precede it.

Such satisfactions cannot be sustained; they require the contrast of desire to be re-experienced. Without this contrast, they are subject to "habituation."[25] The initial satisfaction recedes as the desire that moves you to seek it fades from awareness. The pleasure of sated hunger or lust requires renewed hunger and lust to be experienced again. When you become accustomed to possessing an item, the initial satisfaction of acquiring it diminishes. When you are comfortable, the easing of discomfort is no longer an available pleasure. If you always feel secure, the relief of safety fades from your mind.

Such satisfactions must be "re-stimulated" by the perception or fear of their lack. The initial sense of pleasure is also pushed from consciousness as other matters and concerns, and sometimes memories of comparatively preferable feelings that spark new desires, intrude. This symbiotic relationship between desire and its satisfaction may be among the reasons for the "inexorable" alternation of pleasure and pain. Nisargadatta Maharaj goes further:

"Moments of pleasure are merely gaps in the stream of pain."[26]

Desirable feelings are not necessarily the satisfaction of a conscious desire. We experience unexpected pleasures. Sharing a laugh, getting a compliment, awareness of the beauty of a sunset or a person, hearing a song that recalls pleasant feelings, etc., do not necessarily require active desire to be appreciated. But my focus here is the relationship between desires and their satisfactions. They are the core motives for the steps people take in the pursuit of happiness. And unexpected pleasures do not escape the effects of desiring when the mind returns to its usual preoccupations.

Perversely, satisfactions can be *sources* of pain. In the words of a song by the Indigo Girls, "every pleasure exacts its pain."[27] Even if we could arbitrarily extend the duration of a particular satisfaction, we might not want to. If you closely observed the feeling of a momentary satisfaction, you might find it contaminated with the underlying tension from worrying about what comes after or with lingering concerns about other matters. Disappointment occurs when a satisfaction does not live up to expectation. Even while experiencing them, our minds tend to sabotage our pleasures.

In other words, experiences of satisfaction often contain elements of dissatisfaction. They contain the seeds of their own destruction. Also, having scratched the itch of desire, it may return stronger and less easily satisfied. Pleasure can lead to addiction, experienced as compulsions that nag and itch and diminish our enjoyments. Desire is attachment to what is desired, and attachment bears a cost. Mingyur relates that "The Buddha compared attachment to drinking salt water from an ocean. The more we drink, the thirstier we get."[28] Repeating behaviors that always cost more than you ever get out of them qualifies as irrational.

Such irrationality is often blamed on the artificial concept of self called the ego. The ego is a variable concept of self, a concept that includes "a repertoire of self-images."[29] These images are ever-changing. David Hume describes the difficulty in trying to discover a sense of self beyond ever-changing perceptions: "For my part, when I enter most intimately into what I call myself, I always stumble on some particular perception or other, of heat or cold, light or shade, love or hatred, pain or pleasure. I never can catch myself at any time without a perception, and never can observe any thing but the perception."[30]

The inherently unstable ego images of self cause fear. An unstable sense of self brings insecurity of self worth. A feeling of insufficiency of self worth is the motivational core of ego. This perceived insufficiency constantly drives us to try to bolster our sense of worth with evidence of our superiority over others or of their positive regard for us. Should we temporarily succeed — for example, winning a competition or getting a compliment — the reward is a relatively pleasurable feeling known as an ego gratification. That is, it is pleasurable compared to the pangs of self-doubt.

The emotional hunger for external validation of worth cannot be sated for long. As with the satisfactions of desire that require desire to be satisfying, ego gratifications require perceived insufficiency of self worth to be gratifying. External validation of worth would not be gratifying if you felt no need for it. Every ego gratification is haunted by the certainty that the barbs of self-doubt will return. Unfortunately for our happiness, every satisfaction in which the ego plays a role — and it is seldom completely absent — is contaminated by the fear inherent to its nature.

Not all highly desirable feelings require the perception of lack to be experienced. And some may even be immune to habituation. Unfortunately, most of the satisfactions that glitter in people's eyes are not among them. In order to make the case for the "higher" feelings, I need to unravel some of the complexity of human motive.

Hedonic Pleasures

In one sense, "hedonic pleasures" is redundant, because the word *hedonic* refers to pleasure in general. But I use the phrase here in a narrower sense to identify a rough category of desired feelings. The carnal satisfaction of lust, the enjoyment of food, and other stimulations and comforts of the body are always among the pleasures considered hedonic. The pleasure of sensory stimulation is only partly *carnal*, though, for imagination often plays a bigger role than the senses. Emotional "stimulations" thought to be pleasurable are also usually included in the hedonic category. My main criterion for calling a pleasure hedonic is that it is relatively short-lived and for the most part requires external stimulation of some sort.

Epicurus favored hedonic pleasures, seeing little to be gained from fighting our natural desire for them when nature would but lead us to the "goal of a happy life."[31] His is a minority opinion in the pages of philosophy, but many still defend hedonic pleasure as an innately desirable experience. "In truth, positive emotion is positive emotion" says Lyubomirsky.[32] Wayne Davis maintained that hedonic pleasures and the satisfactions thought more worthy of happiness "refer to the same mental state" in the moment they are experienced.[33]

But hedonic pleasures are not generally held in high esteem. They are considered "evanescent," shallow, without lasting benefit, and "subject to satiety and disgust."[34] They may be the most short-lived of satisfactions, the least satisfying, and the most prone to addiction as they require new stimulative "fixes" to be recalled into experience. Since they "do not build anything for the future," they are also thought to be the least productive in terms of inviting and reinforcing deeper and more lasting satisfactions.[35]

The stimulated pleasures share an attribute: they become increasingly unpleasant the longer they are indulged. Chocolate is delightful at first, but if you were forced to keep eating it for hours, the initial pleasure would turn into pain, both physical and mental. The same is true of sex, physical thrills, and even massages. This applies to all physically stimulated pleasures. They not only habituate, they become painful if you don't take a break from them.

Anything a person enjoys can become psychologically addictive, but hedonic pleasures are most apt to exact a directly physical price. This is obvious with drugs and alcohol. Intense pleasures release dopamine, which in a sense is another form of drug addiction. In fact, drugs such as heroin and cocaine raise dopamine levels, so dopamine-induced euphoria is the actual cause of addiction.[36] Every physically stimulated high comes with the price of a low, partly because the body tries to defend its equilibrium by counteracting the artificial stimulation.[37] The health of the body requires moderation in a person's physical stimulations. In this sense, the pleasures of the body are physically as well as psychologically limited.

On the plus side, hedonic pleasures may be more readily available and more obviously pleasurable while one experiences them. They can be considered the spice of life so long as a person avoids the temptation to over-spice. And most everything people do to entertain themselves aims for short-lived stimulated pleasures that fall within the general category of hedonic pleasures. So long as they last, they must seem worth the effort, because people spend most of their free time engaged in one diversion or another. These include almost all of our daily entertainments — social interaction, competitive challenges, puzzle-solving, projects and hobbies, sports and other physical activities, reading, watching television or movies, playing video games, listening to music, dancing, cooking, and even shopping.

Different activities no doubt bring different pleasures, but they have some motives in common. The most obvious is that we are uncomfortable with our undiverted state of mind. *Boredom* is the word we commonly use to describe this discomfort. But what causes boredom? One theory holds that we fear the unbidden thoughts that arise when our minds are not focused on something. Or perhaps a feeling of existential loneliness begins to grip us when it is not held at bay with diversion. Whatever the cause, this fear is experienced as the restlessness of boredom that demands relief.

Entertainments such as hobbies and puzzle-solving mainly aim to engage our minds. Most entertainments involve stimulating our emotions in some way. The desire to stimulate emotions is a prime motive for playing games, watching sports and movies, reading, and seeking social interaction like hanging out with friends or going to parties. The diversion theory might explain this desire to stimulate emotions. Emotion is a handy and effective distraction. It may also be that the emotions are deemed pleasurable in themselves, which would be sufficient reason to stimulate them. But this does not explain why we want to stimulate *unpleasant* feelings.

At times we want a dose of sadness, or why else would we willingly choose to hear sad stories and songs or watch tear-jerking movies? Hollywood grew wealthy from people's apparent desire to conjure feelings of fear, sadness, and anger. But this is just a modern reflection of the stories told around the campfire and the communal singing that served the same purpose long before the history of our species began to be recorded.

A number of theories try to explain the seemingly universal desire to experience relatively unpleasant feelings. The simplest is the contrast theory: we cannot know pleasure without the contrasting pain of desire. Paul Bloom says some scholars hew to a *catharsis* theory to explain why we "get such delight from unpleasantness": "negative experiences build up, and ultimately bust out, leaving us feeling sated and purified."[38] People obviously seek tension in order to feel the pleasure of release. In order to reach the release of "happy ever after," our stories must build the tensions of challenges, troubles, and anger at evildoers.

The tension-release theory might also explain our attraction to demanding projects and challenges. It feels good when the tension that drives us to complete projects and overcome challenges dissolves with completion or resolution. A related catharsis theory maintains that unpleasant feelings are not so much desired in and of themselves, but are rather necessary precursors to the pleasure of releasing them.

Perhaps, as Eckhart Tolle says, our pursuit of unpleasant feelings has to do with an aspect of the ego that feeds on negative emotions. This has some plausibility to my mind because it offers an explanation for the self-destructive behavior of people. It might explain why some choose to live in a constant state of drama of mostly their own making. Drama creates plenty of food for their egos if Tolle is right.

The diversion-from-fear and ego theories suggest negative motives for our entertainments. We either seek entertainment because we would feel worse if we did not, or we are victims of our ego's perverse attraction to pain. The tension-release and catharsis theories say we are motivated by the reward of relief when we release the tension of our engagement. Other than relief from boredom and tension, these theories say little about the positive qualities of the pleasures themselves. But it would deny the meaning of "pleasure" if it did not feel good while experiencing it. We can reasonably suspect that people are attracted to the attributes of the feelings themselves.

The attributes of hedonic pleasures vary according to their sources, of course. The relaxed feeling you get from a massage is not the same as what you feel when your team wins a game, or when empathizing with characters in a book or movie, or when you hang out with friends. Some pleasures involve tension. When I read or hear descriptions of what people consider moments of joy, I often hear words of energized tension: thrilled, excited, charged, pumped, overjoyed, elated, exhilarated. Such words bring to mind, and seem to exhibit in the stretched faces and expressive body movements of people experiencing them, a state of physical tension.

The words for energized joy describe moments of peak pleasure, so some sorts of tension must feel good. Perhaps tension contributes to the intensity and "aliveness" of an affective experience.

Some pleasures involve relaxation of body and mind. Fishing, going for walks in nature, banter with friends, and listening to soothing music are desired for their lack of tension. Most people seem to like to alternate emotional stimulation and relaxation. Many philosophers considered states of energized, tension-laden joy as diversions from the far more desirable state of peace of mind. Tension and peace are mutually exclusive.

I find parsing the attributes of pleasures difficult because it seems that most of our pursuits have mixed motives and yield mixed feelings. Consider, for example, entertainments of a social nature. People enjoy interacting with friends and acquaintances, sharing stories, repartee, laughs. Some seek to gratify their egos when they try to win arguments and brag about accomplishments. But interaction also offers the pleasures of emotional and mental stimulation, the release of mirth, the joy of appreciation, and perhaps the deeper pleasure of extension of self through sharing. If we could identify some general attributes of these different types of feelings, we could more easily separate the gold from the fool's gold.

Tension and relaxation are felt in the body as well as the mind, but some physical reactions are too subtle to detect without training. When I try to observe the attributes of what I'm feeling, I pay attention to the psychological dimensions of the experience. It seems to me that some feelings are comparatively "lighter" and some "darker." Some feelings seem to psychologically "weigh" more than others in the sense that they are more compulsive and burdensome. Light and easy feelings seem more elusive, flitting in and out of awareness and difficult or impossible to capture with a line of thought or focused intent. Some feelings seem more expansive in the sense of being more open and accepting of circumstances and environment. Negative feelings about someone or something contract my focus and accentuate my separation from others and all other aspects of my environment.

I much prefer the relaxed, lighter, more open and accepting feelings. They are closer to the peaceful joy I have come to appreciate more than any other feeling. Upon reflection, I find my ego involved in one way or another in the darker, heavier, and more contractive feelings. Deep introspection reveals that the latter involve a compulsion to protect or enhance my sense of relative worth. The former arise when I am relatively free from such compulsion.

These are my preferences and, judging by their pursuits, many people do not share them. Yet my preferences are in keeping with what I believe people would want to keep feeling if they could ever experience them uncontaminated by ego emotions. Though it is but one notion of many for what constitutes the feeling of happiness, I present the case for peace and the joy of love.

Flow, Reverie and Peace of Mind

In decades of research into what people consider an "optimal experience," Csikszentmihalyi discovered a state he calls flow.[39] It is akin to what is called "being in the zone." Flow occurs when a person is focused on a meaningful task that engages and challenges his or her talents and abilities. In the state of flow, "one acts with a deep but effortless involvement that removes from awareness the worries and frustrations of everyday life."[40] Further, "concern for self disappears" and "the sense of the duration of time is altered; hours pass by in minutes, and minutes can stretch out to seem like hours."[41]

Csikszentmihalyi quotes a dancer describing her experience of flow: "A strong relaxation and calmness comes over me, I have no worries of failure. What a powerful and warm feeling it is! I want to expand, to hug the world."[42]

The state of flow seems to involve "a loss of consciousness of self," that may entail an extension of consciousness beyond the narrow confines of self as body: "When a person invests all her psychic energy into an interaction — whether it is with another person, a boat, a mountain, or a piece of music — she in effect becomes part of a system of action greater than what the individual self had been before."[43] This state of untroubled awareness yields "a sense of deep enjoyment that is so rewarding people feel that expending a great deal of energy is worthwhile simply to be able to feel it."[44] This state may be energized in the sense of intense present awareness, but it entails a relative absence of tension.

The attributes of Csikszentmihalyi's state of flow can be experienced without the focused engagement he recommends. They can be found in the more disengaged state of reverie as well.

During a period of respite from being harried from place to place due to his heretical writings, Jean-Jacques Rousseau found solace in the reveries of walking alone in the woods and lying in his boat adrift on Lake Bienne in Switzerland. In these reveries he found what he believed to be the key to happiness:

> ...if there is a state where the soul can find a resting-place secure enough to establish itself and concentrate its entire being there, with no need to remember the past or reach into the future, where time is nothing to it, where the

present runs on indefinitely but this duration goes unnoticed, with no sign of the passing of time, and no other feeling of deprivation or enjoyment, pleasure or pain, desire or fear than the simple feeling of existence, a feeling that fills our soul entirely, as long as this state lasts, we can call ourselves happy, not with a poor, incomplete and relative happiness such as we find in the pleasures of life, but with a sufficient, complete and perfect happiness which leaves no emptiness to be filled in the soul. ... The feeling of existence unmixed with any other emotion is in itself a precious feeling of peace and contentment which would be enough to make this mode of being loved and cherished by anyone who could guard against all the earthly and sensual influences that are constantly distracting us from it in this life and troubling the joy it could give us.[45]

Note the similarities with the state of reverie Rousseau describes and the state of flow: the loss of consciousness of self but the focused awareness of "existence" or "Being" as Tolle calls it; the lack of awareness of time; the absence of thoughts of lack, threat, and insufficiency.

People seek reverie in a number of ways. Robert Solomon says "music takes us out of ourselves. It allows us to escape from our worries and desires. ... It transports us to a larger universe and forges a community with our fellow listeners."[46] We also find pause in daydreaming and "spacing out." We sometimes lose ourselves in repetitive tasks, something akin to the flow experience in the fading of self-consciousness, awareness of time, and worry. We pause for a moment of peace and appreciative wonder at meaningful beauty — sunrises and sunsets, peaceful vistas of trees and meadows, flowers and art — and at sights and sounds that gently strum our heartstrings — warm smiles, gestures of affection, laughter.

A similar state, different only in depth, is the goal of formal meditation. The abeyance of worries, distractions, and ego in a thoughtless presence in the now points to a state of mind where we are "self-sufficient like God" in the words of Rousseau. An extended experience of feeling "self-sufficient like God" would certainly qualify as a feeling I would wish to keep feeling.

Peace of mind is the holy grail of many who are considered wise. It implies the absence of fear, guilt, anger, conflict, insufficiency, and desire. Peace implies the absence of emotions that move us to seek a preferable feeling; some believe it entails the absence of *all* feelings. Perhaps an enduring state of peace without the contrast of its lack would cease to be experienced as pleasing and simply constitute an uncaring state of robotic awareness.

I have read that peace is the negation of life, that the desire for peace is the desire for an early death. This is denied by Buddhists and others who claim to have experienced a deep sense of peace. Mingyur relates the insight of centuries of Buddhist experience in explaining that in the blissful experience of a peaceful, open mind "everything you see is made of love."[47] Tolle speaks of the "joy of Being" found in the experience of deep peace. He maintains that "love, joy, and peace are deep states of Being or rather three aspects of the state of inner connectedness with Being. As such, they have no opposite."[48]

Jill Bolte Taylor, the brain scientist who experienced a stroke in the left hemisphere of her brain, relates that "my stroke of insight is that at the core of my right hemisphere consciousness is a character that is directly connected to my feeling of deep inner peace. It is completely committed to the expression of peace, love, joy, and compassion in the world."[49] It may be that deep peace is an inseparable aspect of pure love and joy. If so, it is hardly a state devoid of feeling and a denial of life. Rather it is plausibly an essential condition of the most fulfilling affective experience of life.

Love

Love is widely considered the most desired experience, the most fulfilling feeling. Yet it is the *yearning* for love that compels us to seek it, a yearning that springs from the perception of love denied. We can see this most clearly in the transparent hunger of children, but the yearning for love may be behind all the veils we adults have learned to draw across it.

I have long wondered if in the pursuit of wealth lies the hidden hope of possessing love, whether the pursuit of fame and prestige arises from the hope of inspiring love, if the pursuit of power is a subconscious attempt to compel love. We arouse guilt to demand love. We charm and manipulate to steal love. We seek love in the union of bodies, in making others idols of our desire, in attempts to enhance the attractiveness of our bodies and personalities. We sacrifice in the hope we may thus be worthy of love.

As most people understand it, love is a great enigma. Love is held to be joy, beauty, inspiration, the song of the heart. Love is also thought of as heartache, unquenchable yearning, pain of loss, obsession, and temptation.

Love, it seems, is complicated and, for all its great value, comes at great cost.

It is a folk wisdom that love is not amenable to conscious choice; the mind and the heart can and often do choose differently according to this wisdom. And love exacts a high price. If the experience of giving and receiving love is the most desirable feeling to which we can aspire, the yearning for it seems to condemn us to pain or the fear of threatened pain. Yet the belief that pain is inherent to love, that we are powerless to choose love, that love renders us vulnerable, speaks to people's confusion about the nature of love rather than their experience of it.

Haidt distinguishes between *passionate* and *companionate* love.[50] The former involves the "fire" of intense emotions and obsession with a person. It is the rhapsodized delirium of falling in love. Companionate love is the calmer comfort and appreciation that sustains lasting relationships. Both are included in the common understanding of love. The passionate variety is more like a drug-induced state destined to end, but companionate love can endure a lifetime. The latter is more likely to point the way to an understanding of the essential nature of the feeling we hold in such high regard.

Consider what love *feels* like, the *experience* of loving someone or something. I do not speak of the heartache and longing born of the perception of love denied or absent; that is the *yearning* for love, not the experience. I also do not speak of *needing* someone to feel whole, worthy, safe, and entertained. This includes the passionate love just described. Feelings of need are directed at what we want *from* a person rather than what we feel *for* a person. Feelings of need inherently entail fear. If we could remove all the impurities of perceived lack and its attendant fear, what would be left? I believe that the essence of love is pure, unneedy, undemanding, accepting appreciation. Pure appreciation is the essence of quiet, tension-free joy.

Perhaps appreciation seems too pale a word for love, but I think it lends itself to the distinction between *valuing* someone in and of themselves and wanting them as a means to fill a perceived lack. One meaning of appreciation is to *increase in value*. It is the experience of valuing. We behold what we hold most dear in whom and what we love, and in the loving we *experience* what we hold most dear. Joy is the best word we have to express the feeling. It is what the bestowal of worth *feels* like, and, to the extent it is a desired feeling, it is its own reward. Unconditional appreciation may be the essence of joy, for joy may be the unbounded appreciation of a present experience.

Think of those moments when you simply enjoy someone or something for what they are, rather than for what you wish them to be or what you hope to gain from them. For example, the enjoyment of a sunset, a flower, and the song of a bird need not be conditioned by your demands and expectations. Your enjoyment is greater when it is accepted without condition. You may bask in the glow of a smile, or a grandmother showing affection to her grandchildren, or the simple joy of children at play without further demand. The laugh of a child, the peace of a meadow, the affectionate teasing of a friend can be enjoyed as gifts of the moment, gifts we give ourselves by "allowing" our appreciation of them.

We feel a keener appreciation for family, friends, and lovers when we delight in our experience of them rather than perceiving them through the lens of our preference for who they should be and how they should act. Appreciation unsullied by fears, neediness, and judgment is enjoyment of an experience. Indeed it would be pure joy were it felt in isolation without the usual mixture of attenuating feelings. Pure appreciation, I believe, is pure love.

Love as undiluted appreciation is closer to the Greek word *agape* or the Buddhist expression *loving kindness*, but love is the all-purpose word in the West. Here we use adjectives to distinguish types of love. Maslow made a distinction between "B-love (love for the Being of another person, unneeding love, unselfish love) and D-love (deficiency-love, love need, selfish love)."[51] His "B-love" is an appreciative love.

But the reward of experiencing love may be even greater than what the word joy seems to promise, for the lack of condition avoids the causes of fear and dissatisfaction. The uncontaminated experience of love contains no sorrow, pain, fear, anger, jealousy, or need. It sees no wrong to be righted or provision to be made. Love undimmed perceives no need or lack, places no condition on the future, issues no call for completion, is unconstrained by fear. A state of mind without fear, lack, or condition implies the state of peace.

In the acceptance of what is, love is different from *emotion*, which is a feeling that moves us to seek and do, in other words, to change what is. All emotions reflect a judgment of dissatisfaction with what is, in particular with what we currently feel. Love may be thought to be a state of being or state of mind rather than an emotion, because, in its purest form, it entails a self-sufficient appreciation of what is, including what we currently feel. It does not move us to seek a change. If love undimmed by condition is joy and peace, it may be thought the experience of fulfillment, of happiness.

The experience of love, and thus fulfillment, lies in the love we bestow, or *give*, rather than what is usually meant by love we *receive*, which cannot be directly experienced short of sharing the mind of another. The significance of this cannot be exaggerated, for it would utterly transform our lives and our world if it were understood and believed. It implies that the love we give is its own reward; the more we love, the more joy and peace we experience. Since we are the source of this love, we do not, and by the nature of the experience cannot, depend on circumstance or the presence and behavior of others to experience its blessings. Given that so much of our lives is devoted to gaining love from others, the assertion that the giving is the receiving may seem counterintuitive. Yet it cannot be otherwise. We unavoidably experience what we feel for others. If you feel love, love is what you feel. If you feel hate, hate is what you feel. You immediately reap what you sow in terms of feelings.

People can feel a general love of people, animals, and nature. Love of nation, love of community, love of place, love of one's home, and love of one's job are commonly professed. Such professions of love may be a pretense or greatly exaggerated, an overly grand characterization of an episodic murmur of affection and appreciation that punctuates less positive judgments. Yet the more general love of all that populates one's environment might also be a genuine affective experience, an experience inherent to the purest form of love that does not divide experience into loved and unloved aspects. To so divide experience necessarily denies the full experience of the agape understanding of love. It not only limits our appreciation, it denies the necessary condition of peace as well.

Peak Experiences

Peace and the joy of pure love are combined in a state of mind we might never wish to end. Quite plausibly, the whisper of this state is what we seek in the state of flow, in reverie, in our enjoyment of companions, in creative expression, and in higher purpose and virtue. Though reason commends this state as the full realization of happiness, we might not want to rely on reason alone to define our highest affective aspiration. We might follow Maslow's example. He based his study of self-actualized people — people Maslow considered as having reached their full potential — on the premise that we should look to the highest achievers if we want to identify the attributes of exceptional achievement.[52]

Maslow coined the term "peak experience" and devoted several decades to collecting accounts of such experiences. William James also studied them, calling them "mystical states" and "cosmic consciousness" in his classic *The Varieties of Religious Experience*. Such terms describe states of consciousness in which a person is temporarily transported from the normal perception of the world to a radically different experience of reality to which the word "cosmic" seems an apt adjective.

Such experiences are usually characterized by intense awe and bliss, of super clarity and certainty where often, in the words of Maslow, "the whole universe is perceived as an integrated and unified whole."[53] More lasting states of similar consciousness are known as grace, nirvana, samadhi, and enlightenment according to various wisdom teachings.

What makes them relevant to the consideration of the nature of happiness is that there are pronounced similarities in the accounts of what people say they felt during a peak experience. They usually use words of similar meaning to describe affective states they expressly consider vastly preferable to normal feelings.

We do not have to accept the implication of a transcendent nature of reality to accept such accounts as actual *subjective* experiences. They often occur spontaneously among people of all types of belief. They can apparently be induced by drugs and stimulation to parts of the brain, which materialists see as evidence that they are not true visions of a supernatural reality.[54] Yet those who claim peak experiences are convinced these experiences are real and highly meaningful.

According to James, "Mystical states, when well developed, usually are, and have the right to be, absolutely authoritative over the individuals to whom they come."[55] Whether they depict actual union with the source of universal consciousness or anomalies of the brain, the commonalities regarding superlative states of mind can be legitimately considered glimpses of the higher reaches of affective experience. They may well provide clues to the essential nature of happiness, or at least provide direction for one's pursuit of it. Maslow makes the case for the value of the experience:

There is no doubt that great insights and revelations are profoundly felt in mystic or peak-experiences, and certainly some of these are, ipso facto, intrinsically valid as experiences. That is, one can and does learn from such experiences that, e.g., joy, ecstasy, and rapture do in fact exist and that they are in principle available for the experiencer, even if they never have been before. Thus the peaker learns surely and certainly that life can be worthwhile, that it can be beautiful and valuable.[56]

Both Maslow and James found that a characteristic, though not universal, aspect of peak experiences is what is now known as a "unitive" consciousness or state.[57] James speaks of "a monistic insight, in which the other in its various forms appears absorbed into the One."[58] The perception of becoming one with the observed, of a unity of experience and experienced, of a loss of consciousness of an individual, differentiated self is typical. Bolte Taylor describes her experience of a stroke in the left hemisphere of her brain:

As the language centers in my left hemisphere grew increasingly silent and I became detached from the memories of my life, I was comforted by an expanding sense of grace. In this void of higher cognition and details pertaining to my normal life, my consciousness soared into an all-knowingness, a "being at one" with the universe, if you will.[59]

This unitive consciousness is variously described as unity with God, unity of creation, unity with the universe, unity of life, unity of humanity, and unity with the primal awareness from which all form arises. People have to grope for words to describe the indescribable, but the descriptions of peak experiences point to the same general qualities of experience even though they are recounted by adherents of every faith and none.

One can reasonably suspect that the perception of unity with all existence would mean the abeyance of judgment of all aspects of existence, and this is indeed a near-universal characteristic of peak experiences. For one thing, there is the relative absence of the main source of judgment. Maslow observes that "perception in the peak-experiences can be relatively ego-transcending, self-forgetful, egoless, unselfish."[60] Acceptance of all creation as having intrinsic, equal, and inestimable worth, as being part of the perfection of higher purpose is expressed in several of the examples James cites and is a robust finding of Maslow's studies.

The world seen in the peak-experiences is seen only as beautiful, good, de-

sirable, worthwhile, etc. and is never experienced as evil or undesirable.
The world is accepted. People will say that then they understand it. Most
important of all for comparison with religious thinking is that somehow
they become reconciled to evil. Evil itself is accepted and understood and
seen in its proper place in the whole, as belonging there, as unavoidable, as
necessary, and, therefore, as proper.[61]

This aspect of the peak experiences Maslow collected is reflected in
Sophy Burnham's experience: "I saw that everything was perfect, and all was
composed of love."[62] She speaks of an "unfathomable, unconditional, and in-
superable love" that echoes many accounts of peak experiences.[63] The complete suspension of judgment is consistent with almost all of the accounts of
peak experiences of which I am aware.

I frequently find comments in the reports of peak experiences that the
attendant feelings are far beyond normal human experience, that they are
not in the same league as the feelings of common experience. Nonetheless,
they can only be recounted with words of shared meaning. Accounts are
peppered with affectively descriptive words such as joy, joyousness, ecstasy,
bliss, elation, exaltation, and rapture. The "peakers" often claim that the feelings are quite intense.

At first blush, this does not seem quite consistent with the frequent
claim of the simultaneous experience of peace. Bolte Taylor speaks of "a state
of peaceful grace" amid her joy.[64] Tolle testifies to a state of "vibrantly alive
peace" that is the essence of joy.[65] James quotes J. Trevor: "I felt that I was
in Heaven — an inward state of peace and joy and assurance indescribably
intense ..."[66] Perhaps peace arises less from absence of intensity than lack of
cause for disturbance. Maslow observes that:

> *In the peak-experiences, there tends to be a loss, even though transient,*
> *of fear, anxiety, inhibition, of defense and control, of perplexity, confu-*
> *sion, conflict, of delay and restraint. The profound fear of disintegration,*
> *of insanity, of death, all tend to disappear for the moment. Perhaps this*
> *amounts to saying that fear disappears.*[67]

I can only speculate, but peace may come from the perceived lack of con-
tradictions and threat in the experience of unity. Of this, Maslow says:

> *In peak-experiences, the dichotomies, polarities, and conflicts of life tend*
> *to be transcended or resolved. That is to say, there tends to be a moving*

toward the perception of unity and integration in the world. The person himself tends to move toward fusion, integration, and unity and away from splitting, conflicts, and oppositions.[68]

James described his own experience under the influence of an anesthetic: "It is as if the opposites of the world, whose contradictoriness and conflict make all our difficulties and troubles, were melted into unity."[69]

In the experience of unity as perfection, conflict, threat, and insufficiency are absent. Nothing remains to trouble the peace of one's mind. Joy devoid of all conflict and fear may well be experienced as "intense" in terms of degree without contradicting an underlying awareness of peace.

Feelings described as awe, reverence, gratitude, and worshipfulness may be aspects of the agape notion of love. All these words apply to love understood as pure appreciation. The word appreciation may be inadequate to describe the state, but it nonetheless provides a core understanding of its nature.

It is not clear from the accounts of peak experiences if love, joy, peace, and awe are ever experienced as discrete, separate, and sequential states of mind or are always experienced simultaneously as aspects of the same feeling. Many imply and some expressly claim, however, that the unity of experience entails a simultaneous unity of feeling. Thus, we might conclude that the peak feeling of happiness entails the joy of unconditional appreciation — love — combined with perfect peace. It may be that nothing in the universe can offer more than this, and we have no further to look for the source of this state than ourselves.

This affective state, I believe, can be called an *angel* notion of happiness. It shares the core characteristics of what is called grace, bliss, and samadhi. It is but one of the many notions of the nature of happiness, but students should consider it in their investigation of alternative notions. They should explore both the lowlands of common pleasures and the highlands of peak experiences.

Exploring happiness involves more than comparing notions of the nature of happiness, of course. Students must also explore perspectives on the sources of happiness. The findings of research and observation are more readily available and relevant when it comes to sources. We thus push on with our expedition in search of the wellsprings of felicity.

4

Sources
Of Happiness

*To live happily ... is the desire of all men, but
their minds are blinded to a clear vision of just what it is
that makes life happy; and so far from its being easy to attain
the happy life, the more eagerly a man strives to reach it, the
farther he recedes from it if he has made a mistake in the road;
for when it leads in the opposite direction, his very speed will
increase the distance that separates him.* | Seneca

Most people would be at a loss to explain what happiness feels like, but they are full of assumptions about what *causes* it. I find that the nature and sources of happiness are melded in most people's understanding. This was true of even the great Aristotle:

> *We may define happiness as prosperity combined with virtue; or as independence of life; or as the secure enjoyment of the maximum of pleasure; or as a good condition of property and body, together with the power of guarding one's property and body and making use of them. That happiness is one or more of these things pretty well everybody agrees. From this definition of happiness it follows that its constituent parts are: good birth, plenty of friends, good friends, wealth, good children, plenty of children, a happy old age, also such bodily excellences as health, beauty, strength, large stature, athletic powers, together with fame, honour, good luck, and virtue.*[1]

If I were *x*, had *y*, and achieved *z*, I would be happy. Variations of this formula constitute a common understanding of not only the sources of happiness, but of happiness per se. We each plug in our own favored values and change them from time to time. In moments of doubt, many of us likely reflect on the bets we're placing, but few disregard the formula altogether in placing them. No matter how often your bets prove disappointing, you are unlikely to discard the only formula you know.

But the stakes could not be higher. It does not seem reasonable that people would place their bets on the sources of happiness without deep reflection and thorough investigation. But that is largely the case. It need not be that way for our children, though. A happiness pedagogy would guide students to awareness of alternative sources and an understanding of their comparative merits. The early years should focus on awareness of what students prefer to feel and what seems to cause these feelings. When they are ready, they should begin a multi-year exploration of different perspectives on the nature and sources of happiness. They would consult philosophical insights and the evidence of scientific research.

I rely more on the findings of research in my consideration of sources of happiness in this chapter, though I believe some caution is in order. Most of the research is based on surveys. The answers to such surveys likely reflect common rather than deeply contemplated understandings of happiness, lack of experience in focusing on internal states and discerning among them, great ambiguity in labeling feelings, concern for self-image, self-deception, cultural biases, interpretive ambiguities, and a host of other distortions. Following the advice gleaned from such surveys may be a case of the blind leading the blind. Gary Gutting puts it this way:

> Researchers emphasize that when we ask people if they are happy the answers tell us nothing if we don't know what our respondents mean by "happy." One person might mean, "I'm not currently feeling any serious pain"; another, "My life is pretty horrible but I'm reconciled to it"; another, "I'm feeling a lot better than I did yesterday." … There's no reason to think that the ideas of happiness we discover by empirical surveys are sufficiently well thought out to lead us to genuine happiness. For richer and more sensitive conceptions of happiness, we need to turn to philosophers, who, from Plato and Aristotle through Hume and Mill, to Hegel and Nietzsche, have provided some of the deepest insight into the possible meanings of happiness.[2]

Nonetheless, better some quantitative evidence than none. All the evidence concerning happiness not based on our own experience is based on reported descriptions and evaluations of other people's experience. We have no choice but to rely on other people's subjective reports to some extent.

External Sources

Strictly speaking, there is no clear dichotomy between external and internal sources of feelings. All we perceive, do, and think is an internal experience in the sense that our minds filter and provide the meaning of the raw sensory data that enters our consciousness. We are creatively engaged in determining our experience of the world that appears external to our minds. But there is a difference in focus, in where we look for the treasure of our hearts. Most look without for conditions they believe will make them feel better than they do. Some doggedly pursue wealth, fame, and power. Security, comfort, freedom, the love of loved ones, and the esteem of others are on most everyone's list.

Those deemed wise caution that such things do not cause happiness, but this wisdom goes largely unheeded when it comes to what people choose to pursue. Money is high on the list of many. College freshmen have been surveyed in the United States every year since 1967. The percentage of those who thought it highly important to be "very well off financially" rose from an initial 42 percent to 71 percent over the course of four decades.[3]

The evidence does not support the assumption that wealth and possessions lead to greater perceived happiness. Quite the contrary. Adam Smith, who is hailed as the father of capitalism, observed that wealth had only a temporary effect on a person's usual state of mind. "In prosperity, after a certain time, it falls back to that state; in adversity, after a certain time, it rises up to it."[4] This "hedonic adaptation," or habituation as it is called by psychologists, is well-established. The economist Richard Easterlin observed in what has become known as the "Easterlin paradox" that life satisfaction as indicated in national surveys did not rise with substantial increases in national wealth.[5] Arthur Brooks cites ample evidence from numerous studies that substantiates this paradox.[6] He does say reported happiness tends to rise with perceptions of relative wealth, but believes the data indicates "that richer people are happier than poorer people because their relative prosperity makes them feel successful."[7]

Sonja Lyubomirsky cites robust findings that, "although those with higher incomes report being somewhat more satisfied with their lives, studies of how they actually spend their days find that they don't spend time in any more enjoyable activities than their less prosperous peers and, in fact, are more likely to experience daily anxiety and anger."[8] "How important money is to you, more than money itself, influences your happiness," in Martin Seligman's assessment of the evidence. "Materialism seems to be counterproductive: at all levels of real income, people who value money more than other goals are less satisfied with their income and with their lives as a whole, although precisely why is a mystery."[9]

Seligman echoes many others in reporting signs of increasing emotional distress despite the general increase in wealth:

> *Mounting over the last forty years in every wealthy country on the globe, there has been a startling increase in depression. Depression is now ten times as prevalent as it was in 1960, and it strikes at a much younger age. … This is a paradox, since every objective indicator of well-being — purchasing power, amount of education, availability of music, and nutrition — has been going north, while every indicator of subjective well-being has been going south.*[10]

The spread of depression seems to be speeding up. Stefan Klein observed that "Today the risk of depression for young people is three times higher than it was ten years ago." He warns that "depression is threatening to become the plague of the twenty-first century."[11] "In the heyday of its material splendor," says Csikszentmihalyi, "our society is suffering from an astonishing variety of strange ills."[12] Perhaps this just reflects increased sensitivity to such ills, but if we are to include scientific data in our assessment of sources of happiness, we cannot ignore these trends.

Hedonic adaptation — the wearing off of initial satisfaction — seems to apply to all the favored circumstances of life. Getting what you want in terms of desired circumstances has been repeatedly shown to be "short-lived" in studies that examine the issue.[13] "Human beings adapt to favorable changes in wealth, housing, and possessions, to being beautiful or being surrounded by beauty, to good health, and even to marriage," says Lyubomirsky.[14] In light of the thousands of self-help books that divulge the secrets of "how to get rich, powerful, loved, or slim," Csikszentmihalyi asks:

> ... *what would be the result afterward in the unlikely event that one did turn into a slim, well-loved, powerful millionaire? Usually what happens is that the person finds himself back at square one, with a new list of wishes, just as dissatisfied as before.*[15]

This seems to be the bottom line of an unusual study conducted by researchers at Harvard that attempted to follow 268 men who started at Harvard in the late 1930s throughout their lives. Elite education, elite social status, and worldly success did not propel these young men into particularly happy lives; in fact, many of the life stories suggest the opposite.[16]

Satisfactions that depend on contrast with dissatisfaction cannot be sustained. This observation was simply asserted in the preceding chapter, but it is well substantiated in research. I also argued that this general rule applies to seeking happiness in relationships as well, but it does not apply to the joy of appreciation we may find in relationships that is unconditioned by our desire to escape loneliness and boredom.

Many attest to enjoying interaction with others more than most other activities. Jennifer Hecht offers a rather quirky theory that money can buy some happiness because it facilitates interaction and sharing related to shopping.[17] Lyubomirsky says of the "happiest participants" of the studies in which she participated that "they devote a great amount of time to their family and friends, nurturing and enjoying those relationships."[18] Nel Noddings regards "the domain of human interaction as the principal arena of happiness" and recommends "creating the conditions under which people are likely to interact with others in mutually supportive ways" as a task of education.[19] Relationships based on need, however, come with all the problems noted earlier. Until they advance to appreciation for its own sake, they will be beset by the many ills of relationships.

Marriage is no exception to this rule. It may be, as Jonathan Haidt claims, that "a good marriage is one of the life-factors most strongly and consistently associated with happiness."[20] Seligman elaborates in saying "marriage is a more potent happiness factor than satisfaction with job, or finances, or community."[21] But it is a quite conditional factor, as high rates of divorce seem to attest.

Many find that the emotional haven they sought in marriage is not nearly as secure as they hoped. They discover that the person they projected in their initial enthusiasm is not the person they married. There is also habituation. Lyubomirsky cites the findings of a "spectacular data set" that shows "marriage has only a temporary effect on happiness. It appears that after the wedding husband and wife get a happiness boost for about two years and then simply return to their baseline in happiness, their set point."[22]

Those of us who continue to find joy in our marriages through the decades of our lives, I believe, have found the sustaining joy of appreciation as the yearnings and fires of earlier years abate. This is likely true of lasting friendships as well.

As for other environmental circumstances such as landscape, climate, community, and a large house in a good neighborhood with a two-car garage and white picket fence, the initial enjoyment also wears off.[23] Holden quotes a woman who moved frequently in search of greener grass:

> *Everywhere I moved to I was really happy at first. But then the novelty would go, and the happiness soon wore off. The only problem with each new place was that I kept turning up there! I wasn't happy with me. I can see now that until I'm happy with me, nowhere will be good enough.*[24]

Studies find a positive correlation between political freedom and reported levels of happiness.[25] People who live in societies with rampant crime, internecine war, and repressive regimes face great insecurity. Without doubt, security and freedom are favorable circumstances for pursuing happiness even though they are not causes of happiness in themselves. The jury is still out on whether income inequality per se is an important circumstance. Mexico, for example, once placed high on national happiness surveys.[26]

Beyond basic levels of security, comfort, and freedom, the social environment does not seem to contribute a great deal to perceived happiness. Life in rich liberal democracies is far from bliss. I have talked to many people from poorer countries who said there was a richer communal life where they came from than in the United States, and they missed it. I remember my son, who was studying abroad for a semester in Ecuador, saying he thought that people seemed a lot looser and happier there than in the United States despite their relative poverty. The comparatively high and growing suicide rates in the United States give cause to suspect there may be something to this.[27]

We naturally wish for more freedom, justice, security, and abundance for ourselves and others. But, as is often the case, the cause itself may be more important than any particular attainment, any particular victory in the struggle for social progress. I spent most of my life believing in social causes, and this book reflects a continuing desire for social change, but George Orwell pointed to the flaw in utopian hopes when he observed that "nearly all creators of utopia have resembled the man who has toothache, and therefore thinks happiness consists in not having toothache."[28] The joy of the perfect society is bound to wear off when the pain of imperfection disappears from awareness.

Many who came to America from troubled lands are grateful to be here and are therefore often fiercely patriotic, but that does not mean they are immune to habituation. It is better to have freedom than not, but while freedom removes some obstacles to happiness, it is not in itself a cause. The same is true for justice, security, and abundance. Karl Marx's claim that changing material conditions leads to changes in consciousness may be true in some ways, but improved material conditions alone are clearly insufficient to cause happiness.

Researchers advise that it is not so much our environment per se that is a source of happiness, but rather our *engagement* with our environment. Focused activity such as work, projects, causes, and challenging leisure activities keep our minds occupied and provide opportunities for gratification. Such activities are usually goal-oriented, which is to say endowed with purpose. Haidt says work that involves "connection, engagement, and commitment" is a major source of satisfaction.[29] If one's work is seen as a calling, it is the "most satisfying form of work," according to Seligman.[30] In regard to Maslow's studies, Frank Goble says "Without exception, he found self-actualizing people to be dedicated to some work task, duty, or vocation which they considered important."[31] Whether work or play, what seems important, according to Seligman and a host of others, is "successfully using your signature strengths."[32]

This is key to Csikszentmihalyi's state of flow.[33] He believes, though, that vigorous, concentrated engagement is required for "optimal experience": "The best moments usually occur when a person's body or mind is stretched to its limits in a voluntary effort to accomplish something difficult and worthwhile."[34] Tolle gives an explanation for this: "The reason why some people love to engage in dangerous activities such as mountain climbing, car racing, and so on, although they may not be aware of it, is that it forces them into the Now — that intensely alive state that is free of time, free of problems, free of thinking, free of the burden of the personality."[35]

Richard Taylor believes that it is the exercise of creative intelligence, of "creating from their own resources things original to themselves" that is the source of happiness.[36] He says, "If we think of happiness as fulfillment, then it must consist of the fulfillment of ourselves as human beings, which means the exercise of our creative powers."[37] The felt need for creative expression seems strong in many people. And most types of engagement call for creativity of some sort. There is a creative dimension to almost every human activity: relationships, persuasion, cooking, sports, conversation, and virtually every pastime humans have invented. We can presume the joy of aesthetic appreciation in creative expression, and the relative peace of losing ourselves in deep engagement. Of course, ego-gratification is a prominent motive for creativity as well.

Purposeful engagement promises the satisfaction of achievement. It can lead to the less troubled state of flow. The "action and employment and the occupations of common life," in the words of Hume, can give respite from the puzzles of existence.[38] Work can "draw us out of ourselves and into connection with people and projects beyond ourselves," Haidt observes.[39] Engagement allows creative expression. And it can provide "normative" satisfactions — satisfactions that come from doing what a person believes is good and right — when it aims at the welfare of others. Of course, the sense of accomplishment also feeds the ego's appetite for evidence of relative worth.

Many people believe that the good life consists in setting significant goals and achieving most of them.[40] Graduating from college, success in a career, finding a soul mate and having a happy marriage, building a business, getting rich, winning a title, and inspiring the esteem of one's fellows are thought to add to one's self esteem and sense of a well-lived life. But it is difficult to find a source of such satisfaction other than the easing of the ego's hunger. The need to buttress one's sense of worth implies a lack. The joy of engagement or creative expression may lead to achievement, but here achievement is the result rather than the cause of the joy. "Achievement for the joy of it is healthy," says Holden, "for your motive is love and your worth is never questioned. Achievement because you need it is problematic."[41]

The affective benefits of engagement and achievement reasonably require an environment with which to engage, thus they seem to have an external source. Of course, these benefits also require the internal resources of attitude, intent, talents, abilities, and motive. This fits Haidt's hypothesis that happiness comes from *between*. The need *to do* implied in the drive to be engaged, however, implies a lack, a need that must be met at least partly from without. The feeling you seek to experience is either dependent on doing, and therefore ceases without engagement, or, if independent, action is not inherently necessary. If engagement is considered necessary to your sense of worth, a sense of intrinsic worth is absent by implication. And if you need to use the external environment as a canvas for creative expression, you face the judgments of your fellows.

Lasting peace of mind is unlikely to result from the need for engagement. Many are driven to be purposefully engaged, which does not hold much promise that it will ever bring them peace. The flux of the world is exceedingly inhospitable to this state of mind. The gratifications of engagement may be very desirable, but they are temporary escapes from the pain of insufficiency that motivates pursuit of them unless they are the expressions of what arises from within. When joy is the cause of its expression, rather than expression being the cause of joy, it is less vulnerable to perceived insufficiencies and the vagaries of the world.

Engagement or behavior in service to others can be considered virtue, and studies show that virtue is indeed associated with happiness.[42] The affective benefits are relatively clear. In addition to normative satisfaction — the satisfaction of doing what you believe is good and right — virtue brings cognitive harmony. Ajahn Chah expressed a Buddhist view when he said "living a virtuous life makes the heart peaceful."[43] Mill saw the greatest affective benefit of virtue in "protection from pain."[44] I presume guilt and social censure are foremost among the pains he had in mind.

A virtuous disposition, according to Hume is "that which leads to action and employment, renders us sensible to the social passions, steels the heart against the assaults of fortune, reduces the affections to a just moderation, makes our own thoughts an entertainment to us, and inclines us rather to the pleasures of society and conversation, than to those of the senses."[45] Maslow found a "network of positive intercorrelation" between the various enjoyments that self-actualizing people gained from doing what they believed was right.[46] They definitely found virtue rewarding.[47] Haidt has a point, though, when he says "virtue can be rewarding, but that's obvious only for the virtues that one finds rewarding.[48]

As with engagement in general, it is difficult to differentiate between the external and internal aspects of virtue. Does one need others to be virtuous *toward*, or can virtue that is not motivated by need for praise or escape from guilt simply express an inward inclination? In Buddhism, natural virtue is an expression of "the spontaneous integrity of the awakened heart" according to Jack Kornfield. "Instead of relying on rules and practices, our benevolent actions come from an innate connection. We all instinctively recognize this level of virtue, when people are authentic, kind, and unshakable in their integrity."[49]

In this understanding, virtue comes from within, though it is expressed without. In other words, the source of its joy is internal, though its external expression is important to the harmony that living with integrity can bring.

A great many people, probably a sizable majority, consider God an external source of happiness. Augustine, Thomas Aquinas, and Martin Luther all argued that true happiness is a bestowal of God and cannot be otherwise achieved.[50] This amounts to a tenet of Western religions. The greater reward of virtue in the eyes of adherents is the reward God bestows. There is little we can say in regard to substantiation of this claim except that there is strong evidence that the belief itself seems to contribute to perceived happiness.[51] But belief per se is an internal source of happiness.

Internal Sources

John Stuart Mill maintained that "No great improvements in the lot of mankind are possible, until a great change takes place in the fundamental constitution of their modes of thought."[52] The same can be said of any individual's improvement in terms of happiness. The link between thoughts and feelings is well substantiated.[53] Patterns of thoughts and their associated feelings create new circuits in our brain as "new connections are forged in our network of nerve cells," according to Stefan Klein.[54]

> *These changes are triggered by thoughts, but even more by emotions. This means that with the right exercises we can increase our capacity for happiness. Much as we can learn a foreign language, we can train our natural aptitude for positive feelings.*[55]

Thoughts entail judgments and come with the affective consequences of judgment. If we can learn to exercise some control over them, we gain a degree of control over feelings. As Csikszentmihalyi says, "People who learn to control inner experience will be able to determine the quality of their lives, which is as close as any of us can come to being happy."[56]

Such control is not just a matter of being able to generate more positive feelings; it also provides relief from painful and destructive negative feedback loops. Jill Bolte Taylor explains that "negative internal thought patterns" lead to anxiety and hostility.[57] "For many of us," she says, "these loops of thought run rampant and we find ourselves habitually imagining devastating possibilities."[58] They can lead to depression and health problems.[59] They are a cause of harmful behavior and vulnerability to manipulation. But most of us are seldom consciously aware of the connection between our thoughts and our feelings, or of the possibility of interrupting the feedback loop.

Tolle says, "Not to be able to stop thinking is a dreadful affliction, but we don't realize this because almost everybody is suffering from it, so it is considered normal."[60] The ability to stop or change our thoughts would be among the most valuable we could hope to gain, but it would require awareness, discipline, and diligence. Bolte Taylor makes an interesting point in this regard:

> Unfortunately, as a society, we do not teach our children that they need to tend carefully the garden of their minds. Without structure, censorship, or discipline, our thoughts run rampant on automatic. Because we have not learned how to more carefully manage what goes on inside our brains, we remain vulnerable to not only what other people think about us, but also to advertising and/or political manipulation.[61]

We are not without obvious means to alter the content, and therefore the affective consequences, of our thoughts. Attitudes, beliefs, and purposes shape what we think and therefore feel. The transformative power of attitude is a folk wisdom. It serves as an interpretative filter of perception, and positive attitudes establish positive patterns of thought that can become as habitual as negative patterns.

An attitude of humor, for instance, can help in this regard. Viktor Frankl found that humor offered some relief even from the degradations of life in a concentration camp: "Humor was another of the soul's weapons in the fight for self-preservation. It is well known that humor, more than anything else in the human make-up, can afford an aloofness and an ability to rise above any situation, even if only for a few seconds."[62]

A less judgmental attitude also helps. Maslow noted a "non-judgmental type of perception" in self-actualized people: "As the child looks out upon the world with wide, uncritical, innocent eyes, simply noting or observing what is the case, without either arguing the matter or demanding that it be otherwise, so does the self-actualizing person look upon human nature in himself and in others."[63]

Many recommend releasing judgment by means of forgiveness.[64] Other recommendations are to cultivate an attitude of appreciation, to develop an attitude of gratitude, and to build an attitude of self-esteem.[65] A more discerning attitude may also be important. Csikszentmihalyi maintains that "achieving control over experience requires a drastic change in attitude about what is important and what is not."[66] All of these recommended changes in attitude or disposition are used in contemporary therapies that are widely hailed as effective.

Beliefs also serve as interpretative filters of perception, and they can offer inner solace amidst the troubles of life or deny it, they can provide meaning or obscure it, they can blunt the edges of circumstances or sharpen them. "Acting on the basis of what you believe," says Chris Prentiss, "is what brings about the conditions of your life and the degrees of happiness you have experienced."[67]

This depends on what one believes, though. For example, a materialist-based belief promises freedom from a judgmental God and final release in death. It can also lead to existential "forlornness" due to the ultimate meaninglessness of life. Religious belief can give hope of eternal life, transcendental meaning, and great aid in facing the turbulence of life. But fear of divine judgment can also attend such belief.

What we believe tints the lens through which we regard the world with the hues of our feelings. Positive attitudes can accentuate the warmer colors of the world; negative attitudes can drain the world of color. Belief often informs attitude, and has the deeper effect of imbuing the world with meaning or denying meaning to one's perceptions of the world.

Belief is a framework for understanding, a framework that gives experience an ordered structure to which one can append meaning. This is true to some extent even when the belief posits an underlying meaninglessness and chaos. To presume an understanding of the world, however bleak, offers some firmness of mental ground, of perspective that affords the ability to discern and therefore judge. Beliefs that imbue the world with positive meaning, of course, are far more conducive to positive feelings than those that call for negative judgments.

Beliefs can also provide a guiding purpose. It is through conscious commitment to such a purpose that the full power of belief to aid the pursuit of happiness might be tapped. As Aristotle advised: "Everyone who has the power to live according to his own choice should ... set up for himself some object for the good life to aim at ... by reference to which he will do all that he does, since not to have one's life organized in view of some end is a sign of great folly."[68]

An overriding purpose can unify your desires and pursuits, give them stability of meaning, and "join all experience into a meaningful pattern" in the words of Csikszentmihalyi.[69] He believes "a unified purpose is what gives meaning to life," and, in conjunction with the belief from which purpose arises, that is undoubtedly true in a subjective sense.[70] He is partly right when he says "The consequence of forging life by purpose and resolution is a sense of inner harmony, a dynamic order in the contents of consciousness."[71]

It depends on what the purpose is, though. A purpose that entails conflict is unlikely to produce the peace of harmony though it brings the benefits of clarity. The purpose of a fanatic cause that requires subordinating and oppressing people may bring order to the contents of consciousness, but callous intent exacts a commensurate affective price. You cannot avoid reaping the affective grain of what you sow in terms of what you intend toward others. You cannot intend coercion without reaping inner conflict. Fear and the perception of lack are inherent to the need to coerce, and the inevitable resistance of those you would coerce will feed the fires of anger, frustration, and fear.

The combination of belief and purpose provide meaning. Feeling is a function of meaning. It is an inherent consequence of the meaning we give to any and all experiences. In this sense, it might be said that purpose is the heart of life — it unites the disparate experiences of life into a meaningful whole, or it would if were you so fortunate as to have conscious unity of purpose.

If the value of experience lies in feeling, the underlying purpose in all we pursue is determined by the heart. If you knew the deepest desire of your heart, you could consciously choose a purpose most likely to fulfill it. Should you, for example, come to the conclusion that what you truly desire is peace, love, and joy, and understood that you feel what you intend for others, you would choose a purpose aimed to serve the peace, love, and joy of others. You would thereby gain both the benefits of clarity of purpose and the miraculous blessings of harmonizing the purpose of the mind with the purpose of the heart.

Not all agree that thoughts, beliefs, and purposes in themselves are sources of happiness. Tolle says "not your aims or your actions are primary, but the state of consciousness out of which they come."[72] In other words, actions, thoughts, beliefs, and purposes may all be effects of a deeper cause, of the primal awareness that is the ultimate source of experience and all its aspects.

Buddhists and others who have learned the discipline of inner awareness maintain that happiness already resides within us; we need but remove the noise of our chattering minds and the fog of our external attachments to bring this deeper sense of sufficiency and fulfillment into awareness. Yongey Mingyur explains it this way: "If you don't try to stop whatever is going on in your mind, but merely observe it, eventually you'll begin to feel a tremendous sense of relaxation, a vast sense of openness within your mind — which is in fact your natural mind, the naturally unperturbed background against which various thoughts come and go."[73] The means to awareness of this state is called *mindfulness*.

Evidence of the state of consciousness Buddhists talk about is not solely based on reports of subjective experiences. Western scientists have taken a lively interest in investigating the processes as well as the physical aspects of the brains of Buddhist monks and others who claim to regularly attain this state of consciousness. Lynne McTaggart reports the results of studies of Buddhist practitioners conducted by Richard Davidson, a neuroscientist and psychologist at the University of Wisconsin:

> ...those monks who had been performing meditation the longest recorded the highest levels of gamma activity. The heightened state also produced permanent emotional improvement by activating the left anterior portion of the brain — the portion most associated with joy. The monks had conditioned their brains to tune in to happiness most of the time. In later research, Davidson demonstrated that meditation alters brain-wave patterns,

even among new practitioners. Neophytes who had practiced mindfulness meditation for only eight weeks showed increased activation of the "happy-thoughts" part of the brain and enhanced immune function.[74]

Other studies found greater coherence of brain activity:

At least 25 studies of meditation have shown that, during meditation, EEG activity between the four regions of the brain synchronizes. Meditation makes the brain permanently more coherent — as might prayer. ... During meditation, both sides [of the brain] communicate in a particularly harmonious manner. Concentrated attention appears to enlarge certain mechanisms of perception, while tuning out "noise."[75]

Years of meditation are not required to experience this desirable state of consciousness. Each of us has momentary experiences of this state without paying much attention to it. It can be found in the state of flow while concentrating on an activity, in a momentary abeyance of thought during a pause in activity or a period of reverie, or, according to Tolle, "whenever a gap occurs in the stream of thought."

For most people, such gaps happen rarely and only accidentally, in moments when the mind is rendered "speechless," sometimes triggered by great beauty, extreme physical exertion, or even great danger. Suddenly, there is inner stillness. And within that stillness there is a subtle but intense joy, there is love, there is peace.[76]

Mindfulness entails the abeyance of judgment called acceptance. Rather than trying to suppress thoughts and emotions, one simply observes them without judgment. Christopher Willard explains:

Mindfulness meditation involves practicing meta-awareness of thoughts, feelings, and sensations in the present moment. "Meta-awareness" is a term for watching our thoughts without judgment, analysis, or storytelling. We simply note observations about the mind's current activities as thoughts, sensations, and associations that both come and go.[77]

Even negative emotional states are to be observed without judgment. The cognitive therapist Steven Hayes asserts that "accepting your pain is a step toward ridding yourself of your suffering."[78] "The pain that you create now is always some form of nonacceptance, some form of unconscious resistance to what *is*," Tolle says. "On the level of thought, the resistance is some form of judgment. On the emotional level, it is some form of negativity."[79] Nisargadatta admonishes: "Leave the mind alone, stand aware and unconcerned and you will realize that to stand alert but detached, watching events come and go, is an aspect of your real nature."[80]

Mindfulness is focused on the present, on the "Now." Friedrich Nietzsche wrote that "He who cannot sink down on the threshold of the moment and forget all the past, who cannot stand balanced like a goddess of victory without growing dizzy and afraid, will never know what happiness is — worse, he will never do anything to make others happy."[81] Christopher Willard adds his voice to a multitude of practitioners and researchers in observing that "the actual present moment is often a lot less stressful than the stories our minds invent about the past, present, and future."[82] In Aldous Huxley's Buddhist-flavored utopia, *Island*, the mynah birds were trained to say "Attention!" to remind the inhabitants to stay present.

Mindfulness is a staple of cognitive therapy. Steven C. Hayes relates that "Recent research in Western psychology has proven that practicing mindfulness can have notable psychological benefits. In fact, mindfulness is currently being adopted as a means of enhancing treatment in a number of different psychological traditions in the West."[83] A large number of self-help and therapy books centered on mindfulness have appeared recently.[84] They extol this focused awareness on the present as highly beneficial for everyone and highly effective as a means to deal with depression and an array of related mental ailments.

An impressive accumulation of evidence shows that some simple methods involving various mindfulness techniques can bring a cornucopia of benefits without the stress and pitfalls of looking for happiness without. The consequent practice of mindfulness, even if only for a few months, has been found to significantly reduce stress and anxiety, help manage negative emotional reactions and encourage positive states of mind, enhance cognitive skills and creativity, and further the development of empathy and relationship skills.[85] "To the extent that you can acknowledge the true power of your mind," Mingyur says, "you can begin to exercise more control over your experience. Pain, sadness, fear, anxiety, and all other forms of suffering no longer disrupt your life as forcefully as they used to."[86]

Kornfield reports that "Mindfulness brings perspective, balance, and freedom."[87] He says recognition of the power of mindfulness is steadily growing in the West: "Since 1980 nearly a thousand scientific papers have documented the effectiveness of mindfulness, often studying Western trainings that are based on a Buddhist approach. An important distinction to make, however, is that while Western psychology has focused primarily on the mindfulness of the therapist, Buddhist psychology asserts that the very foundation of well-being is a systematic training of mindfulness in the student."[88] Bolte Taylor contends that "Once you learn to recognize the subtle feelings (and physiology) running through your body when you are connected to the circuitry of the present moment, you can then train yourself to reactivate that circuit on demand."[89]

Deborah Schoeberlein, who teaches mindfulness to both teachers and students, echoes robust findings on mindfulness in reporting that:

This specific approach to paying attention and honing awareness improves mental focus and academic performance. It also strengthens skills that contribute to emotional balance. The best of our human qualities, including the capacity for kindness, empathy, and compassion, support and are supported by mindfulness.[90]

Further,

As you practice and apply mindfulness, you'll gain skills that will help you accurately assess challenges and handle them with greater ease. Having techniques that help you manage your own experiences and emotions is more comfortable than feeling powerless as a result of your emotions and habits or, worse, buffeted about by the changing winds of other people's behaviors and the environment.[91]

The source of these benefits is not a temporary mending of a sense of insufficiency and lack, but rather a greater awareness of inner abundance. Thus the benefits themselves can continue without contrast and possibly without habituation, and there is evidence for this. This inner source is not a cause of either inner or outer conflict, for it entails awareness of a unity and harmony within that colors our perceptions of our environment, frees us from the gain/loss dynamic inherent to the attempt to extract happiness from others, bestows independence, reduces vulnerability, avoids the tension of judgment, and is naturally expressed in benevolent, harmonious behavior.

The awareness of this "natural self" is said to be a source of naturally occurring peace, joy, and love. Each step closer to this awareness can ease the stress of our daily lives, offer temporary haven from emotional distress, buffer the effects of the turmoil in our environment, and foster a fonder, more caring regard for others.

In my own experience, I find mindfulness very useful as a means to interrupt a train of thoughts causing less-than-pleasant feelings. When I become aware of emotional discomfort, I observe what I am thinking and always find there is no compelling reason to stay on that train of thought. In fact, the dialogues and arguments that constitute so many of my thoughts often seem a bit silly in light of the tension they are causing. Becoming aware of them dissipates the compulsion to think them, which I find brings immediate relief. It usually doesn't last long before another train takes me out of present awareness, but the knowledge that I can stop the train at will makes me far less prone to slipping into a funk or worrying about imagined scenarios than used to be the case. Before, I was an unwitting accomplice to holding my feelings hostage to my thoughts. Now I have an easy means of defense.

And, as I exercise my ability to invite relative moments of peace, it gets progressively easier to do. I find the increasing frequency of such moments has a cumulative effect on the underlying tone of my affective experiences, bringing a deeper feeling of peace when I am relaxed and taking the edge off of tensions when I am confronted with demands and challenges.

Practicing mindfulness reduces the power and hold of unpleasant emotions and helps clear the way to awareness of pleasant feelings. Mindfulness brings feelings and associated thoughts to conscious awareness, which is a prerequisite to the ability to realize one's choice of feelings. Mindfulness is an excellent means to assess the merits of alternative sources of happiness. Such assessment is required for discerning choice. Awareness of feelings, discernment in choosing, and the ability to realize your choices are crucial to the successful pursuit of happiness. Mindfulness is the most accessible portal to the internal sources of happiness, and it is among the most potent means to empower students' pursuit.

The Argument So Far

So far I have laid a foundation for my claim that empowering the pursuit of happiness should and can be the primary purpose of education. I know from experience that this is a tough sell. It confronts the belief that education has more important aims than the happiness of students, that this is neither a desirable nor practical purpose. Many believe that feelings are beyond human capacity to control in any significant way. Hume expressed this view:

> *No man would ever be unhappy, could he alter his feelings. Proteus-like, he would elude all attacks, by the continual alterations of his shape and form. But of this resource nature has, in a great measure, deprived us. The fabric and constitution of our mind no more depends on our choice, than that of our body.*[92]

Hume recognizes how eminently desirable a "Proteus-like" ability to feel as one chooses is, but does not believe it is within the reach of human beings. He is wrong. We certainly have some control over the judgments that give rise to what we feel. Realizing this, we can learn how to take steps that make us feel better than we do at present. This ability can be taught and honed in our schools; and as this is the essence of empowering students' pursuit of happiness, it certainly should be.

Before I turn to the question of how to empower students' pursuit, I should summarize the main points of the argument thus far. If we would treat each child as an end in herself, we must serve her happiness first and foremost. This is the moral foundation of the argument. It is fortified by the first key insight: **the subjective quality of our lives is determined by the quality of our feelings.** Serving our children's happiness requires that we take the question of happiness seriously in our schools.

The second insight is that **the pursuit of happiness includes the moment-to-moment steps we take to experience a preferable feeling.** The more we are aware of what is worthwhile to feel and what causes us to feel as we do, the more likely our chosen steps will take us in the desired direction. Seeing the pursuit in terms of steps also focuses our attention on the moment-to-moment causes of what we feel.

This leads to the third insight: **feelings are responses to the judgments reflected in our thoughts.** Patterns of thought and filters that color our interpretation of our perceptions have a dominant influence on what we feel. They can trap us, making us unwitting slaves of the chattering aspect of our minds that tethers us to our fears, insufficiencies, and negative judgments. Or they can free us from dependence on external circumstance to wander more pleasant trails of thought and feeling.

The fourth insight follows from the third: **we have the ability to choose what we think and thereby determine, or at least influence, how we feel.** This ability begins with present awareness of the contents of our consciousness. In realizing this, we change our vista of possibilities. The awareness of the content of our consciousness expands the inner dimension of experience. Awareness also alerts us to the desirability of changing our patterns of thought.

We can ease the burdens of the past by understanding that the influence of the past lies in present thoughts and interpretations that we can change. We can find the "key to escaping the dogmas that have made so many people prisoners of their past," in the words of Seligman.[93] We can release the hold of pessimistic patterns of thought and develop optimistic ones. As we advance in awareness and practice, we will gnaw fewer bones of regret about the past and lighten worries about the future.

Growing experience will reveal that our will is more important than our environment in determining what we feel. We thereby gain a degree of blessed independence from events, circumstances, and the judgments of others. Discovering this power of will enhances our self-confidence and sense of worth. It would transform the subjective quality of our lives.

These insights establish both the importance and the practicality of empowering the pursuit of happiness in our schools. They provide a foundation for a happiness pedagogy.

5

Empowering
The Pursuit of Happiness

*Happiness can be taught. Imagine a world
where we're taught the practices that develop
happiness and emotional intelligence just as we're
taught algebra or writing. It is possible. And it
can change the world.* | Randy Taran

If schools could do far more than they do to improve children's prospects for happiness, I'm pretty sure most people would agree they should. I imagine trying to convince parents that the happiness of their children is less important than other aims of education would be a tough sell if parents realized that schools *could* contribute more to their children's happiness. But those who champion other aims aren't in this awkward position because parents are relatively unaware of the possibility. The prevailing view is that schools don't do happiness, at least not directly, so why expect it?

Martin Seligman poses a quiz:

> *In two words or less, what do you most want for your children? If you are like the hundreds of parents I've asked, you responded, "Happiness," "Confidence," "Contentment," "Balance," "Good Stuff," "Kindness," "Health," "Satisfaction," and the like. In short, you most want well-being for your children. In two words or less, what do schools teach? If you are like other parents, you responded,*

"Achievement," "Thinking Skills," "Success," "Conformity," "Literacy," "Mathematics," "Discipline" and the like. In short schools teach the tools of accomplishment. Notice that there is almost no overlap between the two lists.[1]

The disconnect between what parents want for their children and what they think schools should teach reflects the general ambiguity about what happiness is and how we pursue it. That is why I propose a practical understanding of happiness as a feeling you want to keep feeling and the pursuit of happiness as the steps you take to experience it. Seen in this light, empowering the pursuit consists of leading a child to awareness of the relative desirability of different feelings and providing her with the knowledge, understanding, and skills that improve her ability to feel as she chooses. Educators can do this. They can make a profound difference in the lives of children if they focus on the research-tested means to develop this ability.

Liberal education is already more or less designed to empower each student's pursuit of her external goals. A happiness curriculum would do the same for her internal goals. Research has confirmed highly effective ways to feel better, improve one's outlook, and build resiliency in the face of turmoil. We need to give these methods a central place in school curricula.

Some schools already have courses in happiness and "well-being," but usually they are add-ons at the periphery of traditional subjects. If empowering the pursuit of happiness is the primary aim of liberal education, the methods of such empowerment should form the heart of the curriculum. I believe this calls for devoting at least an hour per K-12 school day to directly addressing this purpose. In fact, the teaching of all subjects should be oriented to contributing to this core aim. A great deal of evidence backs my claim that a well-developed happiness pedagogy would enhance rather than detract from conventional learning outcomes. It's a win-win proposition.

A well-developed happiness curriculum has five main components: inner awareness, social awareness, means to influence feelings, expression and engagement, and inquiry. Together they form a grand strategy of empowerment.

Inner Awareness

Most people no doubt believe education enhances children's chances for happiness. But it is clear that almost all bets are placed on helping them tap external sources. Some of the more promising external sources are neglected. Nel Noddings points to relationships, home life, and sense of place as important matters of life that are shorted in the education of children.[2]

No doubt our schools could do better informing students' external pursuit of happiness, but this implies guiding students to an awareness of the sort of external conditions and experiences most conducive to what each prefers to feel. Awareness of what works best is a prerequisite for discerning choice. It requires inner awareness of feelings, their causes, and your preferences. So even the empowerment of external pursuits should begin with a foundation of inner awareness.

Whatever role the external environment plays in shaping what we feel, internal factors ultimately determine it. The means to influence the thoughts, judgments, and beliefs that give rise to feelings are based on inner awareness. Inner awareness also provides the means to *experientially* weigh the value of what is taught.

The best way to begin promoting inner awareness is to teach mindfulness and have students regularly practice it. I explained earlier that mindfulness has become a favored method in cognitive therapy, and it is finding its way into corporate training and classrooms around the world. There is "an international movement for mindful parenting and education."[3] The mindfulness movement is considered a "revolution."[4]

Mindfulness is nonjudgmental awareness. Willard explains the difference between mindfulness and other forms of meditation this way: "Unlike concentration meditation, in which we direct our mind where to go, mindfulness practice focuses on observing where the mind goes naturally. If concentration meditation is comparable to a zoom lens upon an object, mindfulness is like a wide-angle lens focused on the whole horizon. Mindfulness brings attention directly to the whole present-moment experience — our perceptions and, perhaps more importantly, the stories our minds make out of them."[5]

"The key," Yongey Mingyur says, "lies in learning to simply rest in a bare awareness of thoughts, feelings, and perceptions as they occur."[6] At first, it is extraordinarily difficult to avoid being carried off by the current of the contents of one's mind, so techniques have been developed to help people pull out of the current. Focus on breathing is a core technique used in almost all variations. Most practitioners recommend sessions of five minutes for younger children, which can be increased as they become used to it.

Mindfulness can be easily taught to kids. Linda Lantieri, the founder and director of the Inner Resilience Program, has taught mindfulness to thousands of children of all ages. She says teachers must first regularly practice mindfulness themselves before teaching it.[7] She has children lie down and focus on "belly breathing" and body awareness before expanding their awareness to thoughts and feelings. Ian Morris, who teaches students in their early to mid teens, has them remain at their desks and begins by asking students to "bring their attention into the space of the classroom they are in and then into the space that their body occupies."[8] He then moves to attention to breathing and thoughts.

Deborah Schoeberlein recommends techniques she both practices herself and uses in the classroom. Learning the simple technique of paying close attention to the inflow and outflow of breathing is fundamental. When it comes to teaching awareness of thoughts, she advises:

> The essence of this technique is attending to the process (the experience of noticing) without getting caught up in content (what the thoughts are about). First, simply notice thoughts as they first appear on the horizon of your mind. Keep some distance as you watch them and let them fade away. This is the difference between witnessing thoughts and engaging with them. It's an attitude of, "Oh, here are some thoughts about work (or a relationship or something else), but I'm not going to get into them now." Be gentle with yourself, and patient, and kind.[9]

Schoeberlein also has recommendations for teaching mindfulness of feelings:

> As with developing mindfulness of thoughts, the idea is to notice and feel emotions without specifying what type. The technique involves just acknowledging the fact of feeling or reaction. There's no need to reinforce the internal story by elaborating on details; so for instance rather than describing "feeling bored," "feeling uneasy," or "feeling peaceful," you would just acknowledge all of them as belonging to the category of "feeling." With practice, you'll increase your ability to recognize the presence of emotion without immediately getting pulled into it or automatically acting on it. This is useful because mindfulness of emotions increases conscious awareness of them, and enhances our ability to manage them at will.[10]

Young children are more adept than most adults when it comes to awareness of feelings.[11] They will not yet have mastered the adult art of suppressing emotions, and therefore their feelings are more readily accessible to them. Observing feelings has to overcome decades of inner blindness for most adults; kids carry far less baggage in this regard. And young students are not put off by being asked to participate in mindfulness exercises that some older students find "weird" because meditation is unfamiliar to them.[12]

Maureen Healy, who wrote and taught a curriculum for preschoolers "to plant seeds of peace and calmness in the youngest minds," discovered it was not nearly as difficult as one might expect.[13]

> I got to lead groups of young children through meditation and interactive lessons to understand peace, name it, cause it, and choose it. Such inner calm was captured over and over again by these kids. ... Kids were able to not only identify the feeling of calmness, but really took to the idea that they can cause it.[14]

If preschoolers can be taught to capture calmness, it bodes well for the readiness of primary school students to learn awareness of feelings and the ability to evoke them. The evidence that young students can be readily taught mindfulness and that they thereby gain some control over emotions and cognitive processes is accumulating.[15] According to Patricia Jennings, "We're seeing evidence that children have a natural capacity for quieting their mind and focusing their attention, skills that can build self-control and enhance their ability to learn."[16] Lantieri finds that "Young children ... still have a great capacity to access the inner dimensions. ... They still have the ability to see beneath the surface of things."[17]

Those who teach mindfulness in schools say that times for stillness should be structured into the school day and that exercises in mindfulness need to be a regular routine. Students should learn to be mindful not only in quiet moments, but also in times of active engagement and even stress. They need to learn how to be mindful no matter what they are doing or experiencing. They should be taught triggers that remind them to be mindful in any and all situations. Many of the riper fruits of mindfulness grow from the ability to be mindful during moments that are not quiet and stress-free.

Awareness of feelings also grows from sharing experiences and observations. To build awareness, students need to talk about feelings and hear what others have to say. This means they have to be able to identify and describe feelings, which requires the introduction of an expanded vocabulary of feelings and inner states. Matthew Lipman advises that "a relevant vocabulary is needed to think, discuss, and learn about emotions."[18]

Morris suggests other ways to develop awareness of feelings and the ability to identify them for students advanced far enough in their reading and writing skills. Students can take an "emotional inventory" available for free at www.authentichappiness.org and keep journals describing what they felt during the day and what seemed to cause these feelings.[19]

In addition to verbal descriptions, all appropriate mediums of expression should be encouraged. Drawing, coloring, music, acting, and storytelling easily lend themselves to describing feelings and making associations. Morris suggests getting students to sculpt specific emotions with clay.[20] If a child learns how to pay attention to her feelings while engaging in activities, she will more likely discover her passion. Videos of children expressing feelings and talking about them is another means to provide examples, build vocabulary, and start the process of learning to identify the causes of feelings. Time should be set aside for children to reflect on what they feel, and they should be asked at odd moments — especially when emotions flare — to try to describe what they are feeling and what they think is causing it.

Some 3,000 schools in the United States use "Promoting Alternative Thinking Strategies" (PATHS).[21]

> In one part of the curriculum, kids receive small labeled cards with faces expressing different feelings. They personalize the cards and use them to communicate their emotions throughout the day. Self-regulation is also taught explicitly with the aid of a traffic signal. If students face a difficult or frustrating situation, they focus on the red light, which means "Stop — Calm Down." They are supposed to describe the problem and their feelings about it. Next comes yellow, "Go Slow — Think," that is, make a plan. Green means "Go — Try My Plan."[22]

Choice implies preference, and at some point students should be asked to consider what they prefer to feel. They should be asked to reflect on how different feelings affect their bodies, for this is easier than judging states of mind at first. Teachers should ask "What does it feel like in your chest when you are angry? Afraid? Frustrated? Happy? When you are having fun with friends? When someone smiles at you? When you do something nice to someone? When you are mean to someone?" Both Morris and Lantieri provide specific exercises to make students aware of how the body responds to different emotions. Such exercises not only enhance awareness of feelings, they also help students recognize the relative desirability of feelings of attraction compared to those of aversion.

I stress the importance of motive. Motive must be strengthened as the basis for advancing practice; students must repeatedly experience the benefits. Children should experience the pleasure of temporary escapes from chattering minds. They should be asked to pay attention to how escaping runaway trains of thought can make them feel better, and offers them a chance to choose rather than merely react.

Susan Greenland emphasizes playfulness and enjoyment in her teaching: "Mindfulness practice is serious work with important, long-term implications for overall health and well-being, but above all, it is a pleasure and can be presented playfully and effectively."[23] Lantieri also recommends cultivating "a spirit of play, adventure, and genuine curiosity."[24] As students advance, observing thoughts and feelings becomes easier and, for those who choose to continue the practice, eventually habitual.

Teachers who want to learn the art of teaching mindfulness and other methods of inner awareness have a growing number of resources to turn to. A Google search will turn up quite a few programs such as Innerkids, Mindful Schools, The Attention Academy, MindUp of the Hawn Foundation, and the Garrison Institute that teach mindfulness and help others learn how to teach it. *The Mindful Child* by Greenland, *Child's Mind* by Willard, and *Building Emotional Intelligence* by Linda Lantieri and Daniel Goleman are examples of the expanding genre of literature on teaching mindfulness to children in the home and in classrooms. Educators can also join networks of people dedicated to bringing mindfulness training to schools, such as the Mindfulness in Education Network.

Social Awareness

How you see others is largely a projection of your state of mind. Your perception of others mirrors your judgments, beliefs, and feelings. Understanding that how you regard others is a projection contributes to self-understanding. It also allows you to choose to set aside the distorting mental lenses and see how much your inner experiences seem to be reflected in the inner experiences of those around you. Recognizing what you have in common gives you greater insight into what they think and feel, for you have the well of your own experiences to call upon. This strengthens the bond you feel for others, and most likely what they feel for you, which enriches your relationships. Self-understanding, understanding other people, and strengthening the emotional bond with others are interdependent aims of teaching social awareness.

The means used to enhance social awareness are crucial to a happiness curriculum. Among these means are having students frequently share their thoughts and feelings, getting them to try to identify what others are thinking and feeling, and leading them in trying to see things through the eyes of another person. Teaching students how to be mindful during interactions with other people is enormously helpful. Getting them to actually listen to what others are saying is a huge step toward expanding their social awareness. The practice of attentive listening brings insight and clears up many misunderstandings. It also builds the resonance of a deeper sense of connection.

The next chapter explores ways to enhance students' appreciation of others by emphasizing what they have in common. Here I focus on techniques that expand awareness of feelings and their causes through awareness of others.

One method is to have students in a class share stories of particularly meaningful experiences and try to explain what they felt while it was happening. Students should be invited to ask questions like: "How did it make you feel when such and such happened?" "Why did it make you feel sad, or happy, or mad, or nervous?" "Would you feel differently if x, y, or z happened instead?" Or students might relate how they felt the same way or differently in a similar situation.

Morris suggests a method he calls "identity parade": "Using images from an Internet search, a film clip or an extract from a book, ask students to 'diagnose' emotional states in the characters and justify why they believe it to be a certain emotion. Ask students to look for a range of evidence from tone of voice to facial expression and body language."[25] He also relates an exercise meant to promote listening and empathy:

In pairs, students read fictional stories in the first person containing emotional aspects (e.g., the break up of a relationship, an argument) to each other. The other student in the pair listens and "mirrors" (notices and describes) the emotional states back to their partner once the story has finished (e.g. "you felt sadness when your girlfriend said she didn't want to be with you any more, you felt this because…"). The listener then allows the speaker to correct any points where they have misinterpreted and the listener then corrects him/herself. This activity encourages students to listen to the details of each other's stories first, and then pick up their emotional states and feelings.[26]

Teachers can assign a journal of observations about other people's emotional expressions. Students can write about emotions expressed in movies, in discussions and get-togethers with friends, at home, by people on the street and in stores, on the news, in music, etc. Students can describe the expressions, guess what the people were feeling, and perhaps relate how other people's expressions of emotion touched their own feelings.

Young kids should also learn how to identify motives. They can pick characters in stories, books and movies and try to guess what caused them to act as they do. They can do the same with people in the news, both famous and unknown. They can put on dramas where students try to figure out the motives of the characters they are assigned to play. I like to give scenarios in my classes and have students explain what they would choose to do in these scenarios and why.

Educators can ask students to discuss their feelings about the things that happen in school: issues with popularity and acceptance, insults and arguments, misbehavior, teacher approval and disapproval, rules and punishments, activities, tests and grades, etc. And, when appropriate, teachers should share their own feelings.

Of course, students should hear the stories and perspectives of people who are different from them in terms of race, ethnicity, gender, class, religion, etc. Exercises that have students stand in the shoes of others are powerful for a number of reasons. Role-playing is a fun and effective technique to get students to try out different perspectives. Sometimes I ask students to argue the opposing view of what they believe, and I model this myself quite often. I argue that you don't understand someone else's view until you try to see it through his or her eyes.

The literature on promoting social awareness and sensitivity is extensive. Educators will have no problem locating tested techniques to promote these aims.

Methods to Influence Feelings

Entire libraries of self-help books give advice on how to feel better. Here I point to some proven techniques for getting closer to what you want to feel at present, for relieving emotional distress, and for improving the affective quality of your life in general. Most of these techniques have been used and tested in schools. They have also been used and robustly tested in cognitive therapy.

Educators are increasingly interested in "happiness interventions."[27] Some schools already have well-being curricula or have introduced special courses based on the findings of positive psychology. The number of programs that teach mindfulness and emotional management techniques in schools has grown rapidly over the past two decades. But a curriculum dedicated to empowering students' pursuit of happiness requires a well-designed strategy — one that builds throughout their years of formal education — to develop children's ability to choose and influence what they feel. Kids should learn a wide variety of techniques that strengthen this ability and be encouraged to practice those that work best for them.

Mindfulness has proven the most effective practice we can teach kids for almost all dimensions of emotional, cognitive and even physical well-being. Some who teach various well-being techniques say students really like mindfulness and they use it to reduce stress, enhance their focus in sports and performances, and enjoy moments of relative peace.[28] Mindfulness is foundational, and it promises a host of benefits.

Another popular technique for finding haven from stress and distress is visualization, which is an exercise of imagination. For instance, you can mentally revisit the most peaceful, most happy moment you can recall. Or you can visualize a pleasant circumstance that helps calm your nerves or provides a restful pause. In basic training, I envisioned myself on a cliff overlooking the Pacific Ocean at sunset. It really helped on long marches and when standing in formation for long periods of time. Sometimes I envision forest meadows and lazy summer strolls down tree-shaded lanes between fields of grain. I use such imaginings to interrupt downward spirals of mood or the pressures of stress.

When plagued by disturbing thoughts, Matthieu Ricard advises us to "try to imagine situations that are sources of peace."[29]

> *Transport yourself mentally to the shores of a placid lake or to a high mountaintop overlooking a broad vista. Imagine yourself sitting serenely, your mind as vast and clear as a cloudless sky, as calm as a windless ocean. Experience this calmness. Watch your inner tempests subside and let this feeling of peace grow anew in your mind. Understand that even if your wounds are deep, they do not touch the essential nature of your mind, the fundamental luminosity of pure consciousness.*[30]

Such imaginings soften the edges of hard experiences and allow a brief mental respite to catch your emotional breath, so to speak. Visualization or "mental imaging" has been found to be an effective means to deal with physical pain as well.[31] Most people likely use some form of such mental devices, and they can be easily taught to children. We all daydream, of course, but daydreaming is usually a less intentional escape. Intention is important to the results of our imagining. In daydreaming we often follow our thoughts rather than direct them. Intentional visualization is a means to consciously direct thoughts toward a desired feeling.

One way to introduce visualization to young children is to read descriptions of what characters in stories think are wonderful places. Students should be invited to comment and discuss the merits of such places. They should also be shown pictures or short video clips of pleasant places and landscapes then asked to pick out those that speak most to their hearts. Students who can write should write descriptions of their favorite settings and explain why they favor them. And when a short break in the lessons of any class is in order, students can be asked to "Take a break in your favorite place."

Students can learn to enter the **state of flow** described earlier. Flow offers not only a respite from cares and the chattering of one's mind, but also a certain feeling of wholeness, of momentary sufficiency. Biofeedback research shows that almost anyone can learn to induce mental states at will once they recognize the experience. Attention is the key; you don't need biofeedback technology to learn to associate activities with a state of mind if you can identify and attend to it. Once sensitized to the experience of "being in the zone," for example, athletes learn to induce the state at will.

Flow can be attained during all sorts of activities, including purely mental ones. Lyubomirsky says,

> To increase the frequency and length of flow experiences in your daily life, you need to become fully engaged and involved. Whether it's writing a letter, making phone calls on behalf of a client, or playing Candy Land or a round of golf, seek work, home, and leisure activities that engage your skills and expertise.[32]

These episodes offer not only significant mental respite; they also exercise an important mental ability that is basic to all efforts that require mental discipline. In fact, they might be considered immediate rewards of mental discipline, providing the basic motivation used in most methods of behavior modification.

Morris suggests a way to teach about flow:

> Ask students to pay attention to times during the week when they enter into a state of flow and write about it. Encourage the idea that flow can be found in a variety of areas of life: academic study/games/music/drama and so on. Ask them to pay attention to the conditions that made flow possible and ask them to reflect on how being in flow affected them afterwards. What emotions did it bring about? How did it make them feel about themselves?[33]

One way to deal with perceived troubles is to reach for perspective. This is called "**reframing**." People have a tendency to turn the molehills of current troubles into looming mountains that block all escape. Few of your troubles are as serious as they seem when your mind is focused on them to the exclusion of the larger picture. Reaching for the perspective of the larger picture helps reverse the process.

Many students have entered my office weighed down by their troubles. My natural response is to offer perspective. It may be a little gallows humor: "Life sucks and then you die." Or "I hope the recruiter didn't tell you earth was a vacation planet when you signed up to come here." Humor offers at least a little immediate relief and an opening for a change in perspective. Greenland observes:

> At times a shift in perspective is all it takes to alleviate suffering. Have events in your life ever seemed so ridiculous that you started to laugh? In

that moment, your suffering had ceased. Nothing had changed in the out-side world, but with a shift in perspective you could laugh about what had happened and experience an oasis of happiness, if only for a moment.[34]

I often remind troubled students of all the other times in their lives when they were confronted with seemingly insurmountable troubles that are now forgotten. "Do you ever notice that things tend to work out in the end?" I also tell such students that adversity has a silver lining in the form of lessons about what is truly important in life, which could help them pull out of the rut of superficial pursuits and live a deeper, more meaningful life. Of course, there is always "All things must pass."

Quick and easy perspective is usually a brief palliative though. The most stable and enduring changes in perspective come from new insights about self, others, and the shared journey of life. Life itself teaches most lessons that lead to such insight, but education is an opportunity for broader and deeper inquiry into the dimensions of the human condition. I explain this component of a happiness curriculum in the section on inquiry.

Most of the methods currently used to promote well-being in schools were developed in the context of cognitive therapy and based on research in the relatively new field of positive psychology. Cognitive therapy explicitly recognizes the relationship between thoughts and feelings and targets thoughts and thought patterns as a means to deal with emotional distress and promote positive feelings. Acronyms are common. For example, there is the generic CBT — cognitive behavior therapy — the ABCDE model Seligman has used — adversity, beliefs, consequences, disputation, and energization — and Haye's ACT — acceptance and commitment therapy.[35] Such therapies raise awareness of thoughts and their consequences in order to change habitual patterns of thinking.

These techniques are designed to check pessimism and cultivate optimism, to disengage thought patterns that contribute to stress and worry, to build self-esteem, to fortify positive attitudes and actions toward others, to release anger and bitterness, to gain affective independence from people and events, to release phobias, to savor pleasures, and to find more meaning in life. Practicing these techniques not only relieves emotional problems, it also builds skills that help develop the ability to feel as you choose.

Versions of Seligman's ABCDE method of building resilience are used at Geelong Grammar School in Australia and Wellington College in Britain.[36] In essence, they have students examine the beliefs that shaped their emotional reactions to adverse situations. Seeing the connection between their beliefs and feelings allows them to challenge their beliefs by playing "angel's advocate." They are led to notice pessimistic patterns of thought and look closely at whether such patterns are justified. Students are encouraged to develop alternative ways to look at things and different ways of responding to challenges. Both schools try to build optimism by getting students to think about the blessings of their lives, either by keeping a journal or discussing what went well in their lives in class.

Similar "interventions" are used in helping students learn how to deal with anger and conflict. Remembering to be mindful creates an opportunity to choose a response rather than automatically reacting. Students are also asked to think about what pushes their buttons and what they might do to soften the impact and "neutralize the trap" of their usual reactions by planning ahead.[37]

Encouraging **gratitude** is a favored method in cognitive therapy because it is an effective way to promote positive attitudes and improve relationships. Students in a happiness class at Wollongong University in Australia are asked to keep a weekly "gratitude journal."[38] Evidence shows that people who keep such journals "feel better about their lives and are more optimistic."[39] The instructors of the course also set up a gratitude activity in which they:

- *Introduced research about gratitude.*
- *Asked students to list 5 things for which they are grateful and rank them 1-5 in order of importance.*
- *Allocated students into small groups and asked students to compare their lists and generate an agreed list of things for which we can be grateful.*
- *Asked students to devise strategies to develop gratitude in their lives.*
- *Asked students to write a poem that they can stick on their wall to remind them to be grateful.*[40]

Forgiveness is a powerful means to alleviate anger, bitterness and the "victim mentality" that plagues so many people. It does wonders for relationships and the ability to appreciate others. That is why it is also a favored method in cognitive therapy. Teaching forgiveness in grade school would build on awareness of feelings and their causes. Young students should be led to consciously experience the relief of forgiveness. Older students can be shown a film like *The Power of Forgiveness*: "The film combines character-driven stories of dramatic transgressions with those of more commonplace annoyances, examining the role that forgiveness can play in alleviating the resulting anger and grief and the physical, mental and spiritual benefits that come with forgiveness."[41]

The Campaign for Love and Forgiveness website has teacher resources, including two lesson plans for middle through high school classrooms, that engage students in thinking about love and forgiveness. Ellen Greenblatt, who wrote these plans, uses readings such as Tobias Wolff's "Firelight" and Mark Twain's *The Adventures of Huckleberry Finn* as the focus for questions about love and forgiveness. She also asks open-ended questions like: "What is the difference between asking for forgiveness from another person and forgiving someone yourself? Which is easier? Why?" Such questions lead to self-awareness. The website has links to dozens of stories relevant to teaching forgiveness.

Expressing appreciation feels good for both the giver and the receiver. Chris Barker and Brian Martin describe an exercise they use at the end of a course on happiness when the students have come to know each other well:

> Sitting in a circle, we started with one student: everyone else wrote down what they appreciated about that student and then put their comments, unsigned, in a pile in front of the student. Then we went through the same process for the next student and so on around the circle. Then everyone picked up their slips of paper and read them. This exercise is extremely powerful. It involves both giving and receiving appreciation, both known to build positive emotions.[42]

Some lessons at Geelong Grammar School focus on having students identify "Signature Strengths."[43] Students write narratives about when they were at their best, then compare their scores on the VIA signature strength test on the Authentic Happiness website with the strengths identified in their narratives. They are encouraged to find ways to use their strengths to overcome challenges and to develop strengths where they are weak.

Morris helps students deal with conflict by having them devise a conflict scenario, then "create a tableau (still image) of it."[44] He asks participants in these tableaus to step out and try to figure out the motives of his or her character. The point is to get students to think how people's reactions are shaped by past experiences. In other exercises students think about the words and actions that make them angry and what causes arguments to spin out of control.

Expression and Engagement

Awareness and realization are potent means to improve what one feels, but few consciously pursue these means. People are naturally inclined to try to change what they feel by *doing*, by diverting their minds with some sort of activity or external pursuit. Children are especially so inclined. They are not strangers to reflection, but few children will have developed the patience and taste for it. Their energy and curiosity need to be expressed in action and in exploring the world in which they live. A curriculum devoted to empowering children's lifelong pursuit of happiness must tap these resources.

The trick is to enhance a child's awareness of his feelings as he engages in activities. That way he is better able to discover the intrinsic rewards of what he does and which activities are most rewarding. To my mind, another important aim is to make a child aware that activities are not so much a cause of enjoyable feelings as they are a way to express them. Schools should do more to make him consciously aware that the joy of creative expression comes from within. Recognition and approval are not necessary to feel it. This can be profoundly liberating.

To these ends, schools should structure more opportunities for all types of creative activities. Dance, art, music, cooking, designing, carpentry, engineering and science projects come to mind, but less conventional venues for creative expression should also be encouraged. Many kids prefer sports as a means of self expression, but they should be encouraged to discover other interests and talents. Whether peers and society at large prize a child's particular talent, she should be given more opportunities to discover where her talent and passion lie and recognize the intrinsic benefits of expressing them. This means she should first try her hand at many activities before making up her mind what she prefers to do.

Time, space, materials, and mentors are required, but there are creative ways to provide all of these without a great deal of additional cost. If a certain time of day is set aside, teachers can be freed from normal classroom duties to share their own interests and talents. Volunteers from the community will help fill the need for mentors. Parents, organizations, and businesses could sponsor particular activities to help pay for materials.

As for time, educators, school boards, departments of education, and advocates of longer school days and years may have to rethink their priorities and reexamine their beliefs that the most desirable outcomes of education are a function of the amount of time kids are exposed to content. The belief that torturing kids with a full day of seat-time is in their best interest won't seem all that plausible when happiness is acknowledged as the purpose of education. Opportunities for creative expression should not be relegated solely to the after-school time slot. They should brighten the school-time experience with more opportunities for creative expression.

Educators should encourage out-of-school activities and engagement, of course. A happiness curriculum should especially encourage more fulfilling types of engagement. Asking students to do things that help others and to pay attention to how it makes them feel blesses the hearts of all involved. Morris recommends getting students to perform acts of kindness:

> Ask the students to perform a random act of kindness in between lessons and note how they felt afterwards. It doesn't have to be saving the starving in Africa: just holding a door open for someone or helping someone with a heavy package is a good start. How long does the feeling last compared with other things they do to bring them pleasure (eating chocolate for example?).45

The students are asked to make something and give it to someone outside the school at Geelong Grammar School. Heather, a student who took part in a "Breadology" project that involved learning how to bake bread then visiting a nursing home where they gave the bread to the inhabitants, explained it this way:

> "First, we learned about good nutrition," she said, "Then we learned how to cook a healthy meal, but instead of eating, we gave the food to other people."
> "Did it bother you to not eat the food you'd spent so much time preparing? It smelled really good."
> "No, just the opposite," she declared, smiling broadly, "At first I was scared of the old people, but then it felt like a little light went on inside me.

I want to do it again."

> *Heather's best friend quickly chimed in, "Doing something for others felt better than any video game."*[46]

Older students should be encouraged to volunteer with charitable organizations or form their own "good deeds" or "pay-it-forward" club. Schools can help with a list of service opportunities. Many schools are already doing something along these lines. They just need to make service an integrated, purposeful part of a happiness curriculum.

Creative expression and service engagement are at least a partial antidote to kids' heavy reliance on phones, gadgets, and screens to fill the unclaimed hours of their days. Many teachers complain that these things are filling some of the claimed hours too. They certainly are in my classrooms. We have deep cause for concern. The quick and easy stimulations of devices distract children from inner awareness and the calming beauty of nature. The connection with nature that feeds the soul and calms the mind seems to be growing weaker.

Schools can strengthen this connection by having students practice mindfulness on quiet walks through parks, woods, gardens, fields, and even school grounds. Teachers can take students on safaris to discover flora and fauna, and on treks into the wild to discover themselves apart from the distractions of modern life. As Lantieri says, "Nature provides important moments for stillness, as we connect to something larger than ourselves."[47] Somehow we must find a way to make children more aware of an irreplaceable source of solace and joy for all the generations that preceded them. Their own solace and joy and the health of all life on the planet may depend on it.

Inquiry

Beliefs structure the thoughts and judgments that cause feelings. They define what we think is possible and desirable, and therefore shape our understanding of happiness and how to pursue it. A curriculum designed to empower students' lifelong pursuit of happiness cannot sidestep the question of beliefs. I fully agree that schools should not be in the business of telling kids what to believe. But it is the business of schools to teach awareness, knowledge, understanding, and skills, all of which inherently inform students' beliefs about reality and values. Nothing taught in our schools is neutral in this regard.

Children arrive at school necessarily programmed with beliefs that help them navigate a highly complex social and physical environment. They are moved by emotions they do not understand to seek feelings they only intuit. Most of what children believe is shaped by the received wisdom of parents and other important adults in their lives, by the views and attitudes of peers, and by the incessant voices in the media trying win people's allegiance to their products and views. A core aim of liberal education, which is meant to *liberate*, is to equip a student with the knowledge and understanding that allows her to make her own discerning choices of what to believe. This is an essential component of an education dedicated to her freedom as well as her happiness.

Our task is to design a curriculum that informs a student's choice of beliefs in a way that increases her chances for happiness. This requires 1) expanding her awareness of choices, 2) deepening her understanding of what she wants and what is worth wanting, 3) developing her discernment through knowledge and understanding of the implications and likely consequences of particular choices, 4) strengthening her ability and desire to explore and discover on her own, and 5) developing the skills and cognitive resources that empower her to realize her choices.

These are the elements of freedom and empowerment. When freedom is understood to include the ability to achieve what you choose, they are the elements of freedom pure and simple. Promoting freedom so understood is inherent to empowering the lifelong pursuit of happiness as each sees it.

Philosophical inquiry into the Big Questions of life enhances freedom and empowers the pursuit of happiness by informing a person's choice of beliefs. As I said earlier, these questions include the nature of reality, the nature and sources of knowledge, the meaning of the Good and the nature of the good life, and the nature and means of the social good. I call these Big Questions because they encompass the main dimensions of the human experience. Each of us must live according to our "operating assumptions" about what the answers are, whether or not we are consciously aware of it. Our daily choices imply understandings of reality, knowledge, and the good, however vague and unexamined they may be.

Philosophical inquiry brings your operating assumptions into the open to be examined. It poses open-ended questions with many plausible answers. It invites you to examine these answers in light of knowledge, understanding, and reason. The best approach, I believe, involves examining alternative perspectives on a particular question. I recommend seminar-style classes based on the following elements:

1) An open-ended question implied in the course title that sets the line of inquiry and the search for an answer as the main task of the course.
2) The investigation of alternative perspectives on the question rather than the presentation of authoritative knowledge meant to answer the question. Knowledge should be presented in the context of a particular perspective and be open to the challenges posed by contending views.
3) Open, communal inquiry and discussion rather than lectures.
4) Emphasis on the Socratic Method to guide discussion, which emphasizes asking questions to get students to think more deeply about their answers.
5) Concise readings and frequent written analyses.
6) The use of media such as films, Internet videos, music, art, etc., to introduce complex ideas and viewpoints and provoke emotional responses.
7) A final written assignment in which each student has to explain his or her answer to the main question.

Such seminars are designed to promote all the elements of freedom I just described. They inform a student's understanding of self and what moves him. At some point when students are ready — say seventh grade — such seminars would become the heart of a happiness curriculum that would continue through the remaining years of formal education. They would be designed to bring progressive insights that build on the insights of previous years.

I recommend beginning with the question of reality because it addresses students' beliefs about what they are and to what they can aspire. The Foundation for Developing Compassion and Wisdom recommends a core curriculum that wisely begins with questions about reality:

What is real?
What is the nature of the universe?
How are things connected and why do things happen?

Does everything change?
What are the things that we know?
How do we know things?
What is my potential?
Who am I?
What ascertains reality?[48]

In my honors seminar on the Nature of Reality, I have students explore the materialist perspective, a traditional religious perspective, and a non-dualist spiritual perspective. "Are you only a body, or a soul that survives death, or part of an all-encompassing spirit? What are the implications of each belief for human nature, ways of knowing, purpose, and the source of morality?" Questions of reality can dig deep into human psychology and plug into popular culture: "Is Virtual Reality reality? Is what we believe is reality a dream?" Dozens of films can be used to introduce such questions. They can also deal with the social construction of views on reality. "How do culture and the media shape people's understanding of reality?"

The exploration of the nature of reality leads to insights that frame the inquiry into the core questions of the Good and the good life: "What is the ultimate Good? What is moral? What is our purpose? What is happiness? What is the good life?" Exploring questions about the good life sets the stage for inquiry into the social good: "What is the good society? Should government promote happiness? Should government promote morality? What sort of government best serves the general happiness? What are freedom, justice, and equality and why do we prize these ideals? What ideal is most important?"

Utopian and dystopian literature provide an excellent context for such questions. It also exposes students to great literature. Thousands of excerpts and essays by advocates of various ideologies — Liberalism, Libertarianism, Conservatism, Communism, Fascism, Islamism, Environmentalism, Feminism, etc. — are available online or in compilations. Teachers can tap a treasure chest of movies and other media related to the question of the social good.

Students should understand that the Big Questions are about them. Inquiry into alternative answers broadens their awareness of choices and enhances their discernment in choosing. They may not be aware of it, but they are gaining important insights. And they are plugging into the legacy of human thought, aspiration, and struggle in a way that reveals their personal stake in knowing this legacy.

A good way to help students organize their knowledge and insights into a coherent whole is to have them produce an articulated personal philosophy of life at the end of each year. Each year they would revise their philosophy in light of what they learned. This would continue until they graduated. At the least, each student would graduate with a conscious awareness of what he believes about reality, himself, happiness, the good life, and the social good at that point in time. He will also have a much better understanding of what others believe and why.

This pedagogy of philosophical inquiry not only leads to the many advantages of the examined life, it is also a superior pedagogy in terms of the conventional aims of education. Jim Burke cites a great deal of research that shows that using questions to turn courses of study into a search for answers awakens student interest and engagement, develops critical thinking skills better than other modes of teaching, deepens conceptual understanding and broadens awareness, enhances reading comprehension, improves communication skills including writing, and aids retention of knowledge.[49] Burke concludes that "when students' instruction is organized around meaningful, clear questions, they understand better, remember longer, and engage much more deeply and for greater periods of time."[50] The pedagogy of questions even seems to narrow the gap between high achievers and low.

A question-based pedagogy is also inherently "integrative" in that neither the Big Questions nor many of the perspectives are the purview of any particular discipline. In fact, it is far more integrative than the discipline-based approach often used in higher education that only introduces a few methodologies from other disciplines. The method of open-ended inquiry into overarching questions allows students to connect the dots between subjects and see the larger relevance to their lives.

I go into much greater depth on this pedagogy in chapters to come.

Progression of a Happiness Pedagogy

The progression of a happiness curriculum from kindergarten to graduation and beyond must address both the developmental capacities of children and the logical building of awareness, knowledge, and skills. I turn to the expertise of others in considering the developmental capacities of children. Unfortunately, there's not much to turn to in the way of a recommended progression of a happiness curriculum through the years of formal education. Models of a happiness education exist, but they are short on advice for a multi-year progression.

But we must begin somewhere, so I offer what reason counsels.

Grades K-3

Those who teach inner awareness to young children seem confident that kids in first grade are able and willing to learn the skill. They are able to distinguish between thoughts and external experience, though they have difficulty putting it into words.[51] Children at all ages learn best by actively participating in the learning process, but this is especially true of young children. Structure and repetition are important, though. Speaking of early-year students, Lantieri says "A child of this age likes routines and rituals. Repetitive behavior maximizes a five-to-seven-year-old's learning."[52]

The emphasis would be on inner-awareness exercises and discussions about feelings and what causes them. Almost everything suggested in the section on inner awareness applies to this age group. It is crucial that exercises to promote social awareness start from the very beginning while attitudes toward others are the most malleable. Most of the means to foster appreciation suggested in the next chapter are appropriate for this age group. They won't be able to read and write very well, but most of the methods suggested in the section on methods to influence feelings that do not involve reading and writing can be tailored for beginning students.

Young students should also have ample opportunity for creative expression. At that age they are far more open to trying new things than older students who have grown more self-conscious and concerned about what their peers think. Younger children are more limited in their ability to engage outside the school, but they can perform acts of kindness with family and friends. The early years are also ripe for strengthening kids' connection to nature.

All agree that children learn best through direct experience, but their curiosity and imagination allow some flexibility in dealing with concepts that can be explained in terms of their experiences. The conceptual exploration of happiness might begin with discussing the happy endings of stories or what the characters seem to think happiness is. K-3 students would also begin their exploration of the larger question of happiness through films, discussions, and creative activities. As they advance in their reading skills, they should read stories that provide a context for thinking about feelings, relationships, and happiness.

Grades 4-6

All that began in the first four years of school would continue in the next three. The practices of inner and social awareness need to be continually developed and strengthened as children mature. The exercises designed to teach methods to influence feelings should become more sophisticated, of course. And developing interests and abilities will call for more expanded means of creative expression.

Eight- to eleven-year-olds are known for their enthusiasm, imagination, and relative reasonableness.[53] Lantieri says "While they still have that sense of wonder about the world around them from their earlier years, they also now have the rational skills to better understand that world — and themselves."[54] Simple exercises that involve role-playing and developing scenarios are suited to this age. Self-conducted experiments in inner and social awareness should go along with keeping journals. For example, students can experiment with different meditation techniques or observe how their own and other people's feelings toward a particular experience change over time. They can experiment with music, art, and games.

As reading and thinking skills advance, students would more directly explore the questions of life and happiness through literature, history, the arts, science, civics, economics, etc. They would begin to consider a range of philosophical and religious beliefs, particularly as they pertain to the question of happiness. This will lay the foundation for deeper exploration later on.

Grades 7-12

Adolescence is a trying age of rapid physical, emotional, intellectual, and social change. Adolescents want greater independence from adults as they try to mimic what they understand as adult behaviors. Yet they tend to conform to peer pressure in order to belong. They are more inclined to challenge received wisdoms and are ready to explore new dimensions of thought. But they also yearn for haven in the emotional turbulence of the teenage years.

Teenagers have great need for sanctuaries of calm in the raging emotional storms of this period of life. Mindfulness and others means for managing emotions should remain part of their daily practice in school. "Young people also need time for self-reflection and to turn inward in order to define their own sense of meaning and purpose for their lives, yearnings that are inherent in this developmental stage," according to Lantieri.[55]

A happiness pedagogy suited to teenagers would accommodate their desire for greater independence and their search for meaning and purpose. It would provide ample opportunity for calm and reflection. It would channel their restlessness toward intrinsically rewarding expression and social engagement. It would expand the frontiers of all they did in prior years and introduce them to a more systematic analysis of perspectives on the Big Questions of life.

The approach I outlined in the section on inquiry is suited to aiding teenagers' search for their own answers to the questions that confront them as they approach adulthood. For one thing, it brings these questions into sharper focus. This approach will help them better understand themselves, other people, and the world. It will bring the light of awareness, knowledge, insight, and reason to their pursuit of happiness. And it will hone the skills they need to realize their aspirations. For all these reasons and more, philosophical inquiry is an essential component of a happiness curriculum in the last half of K-12 education.

Higher Education

Higher education has two purposes in the minds of most people. It offers specialized training for a career, and it is also supposed to enhance a student's life by broadening her awareness and deepening her understanding of herself and the world. Happiness does not cease to be a person's primary aspiration when she enters a college or university, but higher education is not expressly designed to serve this aspiration.

This should change. If the subjective value of all experiences is found

only in the heart, the tight focus on the mind in academe seriously diminishes its relevance and value to students' lives. But the winds of change are
blowing, and we can capture these winds to help propel a happiness curriculum in higher education.

The current trend toward a "first-year experience" and cross-disciplinary
"integrated" courses in the core curriculum of institutions of higher education acknowledges a greater need for coherence. This trend is inspired by
the recognition of how important it is for students to be able to see a larger
picture of the reality each discipline tends to break into parts. It aims for
some vague "liberation" meant to enhance students' lives in general and better develop the skills needed in the modern world economy. Most of what I
see so far, though, lacks a clear overarching aim necessary to integrate a core
curriculum into a coherent, meaningful whole. The aim of empowering the
pursuit of happiness would fill this lack.

I recommend a number of changes in the chapter on higher education,
but my main recommendation is to design the core around the exploration
of the Big Questions with the explicit purpose of empowering students' pursuit of happiness. The approach I advocate for the latter years of K-12 education fits well with academic tradition. Colleges and universities can take
students into the farther frontiers of thought and inquiry.

The Fruits of a Happiness Pedagogy

Would the unifying focus on happiness throughout children's educational
experience significantly improve their chances for realizing greater happiness?
Would the effort to change the external orientation of education by teaching
children to "tend carefully the garden of their minds" be worth it?[56]
Ponder the difference it might have made in your life if you had learned
how to observe feelings at an early age and you became increasingly aware of
what caused them. What if you had gained the ability to reduce the negative
emotions caused by your thoughts and your affective dependence on your
environment? Might knowledge of how to find mental shelter from emotional storms have proven a considerable blessing at times in your life? Might
the ability to savor the moment have enriched your experiences? What if
you had been guided to an experience of a deeper peace and joy that revealed
the possibility of making such experiences more prevalent and lasting? And

what if you had explored the nature of happiness, its sources, and the means to experience it throughout your educational career?

At a minimum, your chosen steps in the pursuit of happiness would have been informed with enhanced awareness, with deeper knowledge and insight, and with greater certainty of what you seek. Having surveyed the horizons of feelings, you would have a clearer understanding of the stakes involved in your choices, and this may have strengthened your resolve to realize a deeper sense of fulfillment. You would likely have been more aware of the importance of clear purpose, and therefore have been less beset by uncertainty of direction. As you gained greater clarity about what transpires in your own heart and mind, you would also have gained a better understanding of the hearts and minds of others. Such understanding may have allowed you to lower your defenses and form closer bonds with your companions on the journey of life.

You would also have been more informed about alternative paths to happiness. Your clearer understanding of both the choices and their likely consequences would have made your exercise of freedom more meaningful and reduced your vulnerability to the emotional manipulations of those who want your money and allegiance. This only begins to suggest the difference your education might have made had it been devoted to empowering your pursuit of happiness.

It would also have enhanced your willingness and ability to learn, your mental and physical health, and your social efficacy. Evidence abounds that teaching mindfulness in schools improves students' mental health, their capacity and willingness to learn, and classroom behavior. A study of the effects of meditation techniques in a California school found that they "helped improve mood disorders, depression, and self-harming behaviors like anorexia and bulimia."[57] A comparison of elementary students taught mindfulness with those in the same school who did not receive the training found the trained students reported greater "happiness, well-being, and mindful awareness."[58] "Teachers reported that these children significantly reduced their aggression and disruptive behavior, and showed significant improvements in their social skills and attention levels."[59] Mindfulness training has been shown to increase empathy.[60]

A 2004 Garrison Institute survey of mindfulness programs in New York reported claims that they helped children become "more responsive and less reactive, more focused and less distracted, [and] more calm and less stressed."[61] The results of a study of students instructed in mindfulness and positive thinking skills in six public schools in Vancouver, Canada, indicated the children were "less aggressive, less oppositional toward teachers, and more attentive in class."[62] Mindfulness training has been shown to improve the "attentional capabilities" of students.[63] In fact, a version of mindfulness training helped reduce the anxiety and increased the ability to focus of teenagers suffering from ADHD.[64] Greenland claims "mindfulness is a different way of looking at learning than the approach taught in most schools, and I've seen it foster the love of learning in children."[65]

Daniel Goleman, the author of *Emotional Intelligence*, has helped bring "social and emotional learning" (SEL) programs to tens of thousands of schools. SEL emphasizes techniques based on mindful inner awareness. He asks: "does social and emotional learning make a difference in children's lives?"[66]

> Now we have the answer: a definitive meta-analysis of more than one hundred studies compared students who had SEL with those who did not. The data shows impressive improvements among the SEL students in their behavior in and out of the classroom. Students not only mastered abilities like calming down and getting along better, but they also learned more effectively; their grades improved, and their scores on academic achievement tests were a hefty fourteen percentile points higher than similar students who were not given such social and emotional learning programs. Helping children master their emotions and relationships makes them better learners.[67]

And we should expect those students who continue mindfulness practices to reap the robustly demonstrated affective benefits enjoyed by adult practitioners.

Teaching methods designed to promote well-being enhance curiosity, love of learning, and creativity.[68] They have also increased language arts achievement.[69] Morris points out that "The teaching of well-being helps to close the vacuum and complete what is missing from education and it can transform the experience young people have of education and the experience that educators have of young people."[70]

The evidence supports my contention that a happiness pedagogy would lead to happier lives for our children. If so, even greater benefits await the children of the future as well as the societies they will inherit. The benefits of the reported happiness of adults are well-established in research. Of course, happiness, or subjective well-being, defines the upper range of mental health. Positive thoughts and emotions are both an antidote and a defense against depression and chronic anxiety. As Seligman points out, "positive emotions undo negative emotions."[71] Relatively happy people are far less prone to abuse drugs and alcohol and exhibit aberrant and dysfunctional behaviors. They are also more psychologically buffered from the effects of adversity.

Lyubomirsky says:

> Feelings of joy, satisfaction, or pride can help people see the "big picture" of their lives and provide a sort of "psychological time-out" in the midst of stress or trauma, thus lessening the sting of any particular unpleasant event. In these ways, positive feelings marshaled in the face of adversity can build resilience, by helping people bounce back from stressful experiences.[72]

Research shows people find their lives more meaningful during happy moods.[73] Happier people are more creative, more productive, more successful in their endeavors, and even smarter.[74] They are more spontaneous and enthusiastic.[75]

They are also considerably healthier in a physical sense. Klein says "joy affects the body at least as much as it does the mind. Unhappiness destroys the body. Happiness strengthens it. … Positive feelings counteract stress and its consequences for health. They even stimulate the immune system."[76] Negative emotions have a negative impact on the cardiovascular system, which positive emotions can repair.[77] Happier people live longer.[78] Dramatic improvements in outlook are associated with miracle cures.[79] It is well known that positive outlook aids recovery in hospitals. Many of the findings in regard to physical health are quite dramatic, as are those regarding the relationship between relative happiness and positive attitudes and behaviors toward others.

The presumption that happy people must be more narcissistic and less sensitive to the pain of others is not supported by the evidence. Quite the opposite. According to an "avalanche" of studies, happier people are nicer, kinder, more compassionate, and more altruistic.[80] Klein says "happy people are … nicer people. They are more aware and more likely to see the good in others. They are more likely to act altruistically, and they are more successful mediators in resolving conflict."[81] "Before I saw the data," Seligman concedes, "I thought that unhappy people — identifying with the suffering that they know so well — would be more altruistic. So I was taken aback when the findings on mood and helping others without exception revealed that happy people were more likely to demonstrate that trait."[82] In her reading of the evidence, Lyubomirsky reports "Compared with their less happy peers, happier people are more sociable and energetic, more charitable and cooperative, and better liked by others."[83]

According to Frank Goble, Maslow found that "The healthy individual, because he has great respect for himself, is able to be more respectful to others. This is supported by Erich Fromm's contention that true self-love or self-respect is harmonious with, rather than antagonistic to, love for others."[84] In the higher ranges of happiness "you're ... naturally kind, generous, open, warm, and friendly," according to Robert Holden. "This is because where there's true happiness, there is no fear, no doubt, and no anxiety."[85] He also says "When you feel whole and blissfully happy, you forget to judge other people. This is because you're not judging your Self."[86]

We could expect a more congenial social environment if there were less depression, less inner conflict, less anger and hostility, less dysfunctional behavior. All of this speaks to less crime and conflict. And, if happiness is contagious as many claim, negative elements in the social environment would decline as more positive elements increased. "Whatever it is," says Holden, "your happiness is an inspiration and a gift to everyone. Everyone benefits from true happiness ... everyone benefits from your happiness."[87]

Kornfield remarks that "The suffering and happiness in our world, both individual and collective, depend on our consciousness."[88] Terry Hyland elaborates that "The world can only be changed by people and often the reflective capacity to change ourselves is precisely what is required before any wider social change is possible."[89] Citing personal experience from her stroke, Bolte Taylor relates that "the most fundamental traits of my right hemisphere personality are deep inner peace and loving compassion. I believe the more time we spend running our inner peace/compassion circuitry, then the more peace/compassion we will project into the world, and ultimately the more peace/compassion I believe we will have on the planet."[90] Lantieri agrees:

> *Far from being marginal or irrelevant, attention to building our children's emotional intelligence and inner lives will help us achieve the equilibrium we all need in this chaotic world; we must foster the compassion, insight, and commitment to ourselves and each other that will be necessary to tackle the deep emotional, social, political, and spiritual dilemmas of our time.*

And as Gandhi has reminded us, "We have to start with the children."[91]

Maslow entertained a similar hope:

If we were to accept as a major educational goal the awakening and fulfillment of the B-Values [Being Values] which is simply another aspect of self-actualization, we would have a great flowering of a new kind of civilization. People would be stronger, healthier, and would take their own lives into their hands to a greater extent. With increased personal responsibility for one's personal life, and with a rational set of values to guide one's choosing, people would begin to actively change the society in which they lived.[92]

Perhaps such hopes are naïve. We might not be able to overcome the countervailing aims and influences in our schools. But we don't have anything meaningful to lose by trying, and we at least stand to gain the affective rewards of knowing we have taken our children's best interest to heart and acted in good faith. Whether or not the seeds we sow on our children's behalf flower into the greater happiness of future generations, they will flower in the heart of many a child. This is reason enough to sow them.

6

Fostering Appreciation

*Understanding is appreciation, because what
you understand you can identify with, and
by making it part of you, you have accepted it
with love.* | A Course in Miracles

I'm taken aback at times by the callous, inhumane views some students express in my classroom. But I know the students who express these views are not really callous and inhumane. I have learned to look behind the façade of students' uncaring attitudes to discover warm and tender hearts. This is a tough planet, and we all learn to erect defensive walls to protect our vulnerable hearts. But I have yet to meet anyone I have come to know well who has failed to let a ray of loving light slip through the cracks in their defenses. I believe that hiding behind the coldest demeanor is a wary heart yearning to feel and express love.

Most will accept that we all yearn for the love of others, but there may be an even deeper yearning to experience our own love, to open the barricades and allow it to come forth into conscious awareness. Some will scoff at this, pointing to the obvious darkness in human behavior, but there is good reason and a great deal of evidence to support the claim that the darkness of human behavior springs not from the depths of the heart, but from the fear caused by the beliefs and judgments of the mind.

If true, this insight has profound implications for how we teach values. It points to a superior though neglected source of moral behavior. The practical expression of such behavior is treating others well. As with all we wish to teach, motive is essential. But if you look closely at the deliberate means we use to teach values in our schools, you will see that they appeal far more to fear than love, or they largely bypass the motives of the heart altogether and aim to train students in ethical reasoning. The way values are taught usually fails to acknowledge the central role of feelings in determining behavior. It certainly reflects little understanding of love and its importance as a moral motive.

It is said that if we were all angels, we would have no need for rules, moral commandments and laws, no need for admonishments and punishments to motivate us to treat others kindly. Benevolent behavior would flow naturally from our angelic hearts. We can only speculate about angels, but many claim to have experienced a blissful state of peace, joy, and love in which only pure, unselfish benevolence *can be* expressed. Benevolent behavior is not the source of the bliss, according to advanced practitioners of inner awareness. Rather it is the natural expression of the "loving kindness" that is inherent to our natural state of being when the ego no longer rules us. If so, this source of benevolence is beyond motive, for it does not move us to seek a preferable feeling. We simply express the joy we feel and want to keep feeling.

What "moves" this expression seems to defy common understandings of motive. Among the explanations I have encountered, the one given in the *Course in Miracles* is the most succinct: the peaceful joy of this state must be shared to be experienced, the giving is the receiving, the feeling and the expression are one. You express as you feel, and you feel as you regard.

Advanced Buddhist practitioners and profound wisdom teachings insist that this state of mind is not learned. They teach that it already exists in us, but is obscured by identification with our ego concept of self and the emotions this identification causes. They say awareness of this state comes naturally once the obscuring veils of judgment and ego defense are released.

Those who are aware of the easing of tension and the quiet joy associated with unconditional appreciation and spontaneous rather than calculated benevolent acts have gained some awareness of the love at the core of their being, a source of peaceful joy beyond the satisfactions born of temporarily easing the fears and insufficiencies of ego. A sure indicator of the difference between spontaneous benevolence and ego satisfaction is the peace that attends the former and is absent in the latter.

This suggests that the art of teaching values is essentially the art of making children aware of the love that already abides in their hearts. We can motivate a child to behave the way we want to some extent by appealing to fear and his need for approval, but we thereby block his primary source of happiness rather than tap it. The appreciation of others is not only the prime inspiration for virtuous behavior; it is also joy. So understood, the aim of teaching values and the aim of empowering the pursuit of happiness are one.

Admittedly, getting educators and the public at large to support such a change is a tall order. As with all else we undertake in our schools, we have various purposes for teaching values. Certainly we aim to tame raging egos and render children inclined to orderly and cooperative behavior. Social interests are served when we encourage children to be kind, honest, and responsible. Yet if we embrace empowering our children's pursuit of happiness as the primary purpose of education, we must try to align our efforts to impart values with the purpose of their hearts.

This alignment is natural when we recognize that positive regard and benevolent behavior are sources of desirable feelings. Here we find a far more potent and self-reinforcing motive for treating others well than the ones we usually appeal to in teaching values. And in making our children aware of the benefits, we reveal a primary inner source of happiness. Obviously, this calls for a change in the way we teach values.

I know of six general approaches to teaching values in schools, though there are many variations. The traditional means of promoting virtue through preaching rules, demanding obedience, punishing laxity, and sometimes rewarding adherence live on as means to keep order in schools. This is called "character education." Traditional character education based on religious codes is still in vogue in many private schools. There is not much evidence that it is a superior means to promote benevolent attitudes and behavior, but other methods aren't particularly effective in this regard either.[1]

The main problem with traditional character education is that it tends to emphasize fear as a motive. Fear of violating prohibitions or failing to meet social expectations is deeply implanted in most of us. "Don't" and "you should" are constant childhood admonishments. They are often reinforced with emotional and/or physical punishments, which continue with the sanctions of law and social expectations into adulthood. People fear guilt, so appealing to it is a handy means of control and manipulation.

Fear is considered necessary to socialization. The inhibitions implanted in our childhood mostly steer us away from harming ourselves and others, and the admonitions to respond to others' needs lead to mutually beneficial behavior. Fear may be thought of as a more reliable motive and easier to inspire and reinforce than more desirable emotions. Reason does not work well when trying to persuade a child to forego something he wants now for an abstract good. It doesn't work well with teenagers and many adults either.

But however useful fear may seem as a relatively easy way to make children fit for society, it is a very unpleasant feeling that comes with a great deal of baggage. Fear easily morphs into anger, resentment, and rebellion, and it builds cognitive barriers to more positive motives. Fear contracts and darkens our experiences, and it inhibits feelings of connection with others. Fear and true appreciation are mutually exclusive. Fear contributes nothing to positive regard. Fear too easily leads to callousness and intolerance.

Other approaches to values education aim more at awakening students' natural sympathies. A widespread strategy is to simply make students aware of suffering and injustice in the hope it will inspire compassion. Raising awareness no doubt awakens compassion in the breasts of students already inclined to it. And awareness is a necessary first step to action. But during my years of teaching such awareness, I have seen little evidence that awareness of suffering and injustice alone changes existing attitudes. Many teachers try to awaken students' concern for the plight of others, but so far it doesn't seem to be increasing empathy. Surveys administered over the past forty years indicate declining empathy.[2]

Trying to awaken a student's natural sympathy should make her more aware of the love she already harbors, so it is a logical way to try to inspire benevolence. The problem is, the way we educators go about it also tends to appeal to fear. Raising awareness of injustice, travail, and impending doom accentuates the pain of compassion and fear. Appealing to a students' innate compassion by making her aware of suffering does not make her feel better.

Rather it aims to move her to relieve the pain of her compassion by doing something to relieve the pain of others. Appealing to her anger by making her aware of injustice comes with all the baggage of anger and judgment. Moral indignation is, after all, indignation, which is a judgmental, unpleasant feeling.

Perhaps we cannot avoid stirring these emotions when making students aware of the plight of their fellow human beings and the dangers that threaten the well-being of us all. We should not leave them ignorant of these things. But we should not merely present the darkness of the world and leave it at that. It would be better if we showed students the light as well. And we should present constructive ways to do something about these problems so they can experience the positive rewards of their sympathy. Positive feelings are self-reinforcing motives to treat others well; negative feelings are not. Even involving them in a small gesture helps balance the ledger. Showing students more meaningful ways to make a difference is even better. But I also believe in the power of forgiveness to not only improve students' chances for happiness, but also to improve the world in which we live. Raising human consciousness has deeper, more lasting effects than merely rearranging the social environment.

Another approach to teaching values is called ethical reasoning. For the most part, this involves "the growth and extension of intelligibility in values and the realm of values."[3] It seeks to clarify ethical principles and codes and exercise students' ability to reason out their application to specific cases. The problem is that reason alone does not supply its own motive. As Jonathan Haidt points out, "Trying to make children behave ethically by teaching them to reason well is like trying to make a dog happy by wagging its tail. It gets causality backwards."[4]

But ethical reasoning also involves trying to show how virtuous behavior is in a student's self-interest. The problem with this is that a student's understanding of self-interest may defy the logic. Getting a student to amend his premises about what is in his self-interest is difficult when appeals to reason are the only tools in the pedagogical toolbox.

Appeals to self-interest usually come down to what I call the strategic Golden Rule: do unto others because it is the best way to get them to do unto you. Acting out of a sense of calculated self-interest may result in mutually beneficial behavior — the core premise of capitalism — but it involves the fears of the perception of lack and does not express spontaneous benevolence. To the frustration of my colleagues who teach ethics, students are adept at coming up with examples of how their self-interest as they understand it is better served by selfish behavior. Getting more and being better than others is an all-too-common understanding of self-interest. Enhancing a student's awareness of how his regard and treatment of others affects how he feels can help change his understanding of self-interest.

A related approach to ethical reasoning is called "values clarification." Rather than specifying values and rules of conduct, it asks a student to respond to comments in a way that, in the words of the authors who proposed the approach in *Values and Teaching*, "encourages someone to look at his life and his ideas and to think about them."[5] The point is to get a student to look deeper into what he values. Though billed as "value neutral," the implied assumption is that the clearer a student is about what he values, the more likely he is to embrace more personally and socially meaningful values. This may seem a rather indirect route to *ethical* values and behavior, though the extensive use of something akin to Socratic questioning at least promises some of the fruits of the examined life. Still, this hypothetical yield is meager in comparison to the promise of a more direct approach.

A popular contemporary approach to teaching values involves community service. Service has the virtue of creating opportunities to experience the affective rewards of helping others. Though there's not much evidence that service opportunities and requirements have had much impact on students' attitudes in general, they have other benefits that make them worthwhile. At least they provide a service, demonstrate concern, and deepen students' awareness of community needs. I think service has a valuable role to play in enhancing awareness of the affective benefits of benevolence, but it is not sufficient in itself. Students should first be prepared with enhanced awareness of their feelings.

Practicing what we preach is an oft-recommended means of teaching values, but it may be the least heeded. Though the most persuasive way to teach values, modeling is the most difficult, for it requires consistent and seemingly sincere caring, kind, honest, and faithful behavior. This is a natural way of being for many educators, but for some it would require a serious change in attitude about students, colleagues, administrators, and people in general.

Educators naturally stress orderly and obedient conduct, primarily through threat of punishment. The values of competitive achievement are emphasized above all others; good grades, prizes, and praise reward achievement and obedience while their absence shames relative failure. Obedience to authority and achievement are given clear priority over all other values in our "walk," though we stress more benevolent virtues with our "talk." Complaints abound that children are being spoiled by trivial, unearned "self-esteem" rewards, but these rewards are far overshadowed by the traditional motivators of grades and threats. John Taylor Gatto expresses what many students feel when he insists "Mass education cannot work to produce a fair society because its daily practice is practice in rigged competition, suppression, and intimidation."[6]

In addition to the human foibles of disinterest, pettiness, and even meanness that confront students in our schools, efforts to model caring and kindness are cast in the shadow of institutional devotion to competing values, values embraced and reinforced by society at large. Our schools may be symbols of social caring, but they are not really organized to model the values of caring beyond the dispositions of individual educators. It would require a fundamental change in aims to organize schools to model the values of caring, and this would require caring enough to carry it out. Unfortunately, values education in general is low on the list of priorities at present, and fostering natural benevolence is seldom even on the list.

In fact, we may be moving backward as liberal arts classes are slashed in order to emphasize "practical" skills thought more directly relevant to jobs and economic growth. Basic skills courses are not geared to teach ethical values. Courses that might be better suited to such aims are being pruned. "If the real clash of civilizations is, as I believe, a clash within the individual soul, as greed and narcissism contend against respect and love," says Martha Nussbaum, "all modern societies are rapidly losing the battle, as they feed the forces that lead to violence and dehumanization and fail to feed the forces that lead to cultures of equality and respect."[7]

Schools offer our best chance to nurture caring relationships and feed the heart of humanity, but we are largely blowing this chance. The underlying reason is that, despite the rhetoric, we really do not place much importance on cultivating the virtues of benevolence. Judging by what we do and most consistently advocate, educators and society in general place far more importance on the values of obedience, achievement, and material well-being.

Perhaps we need a clearer understanding of what is at stake.

First and foremost, our children's prospects for happiness are at stake. We may prize the virtues of benevolence — kindness, caring, honesty, faithfulness, etc. — for their benefit to others, but they are most immediately beneficial to those who express them. Appreciative regard and benevolent behavior cause desirable feelings. They are a way to tap the warmth of one's heart in an emotionally cold world. When we see values less in terms of behavioral inhibitions and more as modes of expressing appreciation, we highlight a positive motive to embrace them.

Our children's prospects for happiness depend on gaining awareness of the affective cornucopia of appreciative benevolence, or love so understood. The farther reaches of peace and joy require appreciative regard; you cannot attain these reaches without awareness that your own love is the most valuable treasure of your heart. Enticing children to lower the defenses around their hearts will also enormously enrich their relationships. What you feel, you tend to perceive in others, and others tend to respond in kind. Your appreciation and kindness make you more sensitive to these virtues in others. You will see them with more accepting and appreciative eyes, which diminishes the fear that inhibits the joy relationships have to offer.

Fear obscures the depths of people, and therefore inhibits your ability to understand them. When you lower your guard, you are more open to perceiving the deeper motives of others, which you recognize as similar to your own. You come to understand other people better, which further lessens your fear and may elicit greater appreciation. We can help our children see a better, more joyful world than they now perceive by making them aware of the benefits of appreciation.

Obviously, the values we impart to our children have important social consequences. The fate of our democracies and ultimately humanity as a whole depends to a considerable extent on the values our children take to heart. I believe what historical progress we have made in constraining predatory behavior has been largely achieved by what Robert Solomon sees as "an ever-increasing sense of the importance and dignity of the individual and the radically expanding scope of our concern for others."[8] The growing insistence on at least tacit respect for the intrinsic worth of all human beings has been essential to the progress we have so far made in reducing the threat of harm from each other and at the hands of governments. If we could nurture the seeds of respect for human worth in our schools, they might sprout into a more humane and secure future for all.

The claim of intrinsic human worth captured in the phrase "human dignity" is the moral foundation of the superstructure of freedom, of liberal democracy, and of the modern world order. It is the founding premise of the moral arguments for freedom, and it places the worth of a human being beyond the right of state authorities to judge and the right of anyone to violate. The claim thus founds the assertion of human rights. The recognition of the intrinsic worth of others may be thought of as the heart of all morality, the premise that both moves and obliges a person to do unto others as he would have done unto him.

Since the worth you see in others implies your own worth, and how you regard others has consequences for how you feel, your regard for others helps determine your prospects for happiness. The strength of our children's commitment and the consistency of their fidelity to the principle of respecting human dignity are of vital concern to the cause of freedom. They are of vital concern to the caring and humane treatment of each other that determines our social well-being. And they are essential to our children's happiness. The stakes are high indeed.

Education commends itself as the most feasible means to reach impressionable hearts and minds on a broad scale, but the means must be suited to the end. If human dignity is an abstraction that depends more on commitment of mind than of heart, then it would be a matter of strengthening the appeal to reason in educating our young. But it isn't. To recall Haidt's observation, it gets causality backward. If the strength of commitment depends on how deeply it is rooted in the motives of the heart, reason alone won't yield it.

Appreciating Worth

How one regards and treats others is the heart of morality and justice. It is the intent of the Golden Rule, the object of most of the Ten Commandments, the heart of the Christian injunction to love one's neighbors, the subject of most obligations in the Quran, a requisite of the Hindu and Buddhist paths to enlightenment, the essence of Kant's categorical imperative to treat others as ends, the main concern of virtues, and the focus of the norms of behavior found in every culture. It may be difficult to determine what behavior best benefits others, either generally or in specific cases, or to even agree on the meaning of "benefit." But to more effectively motivate children to well-intentioned behavior — behavior *meant* to benefit others as one understands it — would be a success of great practical consequence.

Lowering barriers to the awareness and expression of innate appreciative love, I am convinced, is the best way to awaken the natural benevolent intent and behavior of our children. It avoids the considerable baggage of ego motives. Fear is always present when the ego is involved. The ego arises from a perceived insufficiency of worth, and it moves us to strengthen our sense of worth by judging others less worthy. The emotions inspired by identification with the ego, however expedient they may seem as a means to control behavior, block awareness of the peaceful joy that may be the highest reach of happiness. They exact a price in the moment of feeling them and dim one's awareness of the treasure within. Perhaps this price could be justified if there were no other way to motivate moral behavior, but that is not the case.

In contrast to motives that use an ego sense of self-interest or the guidelines of a *concept* of the good as reference, genuine appreciation extends the experience of self to others and sees the good in them. Pure appreciation is the experience of valuing the worth of others. The feeling can be understood as an attraction to whom or what one appreciates, but perhaps it is better described as a *resonance*.

The perception of beauty, for example, attracts and elicits a pleasant affective resonance. Though perhaps contaminated with envy, lust, or desire to possess, such resonance entails the experience of expansion and harmony commonly associated with joy. We appreciate more than physical beauty, of course. We admire talents and abilities, treasure bonds of relationship, reciprocate expressions of affection with affection, feel gratitude for assistance, are drawn to fellow feeling, find pleasure in the company of people with whom we share feelings and purpose, and revere what we believe is greatness. The qualities that seem to elicit a form of appreciation are many. But they do not in themselves possess the power to evoke our feelings. We must endow them with this power.

As Kant said, the thing in itself cannot be known. We can perceive others but not experience them in more than a superficial sense. We cannot directly experience the essence of another person, which is what *they* experience, what *they* feel and perceive, through our physical senses. We can only form an idea of the person from the self-interpreted messages of our senses. And this idea, this collection of thoughts and images imbued with feeling, is ever-changing.

Your feelings are creatively engaged in shaping your perception of others. The fact that perceptions are influenced by moods hints at this. Physical appearances reveal little of the larger and deeper reality of another person. It is like having only the evidence of a mirror to determine what you feel. Seeing physical expressions of feelings does not in itself entail the experience of feelings. It is the difference between form and essence. Appreciation of another person is therefore appreciation of the perceived reality of the person based on the projection of your own experiences.

Projection is necessary, for you only have your own experience of selfhood to interpret the experience of others. What others feel, what they desire, the reality they perceive — in other words their experience of self — can only be interpreted from what *you* feel, desire, and perceive. Absent your own experience, you would have no basis for understanding what it means to feel, desire, and perceive. Likewise, you can but give your own meaning to the words and behaviors of others. Your experience of selfhood is thus the source of your understanding of the selfhood of others. What you appreciate in others must be drawn from the well of your own experiences.

Let us take the argument further with a related hypothesis. Consciousness is experience. It entails, at a minimum, the awareness of existence. It may involve the distinction between the experiencer (self) and what is experienced, but this may not be inherent to *awareness*. Babies, for example, are thought to not make a distinction between self and environment in the early stages of infancy. Even when the distinction is firmly entrenched, self-identity — the conceptual image of self — is prone to constant change. It is not far-fetched to suspect that feelings of appreciation subjectively extend the experience of self to others.

The chapter on the nature of happiness cites studies and reports of people who claim direct experience of this extension. Concern for the feelings of others — the apparent inclusion of their well-being in one's own sense of well-being — offers support for the hypothesis. This may be thought a subordination of self, but the feelings that accompany this affective connection with others suggest that it by no means entails a sacrifice or denial of self, since these feelings are the heart of the awareness of what we call self. The affective core of an orientation toward the well-being of others — love, affection, caring, compassion — seems more consistent with the view that it is an affective extension of the experience of self. You behold what you hold most dear in whom and what you love, and in the loving you affectively experience — feel — what you hold most dear. In this sense, what or whom you love is included in your experience of self.

This understanding helps resolve a moral dilemma. The moral rule that we should treat others as ends in themselves is based on the assumption of the innate worth of human beings. This means the worth of a person resides within her; it is not determined by the judgments of other people. But since only minds can bestow worth, only the self-worth of a self-valuing mind is *innate* in a universe of separate minds. The worth you see in another person is bestowed from without, so, strictly speaking, it isn't a worth that resides in her. The psychological extension of your experience of self to include another person, though, extends your self-valuing to him or her. In other words, love brings others into your circle of intrinsic worth.

This is especially true of appreciative love, which is enjoyment of someone or something as they are without qualification. The joy and peace of such love adds a powerful motive to the Golden Rule: Do unto others as you would do unto yourself, *for as you do, so you shall feel.* Also, as you regard, so shall you feel. But appreciative love is free of conceptual guidelines, of rules, commandments, and ethical theories. It simply observes and naturally responds with benevolent regard and benevolent expression. There is no guarantee that such expression would accord with prevailing moral and ethical codes of behavior, but it would spring from the only pure source of wishing and treating others well: affectively valuing others as you value yourself.

A person can acknowledge that the expression of innate peaceful joy would incline human beings to regard and treat others kindly, but yet doubt it would move people to take on the problems and injustices that beset humanity. When you find the source of happiness within, and learn that the experience of happiness precludes judgment and attack, you would be less inclined to fight for justice and less certain that the problems of the world are best solved by merely rearranging external conditions. The shared pain of compassion moves us to reduce our own pain by addressing the pain of others. But when we focus on relieving the perceived external sources of others' fear and pain, we distract them from the internal sources of well-being. Perhaps expressing our love, joy, and acceptance rather than our judgment and anger at the causes of others' distress would better serve those we wish to help.

Gandhi did not "fight" injustice in the sense of condemning and battling the perpetrators; he brought it to glaring awareness so it could not be ignored, and by his example inspired both perpetrator and victim to look within. Seeing the ugliness of our judgments staring back in the mirror of self-reflection can bring a change of heart. A change of heart brings a change of consciousness, and Gandhi was clear that there are no true and lasting solutions to the problems that beset humanity short of such a change.

I know people who ease the pain of others by expressing a warm and sincere joy. One man in particular has dedicated his life to serving handicapped children, but refuses to acknowledge their handicap. He says they have the same chance for happiness as anyone else, and in his effusive smiles, laughter, and hugs, he expresses nothing but his own joy with everyone he meets. It is utterly contagious. I am convinced he helps the children far more with his joy than if he offered them the furrowed brow of sympathy and concern.

I believe the joy of the innate appreciative love within us has a better claim to being a genuine and reliable source of moral behavior and a more effective means to serve the best interests of others than sharing their pain. It is certainly superior to ego motives in every way other than the expedience of immediate control that appealing to fear may offer. Unfortunately, the barriers of fear in our children's minds are formidable. If we are to serve their happiness and foster a benevolence that fear can only inhibit, we must find a way to lower these barriers to our children's awareness of the love that bides within them.

Fostering Appreciation

If we could enhance children's awareness of the supremely desirable feelings associated with appreciative love, we would profoundly inform their pursuit of happiness, more effectively motivate them to regard and treat others well, and strengthen their commitment to respect human dignity. This requires fostering appreciation.

There are a number of ways to do this. Some are infrequently used in our schools and others need to be made more central, explicit, robust, and consistent. Among the relatively rare are those that acknowledge the oft-repeated observation that thinking ill of others has starkly different affective consequences than thinking well of them. The more aware you are of your feelings, the more aware you are of just how stark this difference is. The multi-year endeavor to foster awareness of the link between feelings and thoughts outlined in the preceding chapter is well-suited to encourage awareness of the difference.

This calls for exercises to either elicit or recall moments of ill will and moments of appreciation. Evoking feelings is a rather developed art in literature, film, and other media. Storytelling far predates civilization as a means to inspire feelings. Students should be led to focus on specific people and situations and to observe what feelings arise as well as the reactions of their bodies. Beyond structured exercises in awareness, students should be asked to focus on what they feel when a teacher notices expressions of anger, mirth, or joy. The hope is that students will learn to do this on their own and continue the practice for the benefits it brings.

As practice advances, students should be led on ever more extensive explorations of anger, grievance, resentment, and associated feelings on the one hand and feelings of appreciation on the other. They should learn to recognize and analyze their judgments both experientially and conceptually. For example, students can be asked to pick a target of their anger and to try to identify the apparent causes by observing what they feel when they think about different aspects of the person. They can be asked to try to understand the motives of the person by recalling when they themselves acted similarly and why.

Finding the motives of others in your own heart is a good way to gain perspective and the resonance of empathy. It helps temper rationalizations and mitigate the pangs of judgment. It is a way to become aware of the attitudinal lens through which you see others and learn to adjust it. A change in attitude can change both your perceptions and the responses of your heart. A new perspective on someone can correct your judgment of them by opening a new vista of understanding. Prejudice dissipates with the gaze of understanding, superficial images of people transform with the evidence of unsuspected depths.

If the conceptual lenses through which our children see others can be changed, their judgments of others would change as well. The conceptual lens most likely to elicit the attraction of the heart is one that is focused on the hearts of others, for there the commonality of humanity is more pronounced than our diversity. Differences may appeal to our imagination, curiosity, and sense of adventure, but the feelings of attraction are evoked by perceived similarities. Perceptions of "otherness" are interpreted as "alienness," which is more likely to evoke fear than appreciation. Those whose behavior and motives we do not understand tend to make us feel uneasy.

It is easier to appreciate others when you recognize yourself in them, because it is then easier to understand them. Some aspects of common educational practice help promote such recognition. The shared environment and interaction of classrooms provide opportunities for broadening and deepening mutual understanding, especially when they are arenas of cooperation rather than competition, intimidation, and embarrassment. Hearing other students talk about their feelings and associated thoughts leads to a realization of just how similar one's own inner experience is to the inner experience of classmates.

Yet fostering appreciation of others is currently more a side effect than a conscious purpose of these aspects of education. I believe a more focused, coherent, and consistent aim would make a big difference in promoting students' recognition of how much they share with their companions on the journey of life.

Fortunately, there are a number of apparently successful initiatives that aim to promote awareness of feelings and improve how kids see and treat others. I mentioned "social and emotional learning" programs that enhance students' inner awareness and understanding of others in the preceding chapter. Another promising initiative aimed at developing peaceful, compassionate relationships was inspired by Marshall Rosenberg's *Nonviolent Communication*.

Rosenberg's observations led him to conclude that "creating a peaceful world entails eliminating language that blames, shames, criticizes, and demands — language based on habitual thinking that inhibits compassion and contributes to violence."[9] The core methods of what practitioners call "relationship-based teaching and learning" involve awareness and expression of feelings and needs that promote understanding and reduce the sources of conflict.[10] The program emphasizes awareness of the affective rewards of freely giving and receiving according to the particular talents of each student. Both the ends and means of the project are well-suited to fostering appreciation of others through understanding, recognition of commonalities, and awareness of the rewards of the heart.

Morris describes exercises to build trust and reflect on what it means to trust.[11] For example, a pair of students will take turns catching the other as they fall backwards. Or a circle of students catch a student standing in the middle as she lets herself fall, and return her to an upright position. Students are then asked to discuss their feelings about having to trust as they let themselves fall backward.

Appreciation of others might also be reinforced by focusing on the recurring motivational themes of the human story. Such themes are found in history, literature, art, music, science, social studies, psychology, and philosophy. To discover an affinity of one's own inner experiences with those of all humanity throughout time is to discover the bond that unites humanity in fate and aspiration. The better a student understands the thoughts and actions of people throughout time, the better she understands herself. The human story is ultimately her own story.

Another way to foster appreciation for others is to have people of all walks of life tell their stories. I suggest means that could introduce such storytelling as part of the curriculum in the next chapter. Reading and assignments that place students in the shoes of others are also rather effective means to evoke sympathy, according to research.[12] Expressing gratitude verbally or in writing also helps students take the perspective of others and develops the capacity for empathy.[13]

Many studies show that mindfulness fosters empathy. Greenland explains how:

> By practicing mindfulness kids learn life skills that help them soothe and calm themselves, bring awareness to their inner and outer experience, and bring a reflective quality to their actions and relationships. Living in this way helps children connect to themselves (what do I feel? think? see?), to others (what do they feel? think? see?), and maybe to something greater than themselves. This is a worldview in which everything is seen as interconnected. When children understand that they and those they love are somehow connected to everybody and everything else, ethical and socially

productive behavior comes naturally, and they also feel less isolated — a common problem for kids and teens.[14]

Deborah Schoeberlein recommends "kindness practice."[15] She and many others say that the experience of kindness tends to arise naturally from mindfulness, but the experience can be enhanced through focused intent during mindfulness practice. She explains that,

> *Mindfully engaging in kindness practice does not automatically paint the world with pretty "kindness" colors that distort reality. Instead, you're likely to find that your sensitivity to the presence of kindness — in and around you — intensifies. Not only does this mean you recognize specific acts of kindness more easily, but also you are more likely to notice unexpected opportunities to act kindly. There isn't more ambient kindness; it's just that you become more attuned to it among colleagues, family members, friends, and even strangers.*[16]

She recommends raising students' awareness beforehand:

> *Before asking students to notice acts of kindness, it's a good idea to hold a brainstorming session to reach a shared definition of what they're looking for. Ask students to offer examples. Suggestions typically range from the profound, such as comforting a grieving friend, to the seemingly superficial, such as opening a door for a stranger. What's important is the recognition that kindness, as a quality, is present in many different situations. Its defining characteristic is the intention to express kindness and not the magnitude of the act.*[17]

Schoeberlein makes the same point regarding motivation as I do: "Most likely students will realize authentic kindness feels good — both for the person acting with kindness and the recipient of it."[18]

We educators would also nurture the roots of appreciation in the hearts of our students by modeling appreciative, nonjudgmental, and kind attitudes in our treatment of them and each other. We reinforce the idea that people should be treated as ends by treating them as ends. We are unlikely to convince students of the benefits of appreciation if we act as if we are uninterested in reaping the benefits ourselves. Rather, we are likely to undermine all we aspire to achieve in this regard if we do not walk the talk. Walking the talk, though, requires a major change in the values emphasized in schools.

Forgiveness

Mastering our feelings confronts the formidable challenge of mastering our judgments. The first step to such mastery is the desire for it. Students need to consciously experience what is at stake. Earlier, I suggested mindfulness as a means to make students aware of the emotional effects of negative and positive thoughts. They should be frequently reminded to practice such awareness, but almost inevitably they will face both inner and outer resistance. Anger and resentment of perceived injury or threat of injury and condemnation of "sins" are protected by a pervasive understanding of right, of *justice*. One feels morally *obliged* to judge what he deems wrongful behavior.

Inner awareness often reveals that we are far more prone to negative thoughts than positive thoughts. Negative judgments of people, events, and circumstances are habitual and apparently addictive. Strengthening a student's will to break this habit is a very tall order. But the path to awareness of the joy and peace of appreciative love is blocked at some point unless we can interest students in what lies beyond the barricades of judgment and show them how to pass through them.

Forgiveness is the release of judgment, and exercises in forgiveness provide an opportunity to experience the relief of this release. Students will not be convinced otherwise. This helps strengthen the motive to forgive, but we should not underestimate the emotional resistance to forgiveness. This resistance is protected by the mind's infinite capacity to rationalize long lists of exceptions. If we are to fortify students' decision to lower the barriers to awareness of appreciative love, we must also get them to venture past their bristling defenses to examine their judgments with clear, assessing eyes. We must get them to examine not only the emotional costs but also the validity of their rationalizations.

Students should be taught to look closer at the question of motive when they perceive they have been wronged: Is the behavior of the person who made me feel angry, frustrated, or ashamed due to ill will toward me, or is it based on a different judgment of what is right and fair? Does their behavior have more to do with their own issues than with me? What emotions move them to act as they do? Do I sometimes act the same way? Would I judge them if I understood what they are feeling? And what am I feeling in response? Do I want revenge? Do I wish them harm? If so, are my motives really better than theirs?

Educators should give students ample opportunity to look deeper into people's motives by means of literature, films, storytelling, etc. They should speculate about the motives of people in history. And when they are ready, they should see what psychological and sociological research has to say. They should be led to understand how often initial judgments about people appear less valid upon close inspection. And they should investigate claims that negative judgments have positive outcomes. Is condemnation really necessary to motivate better behavior? Is diminishing the worth of people by condemning them the best way to deter them from harming others? Does getting revenge really make you feel better?

It is important that students learn about alternatives to judgment. For example, Gandhi and Martin Luther King emphasized love and avoided condemnation and hatred to advance causes that inspired — and changed — the hearts of hundreds of millions. They sought change by emphasizing the light rather than the darkness in people's hearts. There are thousands of less famous examples of those who served causes without condemning those who opposed them even in the face of abuse.

We should show students how accentuating the light in the hearts of others can inspire people's better angels. Lack of judgment can lower psychological defenses, open the door to sincere communication, and move people to examine their motives. It speaks to most people's deep desire to be — and be seen as — a good person. Students who learn this will see an alternative to revenge and condemnation that resonates with the deeper aspirations of their hearts.

Students should hear testimony of the power of forgiveness to change lives. They should hear explanations of why people forgive and how they managed it despite the strong emotions that pulled them in the opposite direction. But this is not enough to counteract the social pressure to join in condemnation. Students need to learn not only that forgiveness can serve their happiness by reducing the pangs of negative feelings, but also that forgiveness is justified.

Unfortunately, you cannot simply overlook what you see as an objective wrong and be free of judgment. This merely suppresses the grievance into the subconscious, where it is guaranteed to resurface in the form of negative feelings. As long as the mind clings to the initial belief that an objective wrong occurred, you are not really free of the affective consequences of judgment. The sort of forgiveness that truly dissipates these effects requires a change of perspective, a change of the lens through which you see people. Your belief about what you and others essentially are tints the lens of your regard. It inherently colors your estimation of the worth of others and the roles they play in your life.

Though educators should not tell students what to believe, they unavoidably inform students' beliefs. Palmer observes, "Every epistemology — rooted (as all of them are) in a particular ontology, and manifesting (as all of them do) in a particular pedagogy — has an impact on the ethical formation of learners."[19] Palmer also says,

> Whether the subject is the human or the nonhuman world, we get much more than facts in the classroom. Consciously and unconsciously, we get images of ourselves (for example, as contestants in a win-lose competition or persons of unconditional worth) and images of the world (for instance, as "a war of all against all" or an interdependent community) that help form our inner lives.[20]

A person's understanding of ontology — the nature of being — is the founding premise of her answers to the Big Questions of life. What a student believes she and everyone else essentially is informs her judgments of human nature, human worth, and human purpose and therefore influences what she feels about herself and others. Such belief may not be conscious and coherent, but we all necessarily act according to operating assumptions of the nature of reality. A pedagogy meant to empower students' pursuit of happiness should expand students' awareness of different beliefs and the affective consequences of believing them. Showing students how they can adjust the lens through which they see others, showing them how to see people in a better light if they so wish, gives them choices they would otherwise not see. Thus students need to explore perspectives on reality and the implications of these beliefs for how they feel about people.

But the current curricula of schools do not allow for examining perspectives on reality. Since religious and materialist viewpoints are among these perspectives, introducing them into classrooms faces legal and political hurdles. They cannot be presented in the context of subjects that deal primarily with assertions of fact such as science classes. They can, however, be legitimately presented in the context of philosophical inquiry.

Philosophy asks questions about the core concerns of life — including all questions that involve judgments of value — and opens the door to exploring different plausible answers. Philosophy does not inherently privilege a particular viewpoint, and leaves none unchallenged. Philosophical inquiry invites each student to come up with her own answers to the central questions of life. It is thus well-suited to a liberal education that aims to expand students' freedom as well as empower their pursuit of happiness.

7

Philosophy

*Philosophy belongs back in the streets, where Socrates
originally practiced it.* | Robert C. Solomon

tanley Katz says "We would do better to challenge undergraduates to
ask their most urgent questions about themselves, the world and the
human condition — and to organize their curriculum around these
questions."[1] As the primary human aspiration, the question of happiness —
its nature, sources, and means — is the most "urgent" question. The value
of the answers to all other questions is measured in what they contribute to
feeling as we choose to feel. The exploration of happiness should be the core
theme of education from beginning to end, the hub around which all else
revolves. All the Big Questions of life are attached to this hub.

Students must make their own journey to self-understanding and insight. Like wisdom, understanding and insight cannot be simply handed to
them, or gained by mastering a body of knowledge. Freedom requires that
students come up with their own answers to the value questions of philosophy. Educators can but give them the wherewithal to make discerning choic-

es about what to pursue and how. For these and other reasons, philosophical inquiry is an essential component of a happiness curriculum. I think it is also an essential component of a liberal education aimed at liberating minds and developing the skills of freedom.

A movement already exists that seeks to make such inquiry a more central component of the school curricula. It is called Philosophy for Children. Matthew Lipman started the movement in the 1960s, and it has attracted many adherents and led to the establishment of quite a few centers devoted to promoting "P4C" in schools around the world, though admittedly to small effect as yet.[2] The movement calls for engaging students in focused, communal discussion on philosophical questions from the earliest years of schooling. It emphasizes *doing* rather than *learning about* philosophy.

Advocates see a number of reasons this should happen. Philosophical inquiry is considered the best way to develop critical thinking skills and habits.[3] It builds "Philosophical Intelligence."[4] It brings greater depth of meaning to each subject because philosophical inquiry goes beyond the *what* to the *why*, including the Big Why of the main point of it all. A.C. Grayling explains that "In a curriculum devoted to acquiring knowledge and technique, there has to be time for reflection on what it all means, what it is for, and why it matters, for almost any 'it', and this ... is distinctively the province of philosophy."[5]

Advocates say communal philosophical inquiry, where a class joins in discussion, taps into children's natural enthusiasm and curiosity. Grayling says his experience with philosophical discussions in various grade levels shows "that young minds are naturally philosophical minds."[6] He further remarks that:

> This openness and readiness to engage with ideas that adult minds might resist on the grounds of obvious silliness (which often means: unobvious importance) is a fertile thing. In view of this, and of the instant exportability of the methods and insights of philosophy to almost everything else in the curriculum, the case for placing it at the curriculum's heart makes itself.[7]

The word "philosophy" is off-putting for many people. To them it implies abstruse reasoning to arrive at provisional conclusions with little practical importance, an exercise in conceptual puzzle-solving of merely academic interest. Worse, philosophy as an academic discipline too often consists mainly of learning about the abstruse reasoning of intellectual luminaries, the "canonical study" that deters many students from taking philosophy classes. This obscures the immense practical value of *engaging* in philosophy.

It is true that the Big Questions of philosophy have no definitive answers based on observable evidence. Bertrand Russell explained that "as soon as definite knowledge concerning any subject becomes possible, this subject ceases to be called philosophy, and becomes a separate science."[8] But the vital, irreducible core of the domain of philosophy is all the questions of value that have only subjective answers.

Questions of value are not merely grist for the mill of conceptual puzzle-solving; people imply an answer to such questions in their daily choices as well as with their decisions about longer-range goals. Most people seldom or never consciously ask these questions, but they cannot help but live according to at least an implied working hypothesis of the answers to guide their choices. We all live according to our personal answers to the "unanswerable" questions of philosophy whether or not we are aware of it.

People answer questions of value when they make decisions about the course of their day, their thoughts and behavior toward others, their pastimes, and what they think it worth their time and money to possess. We answer questions of value when we formulate an idea of what we want from moment to moment. We answer these questions in our choice of beliefs, lifestyles, and careers.

When you acknowledge that you necessarily live your life according to working hypotheses that provide at least provisional answers to the "unanswerable" questions of philosophy, the main point of philosophy becomes clear. Philosophical inquiry focuses your attention on identifying the assumptions that govern all you do in life and turns them into questions. It helps bring the light of knowledge, understanding, and reason to bear on finding answers. It allows you to make the crucial decisions about value and meaning in the light of insight rather than living in the darkness of unconscious reaction.

Philosophical inquiry puts the fruits of the examined life within reach. It gives you the opportunity to discover the deeper, enduring aspiration of your heart in order to better align your chosen values with this aspiration. When aimed at the assumptions by which you live, philosophical inquiry can greatly improve your chances of realizing what you really want rather than wandering about in the darkness of vague notions, superficial understanding, and programmed reactions.

Solomon observed "Philosophy is essentially an art. It is the art of living, the search for wisdom."[9] He is right, but it helps to understand where the value of wisdom lies. The essence of wisdom is discovering the deepest yearning of the heart — the primary aim that renders all other aims subsidiary — and living in accordance with what is required to fulfill this yearning. If wisdom is worthy of its reputation as one of the most desirable attainments in life, the measure of wisdom is not how much you know or the depth of your understanding. It is happiness.

The question of happiness is primary among the Big Questions of philosophy. It should be the primary focus of philosophical inquiry in schools, the hub around which all the other questions revolve.

Methods of Inquiry

Cognitive scientists have found that thinking and learning require preexisting knowledge.[10] It may be enjoyable and stimulating for students to jump into a speculative discussion about a philosophical question, but they will not harvest the fruits of a focused, coherent search for answers until they have acquired a base of knowledge and understanding. Philosophical inquiry in the schools must build this foundation in a cumulative process that progressively adds to what they learn each year.

Educators should emphasize building a foundation of knowledge based on experience in the first years of school. This requires awareness of feelings, thoughts, and beliefs. I believe children will find the exercises of inner awareness meaningful. Unlike most of what they are taught, they will come to realize immediate benefits, benefits they can *feel*. Awareness of present benefit grows with awareness of feelings, and this feeds a self-reinforcing motive. Students who feel inferior in academic ability may feel far more confident and enthusiastic about exploring the inner dimension of experience. This exploration does not expose them to easy comparison and judgment. They may discover a freedom not found in the push to master "objective" knowledge.

I have long hoped we could discover a way to inspire intrinsic motivation and move away from extrinsic motivators such as grades, praise, and criticism that are so easily interpreted as judgments of relative worth. A great deal of evidence backs the claim that intrinsic motivation is far superior to the rewards and punishments of extrinsic motivators, especially in regard to education.[11] A philosophy core might be an opportunity to give this hope a chance.

In addition to the experiential exercises, even young children should begin exploring different perspectives on the question of happiness. It can begin with stories in which people express different assumptions about happiness and discussions in which children hear different views about what others think is desirable to feel and what they think it takes to feel it. As young students learn to read, stories and other reading material should be chosen with an eye to the expression of feelings and desires. They should learn about and investigate alternative viewpoints. As the grade levels rise, the investigation of alternative perspectives on happiness and related questions should both broaden and deepen. Investigation of perspectives on reality, the good life, and social ideals should be progressively introduced.

The core methodology should be the alternative perspective approach. It is an approach with a long history and it has been recommended by a host of teachers and philosophers. It is employed to some extent in the contrasting viewpoint method used to get students to think critically about controversial issues. Many books and series provide contrasting views on debatable issues.[12] These views are alternative perspectives on a particular question. For example, I ask "What sort of society best promotes the happiness of its citizens?" The students consider how the proponents of various ideologies such as Liberalism, Socialism, Fascism, etc., answer this question.

I also use the alternative perspective approach in the two honors courses I teach. Each involves an investigation of proposed answers to a particular Big Question of philosophy. The question of the Nature of Reality seminar is "What is the nature of reality?" The question of The Social Good seminar is "What is the social Good?"

First, I have students read a tract by an advocate of the perspective we are investigating. In the nature of reality seminar, I ask them to identify the assumptions of the perspective — the founding premises about reality and value that the advocate assumes in making his case. Such premises reveal the advocate's take on both what we ought to pursue and what it is possible to achieve. A materialist perspective, for example, differs from religious perspectives in regard to the source and perhaps the nature of the Good and therefore morality. These perspectives differ on the essential nature of a human being, what can be known and how, and perhaps to what we should aspire in life. God commands and reveals and heaven beckons in most religious perspectives, but not in the materialist understanding of reality.

It is important to identify the basic assumptions because they are necessary to discovering the implications of each perspective for the questions of how we should live and to what we can and should aspire. Understanding the practical implications allows students to make an informed assessment of the relative merits of each perspective.

I ask students to hand in their list of the assumptions they found in the reading and, when we have advanced to it, the implications they derived from the assumptions. For example, what are the implications of the materialist assumption that we are purely physical beings that cease to exist at death for how people should live and for what they can hope to achieve? These lists are ungraded; their purpose is to motivate at least some thought on these matters. Having to share their thoughts with classmates is the main motivation for taking the matter somewhat seriously, I find, and having to formulate their thoughts on paper noticeably improves the quality of discussion. I guide the students through the unfamiliar process of identifying assumptions and deriving implications, but my guidance becomes ever less necessary as they progress from perspective to perspective. They progressively internalize the method and hone the skill.

At the end of several weeks of exploring and discussing a perspective, I have the students write and present a full analysis of the perspective under consideration. The analysis must include assumptions, implications, plausibility (evidence, logic, etc.), and utility (advantages and disadvantages of believing it). I emphasize *affective* advantages and disadvantages. For example, I ask what they stand to gain and lose in terms of feelings from believing in materialism. The analysis essentially summarizes the thinking and discussion of previous weeks, so it is not a cause for much anxiety. At the end of the semester I ask them to present their own perspective on the question (the nature of reality or the social Good) in the same format, except they must first describe what they believe.

A semester is insufficient to do any Big Question even a modicum of justice, but a philosophy core throughout the years of education would spring such limits. Freed from the strictures of limited time, I would lead students much deeper into each perspective, providing more history for context, using literature and film to enrich their understanding, and bringing in real-life advocates of a perspective to discuss their beliefs. Students should hear the case made by someone who believes it. I would have them read prominent critiques of each perspective, and invite deeper consideration of motive and more extensive exploration of the consequences of a belief. I would look for a way to make each perspective more experiential by means of thought experiments, outings, and even "trying them out" in some way.

Other approaches have merit. Harry Brighouse describes the "method of reflective equilibrium" for exploring moral beliefs:

> We list our considered judgements about particular cases, and look at whether they fit together consistently. Where we find inconsistencies we reject those judgements in which we have least reason to be confident (for example, those in which we have reason to suspect there is an element of self-interest pressing us to the conclusion we have reached). We also list the principles we judge suitable to cover cases, and look through those principles for inconsistency, again rejecting those we have least reason to be confident in our judgements about. Then we look at the particular judgements and the principles in the light of one another: are there inconsistencies?; do some of the principles look less plausible in the light of the weight of considered judgements, or vice versa?[13]

Lipman and others in the Philosophy for Children movement commend the Community of Inquiry approach. Lipman explains,

> …we can now speak of "converting the classroom into a community of inquiry" in which students listen to one another with respect, build on one another's ideas, challenge one another to supply reasons for otherwise unsupported opinions, assist each other in drawing inferences from what has been said, and seek to identify one another's assumptions. A community of inquiry attempts to follow the inquiry where it leads rather than be penned in by the boundary lines of existing disciplines.[14]

The main version of this approach seems to allow discussion for the most part to follow where the students lead, taking up questions they themselves pose. Research has revealed that various versions of the approach have led to a range of positive educational outcomes.[15]

A related approach more focused on discussion of particular readings is called "Socratic circles." Matt Copeland describes it this way:

> The basic procedure for a Socratic circle is as follows: 1. On the day before a Socratic circle, the teacher hands out a short passage of text. 2. That night at home, students spend time reading, analyzing, and taking notes on the text. 3. During class the next day, students are randomly divided into two concentric circles: an inner circle and an outer circle. 4. The students in the inner circle read the passage aloud and then engage in a discussion of the text for approximately ten minutes, while students in the outer circle silently observe the behavior and performance of the inner circle. 5. After this discussion of the text, the outer circle assesses the inner circle's performance and gives ten minutes of feedback for the inner circle. 6. Students in the inner and outer circles now exchange roles and positions. 7. The new inner circle holds a ten-minute discussion and then receives ten minutes of feedback from the new outer circle.[16]

Copeland reports amazing results in regard to enthusiastic engagement, insight, creative thinking, listening, and team-building skills. I am intrigued by the role of the outer circle; it seems to both motivate and inform the quality of discussion.

These approaches are promising and I believe the communal inquiry they employ is crucial, but they are insufficient in and of themselves. Empowering the pursuit of happiness requires an ongoing process for increasing knowledge and understanding, deepening insight, and honing the skills relevant to the effective choice of feelings. This requires channeling inquiry toward an eventual answer. Conceptual dissection, undirected inquiry, and presenting an unorganized collage of views won't do the trick.

Discussion without a substantive focus and a clear end in mind is unlikely to arrive at any particular destination. Reaching a destination — an informed personal conclusion — is the point if we would realize the main value of philosophical inquiry. The considered presentation of alternative perspectives on specific questions for structured analysis is far better suited to reaching the desired destination.

The first years, as I said, should provide the basis of awareness of feelings and associated thoughts. Direct experience provides the essential understandings and motive for what follows. It is here children should be introduced to the overriding importance of feelings and therefore of happiness. They should learn from the beginning that all that follows in the philosophical core is designed to inform and strengthen their ability to experience what they choose to feel, and all else they learn in school is related to this end as well. We should repeatedly emphasize that we aim to help them develop this skill and inform them of what the choices are and how to determine the likely consequences of particular choices. The presentation of alternative perspectives is necessary to this aim as it illuminates a range of choices and their likely consequences. The approach promises many other benefits as well.

The investigation of perspectives necessarily employs the basic methods of critical thinking and is an excellent way to develop the skill. The identification of founding assumptions of an argument or viewpoint is unfamiliar to students in my experience, but it is crucial to understanding and assessing the merits of a perspective. The ability to identify assumptions will also help them weigh the merits of all the claims of truth presented in the media — an extremely useful ability in today's world. Most of what students are taught at present skips over this step, perhaps because it is not considered important, but likely because it is not considered, period. Yet if we are preparing students to choose rather than simply accept pre-digested truths, they must learn to look at the founding premises of every argument and viewpoint. The alternative perspective approach continually exercises this skill, and it takes them to the next step of deriving the implications of the assumptions they discovered.

Deriving implications makes informed assessment and comparison of perspectives possible. Listing the implications of a "carpe diem" — seize the day! — notion of happiness, for example, makes it much easier to assess its desirability and compare it to an ascetic — denial of desire — notion of happiness. These are the essential skills of inquiry that allow informed and reasoned conclusions, and the investigation of alternative perspectives continually exercises these skills.

The approach also makes students aware of their own operating assumptions and invites them to consider the implications of what they believe in light of alternatives. This is one of my deliberate aims in the courses where I use the approach. I tell my students in honors classes that they do not truly understand their own beliefs until they compare them with contrasting beliefs. I tell students in comparative politics classes they do not understand their own country until they compare it with others. As Kant says, "The thing in itself cannot be known." The alternative perspective approach acknowledges this crucial insight.

The inestimable value in this is that it affords students the opportunity to shape the beliefs that guide their lives and render them more coherent and conscious. Exposure to different beliefs also expands students' awareness of choices, of opportunities and possibilities. It expands the world of which they are aware and therefore the world in which they subjectively live. Exploring perspectives on happiness would extend such awareness into the relatively unexplored universe within.

Contending perspectives help illuminate core dimensions of human existence, especially those that pertain to the heart of human aspiration. Gareth Matthews advises that,

> Since the pursuit of happiness is the overall aim that motivates our lives, it is good for us to be as clear as we can about what, for us, happiness consists in. Moreover, since the pursuit of happiness is also the overall aim of other people around us, reflection on what they seem to understand as happiness will help us understand them better.[17]

The alternative perspectives approach to exploring the Big Questions introduces students to a great deal of information about the human condition and puts it in context. Each perspective has a history. It has a history of developing thought and a history of the conditions that led to it. Such history is a deep vein of knowledge and understanding. If we extend the exploration of perspectives to the end of secondary education, there is time to tap into this vein. Students come to learn about the heritage of human thought, culture, and aspiration in a way that makes it relevant, meaningful, and coherent.

Religious perspectives are obviously relevant to investigating the question of happiness, and to much else besides. Religion is a central dimension of the human experience and it exercises a major influence on social and political behavior. "Excluding religion and spirituality from serious study in secular settings is a stunning form of irrationality in itself," says Palmer. "Religion and spirituality are among the major drivers of contemporary life (as one can readily see in any daily newspaper) and of any historical epoch one can name."[18] Yet Americans, at least, are generally ill-informed about these matters. Laurie Goodstein cites survey results to conclude that "Americans are by all measures a deeply religious people, but they are also deeply ignorant about religion."[19]

Knowledge about religions contributes to historical and cultural understanding, which is one reason for growing interest in teaching about religions in public schools. There are other agendas as well. Peter Steinfels observes that:

> *Many conservatives and liberals agree that discussion of religion belongs in the schools, although their reasons for supporting it differ. Conservatives are drawn to the cause by a belief that the absence of religion carries an implicitly anti-religious message, liberals by the belief that learning about religious diversity strengthens pluralism.*[20]

Citing a report issued by the Organization for Security and Cooperation in Europe in 2007 calling for increased education about religion, Charles Haynes explains that Europeans and Americans "are finally beginning to understand that ignorance about religions in religiously diverse societies is a root cause of intolerance and discrimination."[21] Serious engagement with various moral viewpoints is democratically healthier than suppressing it. "A more robust public engagement with our moral disagreements could provide a stronger, not a weaker, basis for mutual respect" according to Michael Sandel.[22]

Introducing religious viewpoints on major questions of philosophy engages students in a far richer exploration of religions than exposing them solely to "academic information," which is widely thought the only legally and democratically safe way to bring religion into public schools. Bringing religious views into schools as elaborated perspectives on the Big Questions is not token inclusion. It allows religious answers to these questions to be presented in their own terms and on equal footing with contending views.

If consideration of alternative perspectives is to lead to more than just a broader awareness of beliefs, if it is to afford the rich opportunity for informing students' own beliefs and understandings, they should hear the viewpoints explained by those who hold them. One must stand in the shoes of a believer to understand a belief in its own terms rather than in the terms of a contending viewpoint. Speaking of moral education, Brighouse says,

> *Exposure to moral views would occur best by allowing proponents of views to address children in the controlled environment of the classroom. While the instrumental argument is connected to the liberal humanism which is*

anathema to many religious sectarians, the implementation of autonomy-facilitating education would probably require a nuanced attitude to the exposure of children to religion in schools. A child cannot be autonomous either in her acceptance or rejection of a religious view unless she experiences serious advocacy.[23]

The chance to hear viewpoints in their own terms is one of many benefits of bringing outsiders into the discussions on alternative perspectives. Students will hear personal stories and witnessing that help humanize the abstractions. They will be able to ask questions about viewpoints and points of fact their teachers cannot — or should not — answer. Students will better understand why people believe as they do, perhaps eliciting more sympathy and tolerance. As Palmer says, "The more you know about another person's story, the less possible it is to see that person as your enemy."[24] In regard to Gatto's complaint that public education cocoons students away from their communities, this is a way to bring the community into the classroom for genuine interaction.

The alternative perspective approach commends bringing advocates into schools. Bringing people in for discussion is very much in keeping with the communal inquiry recommended by advocates of Philosophy for Children. The approach calls for devoting far more class time to discussion than presentation. Focused discussion builds the skills of speaking, listening, and democratic deliberation that are valuable for both personal and civic purposes.

The approach is not just continual investigation and analysis. In the middle years of K-12 education, students should begin working on the elements of their own philosophy of life. Every year they should revise and develop it further. Writing greatly aids clarity of thinking, and it can be revelatory when it comes to what one believes about deep matters of existence, purpose and the Good.

The task of developing a philosophy of life will also bring the point of it all into sharper focus. Having given the fundamental questions of life deep and frequent thought, students' maturing answers will change the lens of perception through which they see the world and thus the meaning of their experiences of the world. And when they leave secondary school, they will have a small work of their own thoughts on the Big Questions, the written record of at least a good start toward an examined life. Students will graduate as philosophers.

The Fruits of a Philosophical Core

What will a student have gained thereby? First, he will have gained an uncommon awareness. He will be more aware of his feelings, of what he prefers to feel, and of the relationship between thoughts and feelings. He will be more aware of the aspirations he has in common with others and the different ways people through the ages have sought to realize these aspirations. He will be more aware of choices, more aware of the paths he can take in the pursuit of what he seeks. And he will have a much clearer idea of what he seeks, or at least of what is worthwhile to seek.

Upon completing his education, a young citizen will have gained a breadth and depth of awareness of vital aspects of the human condition that relatively few people possess at present. Awareness creates the subjective world in which a person lives, thus he would live in a larger world of deeper meaning. He will better understand the patterns and principles that underlie human behavior much better than otherwise, thus his view of the world would be clearer and more coherent. He will have a deeper understanding of himself and others, and greater sympathy for his companions on the journey of life. He will better understand what people believe and why. He will see the relevance of the heritage of human thought and experience far better than current graduates.

The young adult of the future will be more aware and certain of her thoughts, feelings, and choices as she confronts the clamoring appeals for her money and allegiance. Having learned to analyze arguments throughout her education, the manipulative appeals to superficial material wants, prejudices, and vanity will be less persuasive. She will often have use for the balm of perspective when she reads or hears about the unending causes for fear in the news and when she faces the many difficult challenges life presents. She will have learned how to find inner sanctuary from the chaos of the world.

A future graduating student will also be more likely to consider the point of her various pastimes and pursuits. Perhaps she will pause to ponder what it is she is truly hoping to experience when she buys things she fancies, watches movies and plays sports, seeks the company of friends, attends church, and contemplates what she wants to do when she grows up. We may also hope she will have learned a greater appreciation of the beauty and poignancy of life, and the joy of love.

A young citizen will be more adept at the skills of freedom because she had ample opportunity to exercise them. She will have been frequently invited to consider her beliefs in light of growing understanding. She will be clearer about what she believes and, importantly, why. This is the basis for independent thinking. Her commitment to beliefs and belief systems will more likely be based on informed evaluation and decision in light of the common criteria of happiness rather than non-reflective acceptance of received wisdoms. As Bertrand Russell says, "Philosophy, though unable to tell us with certainty what is the true answer to the doubts which it raises, is able to suggest many possibilities which enlarge our thoughts and free them from the tyranny of custom."[25]

Graduates will be more aware of choices and likely consequences, and they will be more aware of the walls in their minds and how to pass beyond them. They will have learned to formulate their thoughts more clearly and communicate them more effectively. And they would have a better shot at wisdom worthy of the concept.

A philosophical core may be less amenable to accountability tests. But should we sacrifice what is reasonably required to empower the pursuit of happiness because progress toward the aim is less easy to measure? This conjures the old joke of the man looking for his keys under the lamppost: he lost the keys elsewhere, but prefers to look where the light is brighter. Accountability is a means, not an end. As Nel Nodding points out, "We may virtually all agree that schools and educators should be held accountable, but we should press the question: accountable for what?"[26] Here we confront our own responsibility to answer this question wisely and morally rather than allow accountability to be turned into an end in itself.

Schools cannot make students happy either during or after their years of education. But we owe it to our children to do all in our power to help them develop the mental wherewithal to effectively pursue this aspiration should they so choose. A philosophy core and alternative perspective approach commend themselves to this purpose.

It would not require a complete reorganization of current curricula to introduce a philosophy core, but I suspect in time much would change in our schools. To everyone's benefit. Teachers willing to be retrained to the requirements of this core and approach might find relief from the ghettos of their subjects and learn it is far more rewarding to be a fellow traveler on their students' educational journey than merely the authoritative transmitter of what they already know. Making school more enjoyable for both students and teachers would constitute a meaningful transformation of education in itself.

Inevitably, stressing the skills and philosophical exploration of happiness will be criticized as a touchy-feely, irrelevant diversion from the basics. "You can't be happy without a job" is the inevitable objection. A great deal of ink and rhetoric are devoted to insisting that we should concentrate on the skills kids need to get a job in a highly competitive global economy. Those who so insist will be quite annoyed to see their priorities challenged on both moral and practical grounds.

Aside from the questionable assumptions about happiness implied in the emphasis on job training, the contention that basic and "21st century" skills would suffer if empowering the pursuit of happiness were our main focus is wrong. In fact, the methods of philosophical inquiry would continually exercise the most important of these skills. Reading comprehension, communication skills including writing, retention of knowledge, conceptual understanding, critical and creative thinking, social skills, awareness of the social environment, the ability to think outside the box, and a broad foundation of knowledge are all required by inquiry into alternative perspectives on the Big Questions of life. In a 2013 survey, United States employers overwhelmingly favor "intellectual and interpersonal skills" and the "capacity to think critically, communicate clearly, and solve complex problems over other educational attainments in their new hires.[27]

Evidence shows these attainments are best promoted by the pedagogy of inquiry into essential questions.[28] The pedagogy provides a far more meaningful context and engaging vehicle for learning. And it taps a deeper motive. Engagement with important existential questions such as the nature, sources, and means of happiness provides a sense of direction and purpose capable of igniting a passion for exploration.

Past and current educational priorities have failed to address the sense of "emptiness," the "existential anxiety," the "apathy" many observers and researchers see in younger generations.[29] Tony Judt echoes a complaint I have heard myself when he recalls, "For thirty years students have been complaining to me that 'it was easy for you': your generation had ideals and ideas, you believed in something, you were able to change things. 'We' (the children of the '80s, the '90s, the 'aughts') have nothing."[30] Emphasizing achievement for purposes of lesser meaning will only exacerbate feelings of hollowness and drift. As William Damon observes,

> *The message that young people do best when they are challenged to strive, to achieve, to serve ... fails to address the most essential question of all: For what purpose? Or, in a word, Why? For young people, this concern means starting to ask, and answer, questions such as: What do I hope to accomplish with all my efforts, with all the striving that I am expected to do? What are the higher goals that give these efforts meaning? What matters to me; and why should it matter? What is my ultimate concern in life? Unless we make such questions a central part of our conversations with young people, we can do little but sit back and watch while they wander into a sea of confusion, drift, self-doubt, and anxiety — feelings that too often arise when work and striving are unaccompanied by a sense of purpose.*[31]

Done wisely and well, philosophical inquiry into perspectives on Big Questions will not be a diversion from the basics and job-related skills. It will be a more promising means to teach them. More importantly, it will inspire our children with a clearer, more fulfilling sense of purpose that will empower their pursuit of happiness.

8

Higher Education

The way to make the university experience more satisfying is to recognize and support its larger educational purpose. | Harry R. Lewis

Empowering students' pursuit of happiness should begin in kindergarten, but this is not cause to delay trying to get colleges and universities to embrace this purpose as well. Not only do institutions of higher education share the moral obligation to treat their students as ends in themselves, they also bear a great deal of responsibility for inspiring changes in primary and secondary education.

Teachers gain their certification during their years in colleges and universities, and they are imbued with the methoads and values they learn there. Public school administrators are also products of higher education. Many of the innovations adopted in K-12 education in America over the past century began in elite universities. If colleges and universities were dedicated to empowering students' pursuit of happiness, their example and innovations would resonate through all levels of public education.

But they are not so dedicated, or even inclined. Higher education is inflicted with greater ambiguity and dispersal of purpose than primary and secondary education. Whether as ends or means, students are the clear focus during the earlier years of schooling. Students must share the limelight with research, money, and faculty prerogative at most universities and many colleges. In light of the hiring criteria, faculty incentives and accountability, and allocation of funds at most institutions, one could reasonably conclude that making a difference in the lives of students is not really among the top priorities. Andrew Hacker and Claudia Dreifus observe,

> In theory, education is supposed to be a public service: like health care, fire-fighting, national parks. And by and large that describes the motivations of teachers from kindergarten through high school. But as we ascend to colleges and universities — the preserve of professors — self-interest, strengthened by a narrow sense of self-definition, begins to set in.[1]

Not many in academe openly agree with Michael Oakeshott that "a university is not a machine for achieving a particular purpose or producing a particular result; it is a manner of human activity."[2] Few side with Stanley Fish when he insists "higher education, properly understood, is distinguished by the absence of a direct and designed relationship between its activities and measurable effects in the world."[3] Harry Lewis points out the obvious when he says that universities "are privileged with independence and public support because they serve society."[4] But the "elitist" attitudes of Oakeshott and Fish reflect the aristocratic origins of higher education that live on in the halls of academe. Scholarship is honored and rewarded far more than good teaching and meaningful service to society. Academe is called the "ivory tower" for a reason.

The bulk of the scholarship in liberal arts disciplines — and often in other disciplines as well — is of only academic interest and is for the main part read by only a few thousand scholars in a particular field to buttress their own scholarly endeavors, which will then be shared with the same few thousand. The result is a rather sterile feedback loop that serves the careers and intellectual stimulation of scholars and, supposedly, the reputation of their institutions, but seldom anyone outside of the academy. That is, unless one counts the pundits who lampoon the pretensions of the ivory tower.

The claim that academic research enriches teaching confronts the counterclaim that it renders what is taught less relevant to students who are not themselves destined to join the priesthood of scholars. Hacker and Dreifus cite evidence that there is an "inverse correlation between good teaching and academic research."[5] Such evidence will not convince many given the lack of a generally accepted definition of "good teaching," but it does throw down the gauntlet to those who simply assert that research enhances teaching, especially in light of the contention that the point of teaching is to make a difference in the lives of students.

According to Mark Taylor, "The emphasis on narrow scholarship also encourages an educational system that has become a process of cloning. Faculty members cultivate those students whose futures they envision as identical to their own pasts, even though their tenures will stand in the way of these students having futures as full professors."[6] Speaking of Harvard, Lewis observes that "Students are unhappy because too many faculty members are not interested in them, except as potential academics, and the curriculum is designed more around the interests of the faculty than around the desires of the students or their families."[7]

The liberal arts disciplines are eminently suited to revealing the vistas of the human condition and to exploring the heart of human aspiration. The humanities in particular not only introduce students to the breadth and depth of human experience; they can also enhance the quality of their *present* experience. Helen Vendler alludes to this in making the case that humanistic study should be centered on the arts.[8] But the humanities offer far more than enriched aesthetic experiences. "[The humanities] lie near the heart of mankind's restless efforts to make sense of the world," says Peter Conn.[9]

The liberal arts could indeed help students make better sense of the world if they had a coherent vision of the world to offer. These disciplines could be readily adapted to explore the Big Questions of human existence, including the questions of the nature, sources, and means of happiness. They could be sequentially organized to lead students toward ever broader awareness and deeper insight. But they are not. Despite occasional claims to the contrary, there is no unifying theme to render what is taught in the various disciplines collectively coherent. The liberal arts exercise critical thinking and communication skills, but they are thematically fragmented and, taken as a whole, present a disjointed view of life, reality, and value. The exception is their common embrace of *scholarly* values peculiar to the academy.

The disciplinary fragmentation that characterizes higher education fosters the impression that the experience of life itself is fragmented into barely related aspects. "Siloed disciplines" suggest siloed dimensions of experience. "Faculty — growing numbers of whom hold fragmented part-time appointments — develop their courses in isolation from one another while students are left to their own devices to discern any possible connections," says Carol Geary Schneider.[10] Speaking of the rapid expansion of universities in the post-World War II era, Gerald Graff says,

> Universities had the luxury to better themselves by simply adding new components without bothering to think about how to integrate and connect what was added. The result was a notoriously incoherent college curriculum that leaves it up to the student body to connect what the university itself does not.[11]

There may have been a time when such questions as life's meaning and purpose were openly explored in humanities classes, providing a thematic context. But it is relatively rare in contemporary academe.[12] Stanley Cavell writes:

> In contemporary American universities, each academic discipline is treated as autonomous and self-defining, so that its practitioners, or at least the most prestigious and influential among them, prescribe to those entering the discipline what its scope and limits are. And in order to excel in any one particular discipline, one need in general know little or nothing about any of the others.[13]

Ivory tower attitudes, emphasis on research, and thematically fragmented content contribute to what is considered a *relevance crisis* in the liberal arts, especially in the humanities. The percentage of students seeking degrees in humanities disciplines has recovered somewhat from the precipitous decline in the early 1970s, but faculty hires in the disciplines are down, departments are shrinking, and funds are being allocated elsewhere.[14] State governments are redirecting their rapidly diminishing support for higher education to "majors that are in demand in the job market."[15]

Martha Nussbaum opines that,

> The humanities and the arts are being cut away, in both primary/secondary and college/university education, in virtually every nation of the world.

*Seen by policy-makers as useless frills, at a time when nations must cut
away all useless things in order to stay competitive in the global market,
they are rapidly losing their place in curricula, and also in the minds and
hearts of parents and children.*[16]

Anthony Kronman believes "The humanities destroyed themselves by
abandoning secular humanism in favor of the research ideal, which for a
century and a half now has been gaining ground as the principal arbiter of
authority and prestige in American higher education."[17] As a result, there is
a big push to establish the economic relevance of the humanities in terms of
skills demanded by the 21st century global economy.

The thinking and communication skills as well as the heightened awareness of the social environment encouraged in liberal arts courses are presented as valuable assets in the fluid global economy. A consultant hired to
help my college revise our core curriculum was fond of saying that business
makes the best case for the liberal arts, and his contention is echoed in many
published discussions of liberal education. The editor of the Association of
American Colleges & Universities' magazine *Liberal Education* maintains,
"while liberal education remains the best preparation for life, it is now widely
recognized as the best preparation for making a living as well."[18]

Yet if business seems to make the best case for the liberal arts, the case
is not very compelling. The appeal to economic utility is considered necessary because the case for a more vital purpose of these disciplines is apparently even less compelling. The case for a more vital purpose of liberal arts is
undermined by the lack of clarity about what the purpose is, which makes
it difficult to argue the benefits of fulfilling whatever it is. Without defining
what, exactly, the liberal arts contribute to life, how can we convince people
they are "the best preparation for life"? Not many will buy the proposition
that being trained as a scholar fits the bill.

One increasingly hears voices within the academy that agree with Kronman that the liberal arts no longer serve their original purpose. Elizabeth
Coleman says "If we assume that the liberal arts are at a minimum defined
by their focus on developing a student's broadest intellectual and deepest
ethical potential, then I think it's fair to say such an education has disappeared."[19] She further opines that, "Given the collapse of liberal learning in
the bastions of education presumably committed to its ideals, it is no sur-
prise that the purposes of education in almost every arena have narrowed

drastically, and connections between the public good and education everywhere have all but disappeared."[20]

The main thrust of efforts to address the relevance crisis of the liberal arts is to redesign them as "practical liberal arts" that emphasize "real-world" professional, civic, and social engagement. Some consider this a matter of survival for smaller institutions: "If small colleges turn inward as opposed to outward," says Karen Gross, president of Southern Vermont College, "they're doomed."[21]

But this presumes that real-world relevance lies solely in the world beyond students' minds and hearts. The fact that all experience of the world is subjective and all value is determined within refutes this presumption. The personal value of education for each student lies in what it contributes to his subjective experience. The ability to experience as you choose is a cognitive skill that requires inner awareness and mental discipline. It requires "tending the garden of the mind." Were this acknowledged, the pervasive external orientation of education would no longer seem so compelling or wise. Practicality would cease to be defined solely in terms of external utility.

Can we truly make the liberal arts more relevant to the core aspirations of students by diverting them even further from awareness of the purposes of their hearts? Will the "21st century skills" promoted by redirecting the liberal arts outward improve their ability to feel as they choose? If we cannot honestly answer yes to these questions, we must rethink the outward thrust of current reform efforts.

Kronman says "We live today in a narcotized stupor, blind to the ways in which our own immense powers and the knowledge that has produced them cuts us off from the knowledge of who we are."[22] Higher education could do far more than it does to awaken students from this stupor. As it stands, though, academe does little to alleviate the inner blindness that robs students of their main defense against the cacophony of competing claims and the superficial lures of modern life. This failure has serious social implications. Parker Palmer warns:

> Higher education looses upon the world too many people who are masters of external, objective reality, with the knowledge and skill to manipulate it, but who understand little or nothing about inner drivers of their own behavior. Giving students knowledge as power over the world while failing to help them gain the kind of self-knowledge that gives them power over

themselves is a recipe for danger — and we are living today with the proof of that claim in every realm of life from economics to religion.[23]

Alexander and Helen Astin agree that "the relative amount of attention that colleges and universities devote to the 'inner' and 'outer' aspects of our students' lives has gotten way out of balance":

> *What is most ironic about all of this is that while many of the great literary and philosophical traditions that constitute the core of a liberal education are grounded in the maxim, "know thyself," the development of self-awareness receives very little attention in our colleges and universities. If students lack self-understanding — the capacity to see themselves clearly and honestly and to understand why they feel and act as they do — then how can we expect them to become responsible parents, professionals, and citizens?*[24]

To be sure, a movement is afoot to remedy the fragmentation of higher education. The push for "integrative education" has inspired general interest and a great many interdisciplinary courses. Advocates admit the movement has yet to coalesce around a coherent philosophy; discussion centers on technique rather than a unifying purpose of interdisciplinarity.[25] From what I have read and heard in dozens of presentations on the subject, most academics think the main point is simply to broaden students' awareness of other disciplines rather than meld them into a common understanding. This is certainly the case in my college. Considering the prevailing practice in interdisciplinary courses of simply presenting different disciplinary perspectives on a given topic, Louis Menand has a point when he claims "Interdisciplinarity is not something different from disciplinarity. It is the ratification of the logic of disciplinarity."[26] Simply importing knowledge and methods from other disciplines to a discipline-based class is the extent of many curricula billed as "integrative."[27]

I think Palmer and Arthur Zajonc offer one of the more cogent views of what the aims of the integrative movement should be: "A truly integrative education engages students in the systematic exploration of the relationship between their studies of the 'objective' world and the purpose, meaning, limits, and aspirations of their lives."[28] Happiness is the primary human purpose and therefore aspiration, and it provides the main measure of meaning in students' lives. So understood, the cause of happiness education dovetails with the aims of the integrative education movement. In fact, I think the combination of the understanding that happiness is the primary purpose of human beings and the insight that all subjective value lies in feelings qualifies as a "general field theory of integrative education."[29] It identifies the core purpose integration should serve.

The Caring Problem

Unfortunately, lack of concern for the personal relevance of what is taught reflects a deeper problem. At the institutional level there is a *caring* problem. Administrators and professors at institutions of higher learning regularly intone that they exist to make a difference in the lives of their students. But consider how well they walk their talk.

Students enter higher education with a great deal of experience in the ways in which educational institutions seem more devoted to controlling than serving them. That certainly does not end when they enter the doors of academe, but they are now adults exercising their right of choice. In America, at least, they and their parents pay dearly for the privilege of continued education, for the bottom line of colleges and universities largely depends on their money. Pretenses aside, this inevitably means students will be viewed more as customers than as the young citizens these institutions supposedly exist to serve. Student numbers and tuition levels are more immediate concerns than service aims, and service is seen more in terms of attracting and keeping students than of making a difference in their lives.

Saddling students with tens of thousands of dollars of debt to complete the education we supposedly want for all our children is stunningly perverse, but this fact has not yet risen to the level of a compelling social concern, so higher education administrators do not feel pressed to do much about it. The impact of burgeoning costs that far outpace inflation on the lives of students and their families is not usually considered their responsibility. Administrators further their careers by promoting the financial health and prestige of their institutions with little real accountability for the actual value of the education their institutions supposedly exist to provide.

Most of the indicators of institutional health used to determine rankings are only indirectly relevant to the educational interests of students. Finances, endowment, number and academic quality of students, faculty accomplishments, facilities, etc., are among the indicators stressed. Even such metrics as faculty-to-student ratios and class sizes that institutions would strive to reduce if the welfare of students were the main aim are too often seen as "productivity measures" that should increase.[30] Administrators naturally give priority to indicators for which they are most clearly accountable to higher-ups and boards. Indicators of the difference made in the lives of students are essentially reduced to job and graduate school statistics, and these are not usually among the more important indicators in terms of administrative accountability.

Contingent faculty — faculty in part-time and non-tenure track positions — now constitute the large majority of faculty in America.[31] Condensed and online courses are growing rapidly. As I have frequently heard and read, this does not *necessarily* mean that educational quality is being sacrificed. But in my experience, backed by growing evidence, the initial claims that quality will be maintained almost always prove hollow. These developments are mostly about money, and financial considerations become the dominant, often eclipsing, priority, a priority fiercely defended when the sham of quality is challenged. Measurements of quality are diffuse, ambiguous, and easily obfuscated. A few inconsequential feints in the direction of quality of instruction are touted as evidence of substantial effort.

Institutions of higher education must be financially healthy to provide a service, of course, but a predominant focus on money inevitably comes at the expense of service aims. Students themselves are not fooled by the rhetoric. They may like the chance to get their degrees quicker, easier, cheaper, and more conveniently. A degree is the main point of higher education in the minds of many students. But they know that the institutions that employ ever larger percentages of contingent faculty teaching increasingly condensed and online courses are more interested in money than the educational bang students get for their buck. In the many conversations I've had with college students over the past three decades, they know that the rhetoric of devotion to making a difference in their lives is not really their college's highest priority. And this difference is even less of a priority in major universities where undergraduates are too often viewed as a means to fund research — the *real* business of the university.

Giving priority to making a difference need not require spending more and earning less. In fact, returning to the heart of education would likely prove less expensive. A great deal — far more than half in large universities

— is currently spent on things that have little or no real educational value. An education deliberately designed to make the most profound difference it can in the lives of students would offer a far superior "product" in this regard. I am convinced this would contribute more to financial stability in terms of attracting and keeping students than the money-focused alternative. It would increase the relevance and value of higher education to both students and society at large.

The signals of relative lack of caring sent by faculty and staff are less directly pecuniary, though job security is usually an overriding consideration in the design of core curricula and major requirements. In my conversations with students, they seem very aware that courses and requirements are more about faculty interests than educational value. Students at most institutions are also aware that hiring and tenure decisions have more to do with research than teaching ability. And they understand that most professors see grades more as objective measures of academic merit than as means to motivate learning.

This ambiguity of purpose complicates discussions about grading and grade inflation. Lewis says "faculty members cannot decide how to grade because they do not agree on the purpose of grading — is it meant as an objective measurement, a credential for the benefit of graduate schools and prospective employers, or is it meant to motivate students to learn and to reward them if they do? With no consensus on the purpose of grading, there is likely to be little consensus on the standards to be used."[32] The distinction has moral implications: one purpose of grading sees students as means, the other as ends.

If motivation is the purpose for grades, then the question of motive naturally comes to the fore. With such clarity of purpose, we educators would be more interested in finding ways to inspire intrinsic motives to learn, as they are widely acknowledged as superior to extrinsic motivators such as grades.[33] We would think more deeply about the intrinsic value of what we want students to learn and conclude that what serves their deepest aspiration has the highest value. The more students experience the personal benefits of what they learn, the more intrinsically motivated they will be.

Clarity of Purpose

Dedicating higher education to making a difference in the lives of students would offer some benefits of clarity of purpose, but the full promise lies in uncommon clarity about what difference it is most worthwhile to make. If happiness is the universal primary purpose of human beings, empowering students' pursuit of happiness is logically the main difference educators should strive to make in the lives of students. If we explicitly acknowledged this, we would reconsider all we teach and do in higher education.

Taking this purpose seriously calls for significant changes in what is taught and how. All presumptions of the usefulness of what is currently taught would have to be reexamined, as would the underlying motives for teaching it. This would no doubt inspire fear that some areas of expertise may not be easy to rationalize in terms of their contribution to students' chances for happiness, and that some traditional methods of teaching would be found wholly wanting. Expounding dogmatic "truths" would give way to exploring alternative perspectives. The embrace of this purpose would definitely challenge the priority of scholarship and the rewards, privileges, and status that come with it.

I know that being held more strictly accountable for service to students would not be popular with many professors. But sacrificing the higher interests of students to protect the role and privileges of "drones" has no higher *moral* cause to justify it. This is heresy in the eyes of the adherents of the religion of Truth, but the value of what little Truth the academy is capable of revealing is determined by the human heart. The heart establishes the subjective relevance, the experiential value, of Truth. To sacrifice the hearts of flesh-and-blood students to the pursuit of an unrealizable abstract ideal is a moral failure.

The privileges of the priesthood of scholars are already under attack and are unlikely to survive in their traditional forms. State governments are less willing to pay for these privileges, as are the parents of students. Fortunately, the dedication of higher education to serve the hearts of students holds promise for making the lives and work of educators who genuinely care better rather than worse. It will make educators' work more meaningful, for it actually has some prospect of making a real difference in someone's life other than their own. The methods of communal inquiry would make their jobs more interesting and fun as well.

Empowering the pursuit of students' happiness would provide a clear point to all that is taught. This focus would integrate and bring much-needed coherence to disparate fields of study. It would provide a clearer measure of relevance to guide the revision of curricula. The focus would reorient educa-tion to give the inner dimension of experience its due, revealing the heart that gives meaning to the manifold activities of the enterprise. As happiness is the prime motive of students, it is also crucial to demonstrating an institu-tion's intent to treat them as ends. And the thematic focus could invigorate the liberal arts with a sense that their purpose truly is more vital to the lives of students than preparing them for the job market.

At present, liberal arts disciplines take a rather eclectic, shotgun ap-proach to enriching, broadening, and freeing minds. They tend to present narrow perspectives of the larger human enterprise because there is no ex-plicit theme to unite them in a broader perspective. Happiness provides the natural theme and establishes the greater relevance of these disciplines. Were the courses of study redesigned toward cumulative insight into the nature, sources, and means of happiness, they would have a far stronger claim to practical relevance. Nothing has greater claim to practical importance than that which contributes to fulfillment of the heart of human aspiration, and the liberal arts can be readily adapted to contribute far more to such fulfill-ment than they do at present.

It is easy to see the theme of happiness in history, the social sciences, art, music, literature, philosophy, and the other liberal arts disciplines. They all provide vistas on this universal pursuit. They could all contribute to relevant perspectives and insights if they were designed with this purpose in mind. Students would be more likely to see and *feel* the relevance. Advocates of the liberal arts would have less need to strenuously emphasize economic util-ity, for contributions to students' happiness would be recognized as more important.

Students and faculty yearn for a more vital purpose. In a five-year survey study of over 100,000 students in 236 universities and colleges, Alexander and Helen Astin of UCLA reported that students have "high expectations for the role their institutions will play in their emotional and spiritual de-velopment."[34] Two-thirds considered it "essential" or "very important" that their higher education contribute to their self-understanding and the devel-opment of personal values.[35] It is an understatement to say few institutions of higher learning are currently geared to meet such expectations. Few insti-tutions are all that concerned with such aims.

A focus on empowering students' pursuit of happiness could transform higher education into a more uplifting, meaningful, coherent, effective, and exciting experience. Such a transformation does not require tearing down the current edifice to build from scratch. It requires a shift in priorities to match the humanistic rhetoric about making a difference, and the redesign of core curricula, courses of study, and courses with empowering the pursuit of happiness in mind.

Approaches

An obvious place to start the redesign of higher education in America, at least, is the core curriculum. In Europe, entering students have met somewhat more rigorous requirements to gain entrance to a university. Rather than general core requirements, they face only the requirements of their chosen major once they gain entry, though I've heard this is beginning to change. American cores might be considered "remedial" from a European perspective, but they offer a rich and ready opportunity for direct and sustained engagement with the Big Questions of life that are otherwise ignored.

The most common type of core curriculum in America is based on the distribution model.[36] Students are required to take courses in an array of liberal arts disciplines: arts, literature, history, science, language, etc. A required course or two with an international focus is an increasingly common nod to global awareness. But some colleges and universities have designed a "freshman experience" not housed in a particular discipline, usually a first-year seminar or a two-semester sequence of seminars.

I believe the freshman experience is an excellent place to start the college-level exploration of questions related to happiness. I obviously favor the Big Questions approach over the Great Books, highlights of Western civilization, and methods of inquiry models. The Big Question approach better serves the aim of imparting the heritage of human thought and accomplishment because it provides a meaningful focus of inquiry and context in exploring it. When a student is led to ask what this heritage can teach her about the nature, sources, and means of happiness, it becomes a conscious resource to inform the pursuit rather than merely a hurdle to clear on the way to a degree.

My preference would be a sequence of seminars from the first semester to a capstone course in the last semester, but most institutions would likely see this as too great a departure from current practice at first. If direct and sustained engagement with one or more Big Questions is limited to a freshman experience, I recommend that it be two seminars focused on the question of happiness. The alternative perspective approach I described in the last chapter should be used to structure the inquiry of the first seminar, which, of course, should be communal inquiry employing some variation of the Socratic Method. In the first seminar, I would begin with the nature of happiness, asking students to formulate their own thoughts to begin a dialogue of initial ideas. After a couple of weeks of discussion, the students should put their thoughts about the nature of happiness in writing. This provides a handy measure of the change from initial to final insights, and it helps students congeal and formulate their thinking.

Then I would proceed to what can be gleaned about the nature of happiness through reason and evidence. Students should ponder definitions of happiness, the attributes of feelings, and the findings of scientific research. Analysis of perspectives requires a foundation of knowledge and conceptual frameworks. It would be wise to devote a third semester to this purpose.

At some point, the analysis of perspectives should begin. I locate perspectives on a spectrum. Though I have not been given the chance to teach a seminar on happiness per se, I would probably choose a spectrum from the most hedonic — pleasure-focused — notions of happiness to the most spiritual. In my honors courses, I try to use concise readings that most clearly capture the gist of a particular perspective without wandering into tangential issues. Papers from the Internet, chapters or sections of books, or articles usually fit the bill. If I assign a book, it must be a short book. Aside from the problem that most students will not read or will merely skim longer works, it is often more difficult for students to identify the main points and assumptions in lengthy discourses.

The readings should also be rather consistent in advocating a particular perspective. A Shakespeare play might provide a great deal of grist for the mill of reflection about the nature of happiness — existential agonizing, the pitfalls of power, abundant examples of human folly, lust, remorse, rejoicing, etc. — but it is difficult to find clear advocacy of a perspective in his plays. The alternative perspective approach is meant to provide awareness of choices and their comparative merits. The choices must be as clear as possible. Digging for gems of relevant insight in literature would be appropriate in literature courses, but such digging is ill-suited to the clarity required for focused analysis of perspectives in seminars devoted to answering a difficult question.

Frequent writing helps to congeal thoughts into coherent insights, hones analytical and writing skills, and motivates reading. A short, structured analysis is my preferred assignment. Once students have mastered the art of concise analysis, they are better prepared to fruitfully extend their imaginations with more creative assignments. I say "fruitfully" because they will be far more aware of what they are looking for when they have had plenty of practice identifying and assessing the practical implications of believing in the assumptions of perspectives. I would also have the students summarize and analyze their own thoughts on the question we are exploring in the seminar at the end of the semester. After all, the point of the inquiry is to inform their answers to the question, and the summary analysis ensures they will at least attempt a coherent, informed answer.

The second seminar of the freshman year should focus more on the means of happiness, engaging students in the methods of well-being such as mindfulness, forgiveness, gratitude, etc. Chris Barker and Brian Martin describe the methods they used and dilemmas they encountered in a class on happiness at the University of Wollongong in a paper titled "Dilemmas in teaching happiness." They were advised to change their original title — "How to be happy" — to "Happiness: investigating its causes and conditions" to make it sound more academic.[37] But they still stayed true to their original intent: "We agreed that our goal in the class was not just to help students to learn *about* happiness but also to develop understandings and skills that would enable them to *become* happier during the semester or, more probably, over the long term."[38]

In a multi-year sequence of seminars, I would begin with an exploration of perspectives on the nature of reality and continue with the same sequence I recommended for secondary education in Chapter Five. The sequence is meant to lead to progressive insights relevant to students' pursuit of happiness. Higher education is an opportunity for broader, deeper, and more sophisticated inquiry. It also springs many of the limits of secondary education in terms of controversial perspectives and materials. This sequence is broad enough to present all that is considered of value in Western-civilization cores. The Big Question/alternative perspective approach need not involve an either/or tradeoff. Rather it reveals the relevance of the heritage of human thought and experience to students' own pursuit of happiness. This would make the heritage both more coherent and more meaningful.

Seminars devoted to direct and sustained inquiry into the Big Questions would provide the heart of the core curriculum, but inquiry into these questions should be designed into all liberal arts courses of study. To point students toward happiness and then ignore the question in discipline-based courses implies either that we do not really believe happiness is the point of study or that the disciplines are irrelevant to happiness. Either conclusion would be unfortunate and place the disciplines in constant need of defense against justified charges of irrelevance. As I said earlier, it would not be difficult to redesign liberal arts courses with empowering the pursuit of happiness in mind.

Institutions of higher learning should also create opportunities to learn and practice the arts of inner awareness. Though it is difficult to imagine required courses on the techniques of inner awareness in higher education, it is not unthinkable. Such techniques could be embedded in core seminars, which would ensure all students gained at least the rudiments of awareness and might spark interest in further training. Elective courses that lead to the progressive practice of mindfulness and techniques for evoking particular feelings are also highly advisable. We speak here of what is required to gain the ability to exercise independent choice of feelings. No skill taught in higher education is more important and many are decidedly less so. Fortunately, mindfulness and other "contemplative methods" are gaining traction as hundreds of professors have introduced them in their classrooms.[39]

The consequent dedication of higher education to empowering students' pursuit of happiness would send a strong message of caring, as it is more obviously about them and their well-being. But the message is garbled if much else that occurs sends a contrary message. Both human nature and the nature of large organizations stand in the way of orienting all who work at a college or university to caring attitudes and behavior. Personal interests and contrary attitudes always intrude. But the modeling of caring is crucial to teaching and cultivating caring. We must demonstrate caring if we would awaken it in students' hearts. To this end, I offer some suggestions on how the academic experience could be a more caring experience.

First, the overriding purpose of making a difference in the lives of students should be made explicit and the academic community should see and hear constant reminders. Effective means to challenge any policy or practice that seems to depart from it should be created. The shadow of prerogative and personal agendas darkens too much of what we impose on students and we should make it more difficult to hide such motives.

I would also recommend an explicit embrace of the purpose of demonstrating and promoting respect for human dignity. Such respect requires treating people as ends rather than means.

A culture of friendliness should be encouraged. Friendliness is easily reflected in casual encounters. Friendly greetings, offers of help, and stopping to chat may seem of small import, but people tend to respond in kind, and at least a superficial culture of friendliness can become pervasive. The roots of deeper caring are nurtured in such soil.

Even more important than casual friendliness is fairness. To trumpet caring while treating colleagues, subordinates, and especially students unfairly and callously creates cynicism, resentment, and fear. Those in positions of authority bear the larger responsibility in this regard, but one does not have to wield authority to be callous and unfair. At any rate, it is nearly impossible to get more than perfunctory compliance with caring behavior when employees believe they are being treated unfairly. I emphasize the treatment of staff, for they are the most vulnerable employees in higher education.

Institutions of higher education should also consciously demonstrate generosity. There is probably no more convincing demonstration of caring than lending a hand to those in serious distress. When students and colleagues suffer the loss of loved ones, debilitating sickness or emotional crises, campus communities should offer more than just counseling services. All should be ready to offer a shoulder when wanted and help with mitigating academic and financial worries. If the distress is financial in nature, students should be helped with an available hardship scholarship or perhaps a relaxed schedule of payments. If more systematic and generous ways to respond to such distress are in place, the easier it is to do this.

To this end, members of the community should be able to report distress to a person or office responsible for formulating a sensitive and appropriate response. Those with such responsibility could express condolences, offer assistance, and alert professors and administrators who might be in a position to offer personal sympathy and help. I would also recommend the creation of a "generosity" fund of donations to make it easier to offer help in cases of financial distress. And, of course, students should be afforded opportunities to express their own generosity as well.

Students always have problems with some aspects of a college or university. Dorms, food, bureaucratic hassles, security, and perceived unfair treatment haunt the complaint list of every student body. Many problems cannot be satisfactorily solved and certainly many expectations are not realistic, but active interest in learning about problems and attempting to minimize or solve them will go a long way toward reducing discontent and to demonstrating a caring approach.

There is always some sensitivity to inviting complaints. The targets of complaints see them as a personal rebuke and fear that the public disclosure of problems will taint their image. Yet, beyond personal discomfort lie the many benefits of knowing where the shoe rubs. Some problems are easily solved, others can be ameliorated without much effort, and the simple willingness to listen is itself a salve. To this end I recommend the appointment of an *ombudsman*. The role of the ombudsman would be to hear complaints about treatment and problems, contact those involved or those with authority to address the problems, and pass on a response — or lack of response — to students. The ombudsman would also report patterns of complaints and responses to both responsible administrators and an appropriate faculty committee. This would help administrators identify ongoing or recurring problems and it would enhance accountability.

Those responsible for policy should be very sensitive to the consequences of their decisions. Such sensitivity is heightened when faced with the certainty that the consequences will be general knowledge and subject to open questioning. There is an almost universal human tendency to address perceived problems by promulgating ever more draconian policies, constraining rules, and inconvenient procedures. It is usually apparent that such controls are designed primarily to serve the interests and convenience of the controllers at the expense of the controllees. Independent means to acquire and share awareness of the consequences of decisions is a healthy first step to motivate more careful and caring decisions.

Caring is not the same as *carrying*. Caring parents do not serve their child's best interests by relieving them of the burdens of initiative and responsibility, and the same is true of caring schools. As long as requirements are genuinely designed with the higher interests of students in mind, they reflect caring. Yet we should never cease asking whether specific requirements are living up to expectations. We should never allow requirements to become ends in themselves.

Appreciation is inherent to caring. Every human being has facets worthy of appreciation. I think institutions of higher education should make greater efforts to showcase and celebrate the talents of students, faculty, and staff and thereby cultivate a livelier, richer, and more appreciative campus environment. People in academe need to be reminded that the life of the mind has no meaning apart from the life of the heart. A more celebratory campus culture would be a pleasant reminder. And it might help alleviate some of the alienation many students, faculty, and administrators experience in the halls of academe.

Awakened Hearts

I am well aware of the tendency to make token change and present it as substantial progress. Members of boards of trustees are prone to nod approval of bulleted lists of accomplishments and initiatives without digging deeper to discover the reality obscured by the claims. It would be too much work, and signal distrust of chief administrators. Much depends on whether there is pressure from the faculty to live up to the rhetoric of making a difference in the lives of students.

But winning faculty to the cause will not be easy. Many academics will indignantly resist the claim that the value of the life of the mind is determined by the heart. Their sense of comparative worth depends on their mastery of a body of knowledge and scholarly skills as well as the prestige accorded degrees, titles, and lists of publications. Many professors will not willingly entertain the idea that in the accounting of the heart none of this is particularly meaningful.

But greater rewards beckon. Professors will "profess" less and serve more as guides of expeditions meant to show students vistas of choice rather than bodies of authoritative knowledge. Higher education would be more the Great Hunt than the Finishing School of Mind and Career Preparation. I have found the hunt far more fun, intellectually invigorating and meaningful. The prospect of guiding students toward insights that would actually make a difference in their lives is a source of considerable satisfaction.

It takes awhile for students to realize the larger point, but they definitely enjoy the hunt more than the passive consumption of facts and predigested insights. And professors will gain their own insights. As they lead students on expeditions into the relatively unexplored territory of the heart, they may well discover just how possible, liberating, and satisfying the skills of happiness can be.

All this may be a long time in coming, but I am confident growing numbers of people will not only hear, but *feel* the message that education can contribute far more than it does to enhancing students' prospects for happiness. As awareness of a promising alternative grows, the status quo will be deprived of the moral and the practical pretenses that sustain it. Sometime, somehow, the transformation of the enterprise of education will begin and gain traction. Awakened hearts will not forever be denied.

9

Transformation

*Let us dedicate ourselves to what the Greeks
wrote so many years ago: to tame the
savageness of man and make gentle the life of
this world.* | Robert F. Kennedy

"Dreamer" may be among the kinder epithets for someone who
calls for a fundamental reorientation of education and then
titles his last chapter "Transformation." Anyone familiar with
the history of attempts to reform education in America knows how daunting
the obstacles to change are in this country, and I call for not just the reform
of American education, but a transformation of education in all democracies. I am well aware of the barriers. I have personal experience with many of
them. Yet I see ample cause for hope.

The ardent wish of parents for the happiness of their children will en-
ergize the cause when parents realize that the greater prospect of happiness
for their children is at stake. The idea that the pursuit of happiness can be
empowered by nurturing awareness, perspective, and insight in our schools
will strike an intuitive resonance in the minds and hearts of many. This resonance will grow as the idea takes a firmer hold on the public imagination.

That we should strive to harness our core values to the deepest aspiration in children's hearts will also have the ring of common sense. Why not foster the motives for treating others well in our schools?

Those who stand in the way will stand on shaky moral ground. Even those who claim a greater good is served by downplaying children's emotional well-being in schools will face the counterclaims that treating children as means rather than ends is morally dubious and that ignoring the question of happiness is unlikely to serve a greater good that consists of the happiness of citizens. People who claim that happiness is best served by the current state of affairs will confront abundant evidence to the contrary.

The idea that education should aim more directly at the happiness of children is gaining traction. Many states in the United States have standards aimed at social and emotional learning.[1] Such learning has been part of the curriculum of tens of thousands of schools in the United States, Canada and worldwide.[2] Project Happiness champions the cause globally by offering free educational materials and a curriculum that "fits any classroom environment."[3] Their programs are used in schools in forty-nine states and over fifty-five countries. Interest in "happiness interventions" in American schools is growing.[4] Happiness classes are popping up in American as well as in European and Asian universities. Well-being classes and methods are appearing in all school levels in America and in many North European countries.

In Bhutan, the whole school system is dedicated to promoting "Gross National Happiness."[5] Cushing Academy in Massachusetts hosted the education minister of Bhutan during their August 2012 symposium on "Educating for Sustainable Happiness."[6] This was one of many gatherings in the United States and other countries with themes related to happiness education.

Teaching happiness and well-being have particularly caught on in the United Kingdom, Australia and New Zealand. Wellington College in the United Kingdom got the ball rolling with a course with these aims in mind in 2006. Their experiment has garnered sustained national and international interest.[7] The idea has spread to a number of other schools in the country, such as Gooderstone primary school and Shenley academy, a secondary school.[8] The Prime Minister of Britain, David Cameron, established the National Wellbeing Project in 2010 in his broader effort to promote national happiness.[9] Well-being became part of the Ofsted Inspection Framework — part of the education accountability regime in Britain — in 2009.[10]

British educators partnered with the National Children's Bureau to create Action for Happiness in Schools, which seeks to champion the cause of happiness education by sharing research findings, creating an engaged network of educators and experts, and raising public awareness.[11] A broad range of education-related organizations are taking part in the initiative. A partnership of fourteen education bodies in Britain called the Whole Education Campaign is also pushing the teaching of "social and emotional competences."[12]

Official education policies in both New Zealand and Australia also embrace teaching well-being.[13] Australia in particular has a vibrant Positive School movement for developing mental health and well-being in schools.[14] The World Health organization and the United Nations Children's Fund also call for teaching well-being. The happiness education movement is globalized and favored by prestigious international institutions.[15]

Teaching mindfulness is a growth industry. The Garrison Institute and the OASIS Institute associated with the Center for Mindfulness in Medicine, Health Care, and Society are among the many organizations that train educators in teaching mindfulness. These include the MindUp program of the Hawn Foundation, Mindful Schools, InnerKids Foundation, the Impact Foundation, the Lineage Project, and The Attention Academy. These organizations have brought mindfulness programs to tens of thousands of elementary school children and hundreds of schools.[16] The Center for Contemplative Mind in Society encourages mindfulness and introspection in higher education with notable success.[17]

The Foundation for Developing Compassion and Wisdom provides resources for a "Universal Wisdom Education" in schools and other venues.[18] Fetzer Institute's "Campaign for Love & Forgiveness" provides training and resources for educators.[19] The campaign recommends methods closely associated with positive education. The "Kind Campaign" that tackles bullying in schools is among the many efforts to teach awareness of the effects of one's words and actions in schools.[20] The "Democratic Schools" movement that advocates giving students a greater say in their education is growing.[21] These and other initiatives are compatible with the goals and methods of the happiness education movement.

The cause of reorienting schools to empower students' pursuit of happiness is aligned with a number of other education reform movements. The voices calling for more meaning, more coherence, more integration, more caring, and for greater recognition of the importance of the liberal arts will find a natural ally in the cause. Movements that push more critical thinking and philosophy in schools are served as well. Children who languish in the drudgery of school and teachers who dream of touching their hearts more deeply than current constraints allow will find cause for hope. Empowering the pursuit of happiness can unite all these aspirations in common cause. All these tributaries will feed the river of the happiness education movement.

But these efforts are still on the periphery of public discourse. They have yet to capture much public interest. When they do, many of those vested in the current economic orientation of education will feel the need to defend the status quo. They will be joined by other stakeholders in the education "establishment" in opposing any far-reaching reorientation of education. Reform efforts aimed at far less ambitious goals have been stymied by the resistance of the establishment. We who would "make gentle the life of this world" by empowering children's pursuit of happiness must be clear-eyed about the challenges.

Challenges

Any movement advocating large-scale change confronts the entrenched status quo interests of the establishment. The establishment of any major social enterprise consists of power-holders, stakeholders served by the status quo, and a "dominant paradigm" of core beliefs and attitudes. So it is with the establishment of the education enterprise. The various participants have different interests and aims, but the belief that the economic mission of schools should be given priority dominates public discourse and the politics of education. The many educators who disagree with this priority do not yet command the public's ear.

Even many ardent defenders of liberal education are enthusiastic supporters of STEM, programs that emphasize science, technology, engineering, and mathematics in schools in order to strengthen national economic competitiveness. And there is a strong tendency to defend the liberal arts as the best way to prepare students for jobs rather than for life in general. The education establishments in America and countries around the world want schools to be engines of economic growth first and foremost. Political leaders proclaim this loudly and often as the consensus purpose of education.

This is the dominant paradigm of the education establishments in almost all countries in the world at present.

The stakeholders of this paradigm are not united in their opposition to particular means of reform. What should be studied and how are open to debate, as are the specifics of the accountability regime imposed on schools from above. But a challenge to the goals themselves, especially a challenge to the *morality* of the goals, is not easy to accommodate. You cannot question the morality of someone's ardent advocacy without hitting a major ego nerve. Defense shields go up, battle ensues.

It is tempting to downplay the moral challenge to the economic paradigm of education by stressing that a happiness pedagogy would do more to strengthen the skills needed in the 21st century global economy than the current pedagogy. But it is unwise to make this a prominent selling point. We should indeed try to ease the fears of those focused on economic needs, and there is plenty of evidence that such fears are unjustified. But a better way to serve economic ends does not pack much of a moral punch. It sidesteps the issue of treating kids as means rather than ends. It has no special appeal to the heart. Without a strong appeal to the heart, we stand little chance of overcoming the inertia of the status quo.

What enduring progress humanity has made in the cause of freedom is due more to changes of heart that expanded moral understandings than to appeals to reason. The success of the struggle to reorient education to serving children's deepest aspiration depends on its appeal to people's better angels. Moral appeal can penetrate defenses that reason alone cannot even dent. We cannot afford to water down this appeal. It is our chief asset in the struggle to come.

But we must be true to the spirit of appealing to peoples' better angels. Gandhi and Martin Luther King did not question the essential goodness of opponents, and neither should we. After all, few who are involved with education reform have a direct material stake in the outcome. Almost all of them, I'm sure, believe they are working for the greater good of the children and society. Most are unaware of a realistic alternative to the economic paradigm. They may well have an initial knee-jerk reaction to the proposal that we should reorient education to empower the pursuit of happiness, but the realistic prospect of improving children's chances for happiness will eventually win many hearts to the cause. Many who at first opposed the extension of equal rights to women and racial minorities had a change of heart when they came to see the justice of these causes.

We face a difficult political struggle, though. The progress made toward teaching happiness and well-being in Britain has provoked a political counterattack. Well-being measures have been removed from the education inspection framework for the time being.[22] "The education secretary, Michael Gove, said the new framework will allow inspectors to concentrate on what matters and forget the 'peripherals.'"[23] Nick Gibb, the Conservative schools minister, strongly rejects bringing social and emotional learning into classrooms: "This kind of stuff is ghastly. Schools have really got to focus on the core subjects of academic education and teaching children how to learn."[24]

Terry Hyland summarizes a view I have often encountered: "The emphasis on therapeutic objectives such as self-esteem, emotional intelligence, confidence and the like, is said to marginalize traditional goals linked to knowledge and understanding thereby disempowering learners."[25] This, of course, presumes that other goals of empowerment are more important than affective well-being. I agree with Hyland: "I would argue that most educational activity — both at school but especially at post-school levels — is affectively impoverished and grossly deficient in its treatment of humanistic as opposed to economistic matters."[26]

Economic interests are hardly the only grounds for opposing happiness education, of course. Many pose contending moral claims. I addressed the understanding of morality as sacrifice of self-interest in the first two chapters. But many see a threat to parental prerogative in imparting values. Seligman et al. point to a major political issue when they relate that, "Many parents are concerned that programmes will teach values that are determined by educators or politicians and that bear little resemblance to the values they hope to instill in their children."[27] A declaration of the platform of the Texas Republican Party opposed teaching "Higher Order Thinking Skills" that include critical thinking skills because they "have the purpose of challenging the student's fixed beliefs and undermining parental authority."[28]

Concern with politicians and educators pushing their own views is justified. But the idea that schools should teach nothing that might challenge a student's "fixed beliefs" negates the very premise of liberal education. Educators should not tell students what to believe or what path of life to choose, but informing beliefs and choices is at the heart of the very idea of educating free citizens. A happiness pedagogy should expand a student's awareness of choices and consequences while making it clear that the choice is up to her. But this will not assuage those who oppose the idea of free choice of belief.

A sizable percentage of Americans and citizens in other democracies are convinced that happiness can only be found in believing and practicing a particular religion. Many traditional Christians "maintain that only those who worship the Lord and explicitly affirm Christ as lord and savior will find joy in this world and eternal happiness in the next," observes Sidney Callahan.[29] "Full and eternal happiness can be found only in Christian faith" according to the doctrines of many Christian churches.[30]

A happiness curriculum would allow such views to be presented in schools. Of course, it would also allow these views to be examined in light of contending perspectives, which would no doubt displease many. Yet the current situation in public schools is even less favorable to religious values and beliefs. Religious views on happiness would at least get a fair hearing in the happiness education I describe. Helping children experience the benefits of inner awareness, gratitude, and forgiveness surely is in keeping with the core values of the mainstream religions.

Some insist that happiness does not, or should not, consist of positive feelings per se. Such feelings should be "earned" or spring from objectively good reasons to be happy. Many are uncomfortable with allowing a beach bum or couch potato to claim happiness. Frank Furedi contends, "In our vapid emotional era, it is worth recalling that a good life is not always a happy one."[31] He also says "Students need to understand the moral meaning of good before they can feel 'good' about themselves."[32]

Alex Michalos holds that good feelings should not be divorced from objective conditions: "The good life that we must want and achieve for all people is not, I think, just a life in which people feel good, no matter how terrible their real life conditions are, but one in which they feel good with the best of all reasons, because the objectively measurable conditions of their lives merit a positive assessment."[33] David Sosa agrees:

> Take someone really flourishing in their new career, or really flourishing now that they're off to college. The sense of the expression is not just that they feel good, but that they're, for example, accomplishing some things and taking appropriate pleasure in those accomplishments. If they were simply sitting at home playing video games all day, even if this seemed to give them

a great deal of pleasure, and even if they were not frustrated, we wouldn't say they were flourishing. Such a life could not in the long term constitute a happy life. To live a happy life is to flourish.[34]

These are value judgments about what the sources of happiness ought to be. Though I do not agree with them, such views would receive a fair hearing in the curriculum I propose. But they would not be privileged. Children would not be denied the skills to tap the inner sources of feelings because some do not deem feelings per se important. Feelings are the experience of value. Enhancing the value of experience is a reasonable and ethical aim. Students can decide for themselves whether good feelings should be rejected because some regard them as unearned and inappropriate to "objective" conditions. Inner awareness will allow students to assess the desirability of being able to feel as they choose at will, based on conscious experience.

Some critics of promoting good feelings in school think we are doing students a disservice by emotionally buffering them against the harsh realities of life. Schools should "develop the grit to live in life's tensions — the confidence to learn from conflict, mistakes, disappointment, failure, loneliness, and losing," according to Rick Ackerly.[35] Furedi criticizes the concern with emotional well-being because it serves to "anesthetize" people in difficult social and economic times.[36] He says, "How to feel well is not a suitable subject for teaching. Why? Because genuine happiness is experienced through the interaction of the individual with the challenges thrown up by life."[37]

Contrary to these critiques, happiness education would make students more resilient in the face of challenges, more able to call upon inner resources to deal with adversity. Kids will have plenty of experience with challenges and emotional turbulence regardless of what we teach in schools. This is a tough planet. Teaching better ways to deal with life's problems does not cocoon or coddle them. It empowers them to achieve their aspirations regardless of the events and circumstances of their lives. To my mind, this is the main point of everything we teach in schools.

I addressed the contention that teaching kids to look inward would diminish their concern for social problems and injustice in previous chapters. But this is a widespread fear of those who want to orient students to being socially engaged. The implication is that inner experience is not all that important to addressing external conditions. I argued this profoundly misjudg-es the most potent motives for treating others well, which naturally leads to gladly helping others. Even if this were not so, though, I would ask: "If we really could improve children's prospects for happiness by making them aware of the inner sources of happiness, are you willing to sacrifice these prospects for increased ardor for social causes? Is it moral and just to ask this sacrifice of our children?" I would also ask: "Is there evidence that the current external focus of education is more effective in increasing students' ardor for social causes?" I say, let's give inner awareness a chance.

Happiness education faces practical as well as moral challenges, of course. Two of the biggest practical obstacles are the accountability crusade and the lack of teachers trained in the methods of a happiness pedagogy. The main problem with the accountability regimes is that they are primarily focused on job-related outcomes. But even if we could introduce well-being outcomes to these regimes, we would still face the human propensity to be-come so mesmerized by the means that we lose sight of the end. Simplistic measures of achievement and comparative performance judged on the basis of these measures become ends in themselves when jobs, the allocation of money, and public support depend on them. The means to assess and moti-vate "performance" all too easily obscure the main point of performing.

I am amazed at how often my colleagues object to meaningful changes to learning outcomes because such outcomes are not easy to assess. They do not see the irony because the pressures of the accountability regime make as-sessment of education seem like a more pressing need than education itself. Diane Ravitch, who was once a prominent champion of the accountability movement, opines that,

> I saw my hopes for better education turn into a measurement strategy that had no underlying educational vision at all. Eventually I realized that the new reforms had everything to do with structural changes and accountabil-ity, and nothing at all to do with the substance of learning. Accountability makes no sense when it undermines the larger goals of education.[38]

Accountability is laudable when it focuses endeavor on a worthwhile purpose, but schools should be accountable for making the most meaningful difference in students' lives, not the difference that is easiest to measure or for accreditation bodies and employers to assess. We cannot emphasize accountability for math and science and presume the other aims of education do not suffer from the relative lack of attention. The evidence and the testimony of a great many teachers show that they do. And we cannot emphasize economic skills over all else and plausibly insist we are treating our children as ends in themselves.

I add my voice to the large and growing chorus of complaints that teachers are being forced to teach to accountability tests and sacrifice the substantive outcomes of education. Administrators often feel they have no choice because such tests are the primary measures of their own performance in the eyes of school boards, education departments, and the media. Those pushing such tests deny that replacing substance with test performance is the intent. But a great many teachers insist this is nonetheless the consequence. Most accountability crusaders do not deny that the tests are primarily meant to encourage career-related skills that serve national economic competitiveness. That is the foremost rationale for them, and fear of falling behind other nations in math and science scores seems to be a prime motivator. Liberal arts subjects, including civics, are being whittled because comparisons center on reading, math, and science scores.

I find it interesting that Finland, whose education system is consistently at or near the top of international rankings, does not use the evaluation-driven approach that characterizes the systems in the United States and most other developed countries.[39] Pre-teenage Finnish children rarely have homework or take exams. The only mandatory standardized test is taken when students are in their mid-teens. The national curriculum only sets broad guidelines. Yet, Finland far outperforms the United States and other European countries — including demographically similar Norway that has much the same evaluation-driven strategy as the United States — in terms of graduation rates and percentage attending college. In an international standardized measurement conducted every year since 2001, Finnish kids have placed near the top in science, reading and math.[40] Perhaps the merits of the current accountability regime have been oversold, especially in light of all the stress and unintended consequences it causes. From what I have read and heard, most teachers seem to think so.

Assessing how well schools, teachers, and approaches serve the purpose of education is quite legitimate. But this presumes clarity about the purpose. It also presumes the means of assessment are tailored to the purpose rather

than the other way around. The first task of the happiness education movement is to change people's minds about the primary purpose of education.
To do this, we must ease their reasonable concerns about how the impact of
such an education would be assessed. We should not aim to get rid of accountability; we should aim to revamp it.

Fortunately, researchers trying to assess the effects of teaching mindfulness and social and emotional well-being in schools have devised a wealth
of measures. Many of these measures have been soundly tested for validity.
Some are based on questionnaires developed for use in positive psychology
research that measure subjective progress in developing positive outlooks
and feelings. Others are more "whole school" measures such as number of
visits to the principal's office, academic achievement, and graduation rates.
The relative number of students being diagnosed for emotional problems
such as depression and anorexia are among these measures.

The governments of Britain, Australia, New Zealand, and Finland have
encouraged the development of student well-being indicators for use in evalu-
ating their schools.[41] Ofsted, Britain's school inspection framework, has used
questionnaires to evaluate children's subjective assessments of their happiness
as well as whole-school measures. A number of Internet-based assessment
instruments are available. Educators looking for whole-school assessment can
use the School Well-being Profile funded by the Finnish government.[42] Private companies are also getting into the well-being measurement business. For
instance, New Philanthropy Capital in Britain developed a "Well-Being Measure" that tracks subjective assessments of happiness over time.[43] Accountability per se is therefore no impediment to introducing happiness education.

In-course evaluation is another issue. Those who have taught happiness
or well-being courses speak of the tension between the personal improvement goals of the courses and the traditional means of academic assessment.
Barker and Martin, who taught a university course on happiness, put it this
way:

> A class about happiness raises a fundamental question: what is education
> for? In particular, is the purpose of a happiness class the gaining of for-
> mal knowledge, by which we mean "traditional content" such as research
> findings and an understanding of the key debates in the field? Or is it the
> achievement of insights and skills through which students can transform
> themselves and the world around them? In short, is the purpose of the class

to learn about happiness or to become happier?[44]

Barker and Martin found they had to adjust the balance more toward traditional academic means of assessment due to the expectations of both their university and students concerned with grades. They decided not to assess students "outside of the information gathering, presentation and evaluation tasks" they set for them.[45] But Ian Morris thinks "Well-being should be exempt from the obsessive desire to quantify and grade that permeates education."[46] He thinks there should be some kind of measure of progress of the course as such rather than students, though. "In terms of summative (and also formative) assessment of the course, one approach could be a nongraded dialogue where each student is given a particular well-being-related problem to solve and they have to apply what they have learned throughout their lessons to that problem."[47]

The need to train teachers in the requisite skills and methods has proven an obstacle to all efforts to bring about substantive change in classrooms. One might despair of confronting the need to scale the ramparts of existing teacher-training institutions, but I suspect we will find a growing number of allies within those ramparts. Many are dissatisfied with the status quo and would dearly welcome a chance to make a greater difference in children's lives.

Colleges and universities have a long tradition of incubating rebellion, and education departments and teachers colleges are not immune. Some schools dedicated to the preparation of teachers are famous — or infamous in the eyes of some — for being incubators of educational change.[48] But I believe there will be need for independent centers dedicated to developing curricula and methods and gathering the fruits of real-life experience needed to focus education on empowering the pursuit of happiness. Such centers could handle the initial training of teachers. Easing the transition of any institution willing to attempt it must be a core mission of the happiness education movement. A growing cadre of trained teachers and consultants is essential.

A good many teachers in higher education already use some version of the alternative perspective approach in the classes they teach, but relatively few have had occasion to apply the approach to inquiry into the Big Questions of philosophy. This speaks, of course, to the relative lack of philosophy in schools. The questions and perspectives are unfamiliar to most teachers, but this is a minor hurdle. Resources already exist and they need only be adapted and made readily available.

A philosophical core that spans the curriculum would also require a great deal of thought and experimentation to coordinate the efforts of each grade level toward cumulative knowledge and insight. But there is a large pool of experience and imagination to call upon both within and outside the teaching profession in devising such curricula.

The more serious bottleneck is the lack of people with experience in teaching inner awareness to children. Such awareness is crucial to empowering the pursuit of happiness, but it is only beginning to be taught in schools, and relatively few teachers are trained in the art as yet. Deborah Schoeberlein says there is a "paucity of curricula and training programs accessible to individual teachers."[49] Susan Greenland admits "Practicing mindful awareness with kids is still uncharted territory."[50] Fortunately, this deficit is starting to be addressed as programs offering training in mindfulness to both students and teachers spring up in the United States and other countries.[51]

A pedagogy must be developed if we are to train a sufficient number of teachers in the art of inner observation. Collecting the fruits of what experience there is, honing the art through experimentation, and sharing the most promising methods is a first-order task. The fruits of such experiments must be fashioned into a focused, coherent, well-tested pedagogy that can be made available to willing schools and teachers everywhere. Groups of skilled and dedicated people should be brought together to work on these tasks.

I see no way around the need for a "Happiness Education Academy" where both faculty and students will learn, practice, and hone the arts of guiding students in inner awareness and the exploration of perspectives on happiness. Such an academy must be an accredited degree-granting institution. I envision this as the seed that will grow into a seed-producing tree. Education departments looking for professors with the requisite academic credentials and expertise in the arts of teaching happiness must know where to find such rare birds.

The fact that the demand will far outstrip the supply of education professors and K-12 teachers will make the specialty very attractive. And the education departments who hire professors trained in happiness education will become seed-producing trees themselves. The magic of the market, the moral and creative appeal, and the lure of pioneering are my answers to those who say it can't be done. I believe the moral appeal of the cause will help raise the funds to create such an academy.

First, though, we must make inroads on the dominant educational paradigm.

Sowing the Seeds of Change

Movements are the agents of change for any major social undertaking, and orienting schools to the explicit embrace of empowering the pursuit of happiness as their purpose certainly qualifies as such an undertaking. Movements to change educational practice usually set their sights on educational institutions, but such change always has a broader political dimension. Institutions are notoriously resistant to change from within; such change usually requires external pressure. Parker Palmer offers some relevant insight:

> *The civil rights and women's movements would have died aborning if racist and sexist organizations had been allowed to define both the battleground and the rules of engagement. But some minorities and some women performed an inner alchemy on organizational resistance, transforming it from social discouragement and defeat to personal inspiration and power. In both of these movements, advocates of change used organizational resistance as a trampoline to spring themselves free of organizations. They found sources of countervailing power outside of those structures, then consolidated that power in ways that eventually gave them leverage on the structures themselves.*[52]

Palmer identified four stages that more or less describe the dynamics of movements:

> *Stage 1. Isolated individuals make an inward decision to live "divided no more," finding a center for their lives outside of institutions. Stage 2. These individuals begin to discover one another and form communities of congruence that offer mutual support and opportunities to develop a shared vision. Stage 3. These communities start going public, learning to convert their private concerns into the public issues they are and receiving vital critiques in the process. Stage 4. A system of alternative rewards emerges to sustain the movement's vision and to put pressure for change on the standard institutional reward system.*[53]

Movements take shape when those who aspire to similar changes "discover one another." I have personally experienced that "People involved in movements often have more friends far away than they have at home; the reform agenda that is so inspiring on a national scale turns out to be threatening locally."[54] If there is to be a movement to reorient schools toward empowering the pursuit of happiness, it will necessarily start with a group of people committed to this end. But first we must find each other. As Palmer says, "The lost will never be found until they send up a flare."[55]

The Internet and other rapidly evolving means of communication make it easier to catch the attention of distant allies, to form networks, and to organize movements. They have provided modern political movements the means to coordinate efforts beyond national borders. Of course, it will take knowledgeable and talented people to utilize these resources. I believe a sound strategy would be to try to duplicate the Action for Happiness in Schools initiative in Great Britain, which grew out of discussions with representatives of the foremost governmental and private organizations concerned with education. It has three main components:

> **Knowledge hub.** *Creating a central hub of knowledge to highlight the latest research on evidence-based approaches and case studies of practice (both national and international) that is proving effective in improving children's happiness and well-being in schools.*
>
> **Connecting people.** *Helping schools connect more effectively with practitioners and experts in the area of happiness and well-being. This will include online communities to develop and share ideas and organizing events and workshops for participating schools.*
>
> **National campaign.** *Providing ideas and campaign materials for use by participating schools to inform discussions with pupils, staff and parents, and to raise wider awareness within the local community of the actions being undertaken by the schools.*[56]

An American Action for Happiness in Schools would have a natural ally in the British initiative. And there is fertile ground for similar initiatives in most European countries. A Europe-wide happiness-in-schools initiative is plausible. Happiness education movements exist in Australia and New Zealand, and Bhutan's philosophy of Gross National Happiness has captured the imagination of many people in Asia and elsewhere around the world. The philosophy has roots in traditional Asian cultures, especially those that have been influenced by Buddhism. Tsunesaburo Makiguchi, Japan's most influential philosopher of education, is among the first to assert that the purpose of education is the student's "realization of happiness."[57] Daisaku Ikeda promotes Makuguchi's philosophy in the Soka — value-creating — education movement throughout the world, but especially in Japan. We thus have the makings of a global happiness education movement.

A grass-roots strategy could help build support. Palmer and Zajonc recommend a "conversational strategy of change" whereby colleagues in institutions of higher education find ways and venues to engage each other in meaningful dialogues to "pursue issues in the philosophy of education, their implications and implementation, in ways that could move higher education closer to the integrative ideal."[58] This applies as well to the happiness ideal. The strategy should include primary and secondary educators, of course. Modern technology would extend the conversation across borders.

To succeed, the cause must capture the imagination and hearts of a decisive portion of the public. It must directly appeal to the heart with a simple and compelling moral argument, personal testimonies, and stories of how the lives of individual children were improved. The cause should be presented in a conceptually sound, coherent, and easy-to-understand vision. For this reason, I think an umbrella organization is necessary to shape and coordinate the message of the happiness education movement.

Final Appeal

Can the cause of dedicating our schools to empowering students' pursuit of happiness inspire sufficient commitment to succeed? I think so, but I'm biased. Until the movement gains momentum, I can only seek to persuade. So I will end by once again painting a vision of need and possibility.

The past several centuries have seen some remarkable progress in the improvement of the material, social, and political circumstances of a large portion of humanity. What began as struggles for freedom that benefited a few has come to benefit ever-widening circles of people both within and among nations. The hope that growing freedom would lead to an enduring change in consciousness has proven warranted. The hope that it would open the floodgates of happiness has not. The cause of freedom has so far found only shallow resonance in the human heart, and the cause of freedom *is* ultimately the cause of happiness. The fruits of freedom ultimately lie within.

Until we acknowledge and honor this truth, the cause of freedom will have a hollow core and fail its larger purpose.

However far the benefits of external freedom extend, the cause cannot be considered won until we find a way to help those freed from the locked doors of the world learn to unlock the doors to the potential of their minds and hearts as well. If the key is not to be found in external circumstance, we must help them find it within.

We can afford the children we bring into this world an understanding of happiness beyond our own. We can lead them to a clarity of purpose and meaning uncommon at present. We can foster an awareness of inner experience that leads to their ability to experience what they choose to feel. We can expand their awareness of choices and deepen their understanding of the consequences of each choice to make their freedom more meaningful. We can offer our children comforting perspective and inner haven in the face of life's challenges. We can encourage a deeper understanding of themselves and others than most of their elders achieved. We can help them realize the rewards of appreciating others and the price of judgment and thereby make their lives more joyful and gentle. We can bequeath all this and very much more to all the generations to come.

Thus I join my voice to those who share these aspirations. Dreamers we may be, but our dream will make a difference despite the obstacles that confront us. Even if we fail to transform education in general, we will bring light into the hearts of many children. It is not given us to determine how many lives we touch for the better or how deeply. It is given us to make what difference we may with the opportunities we have. Whether or not we can make gentle *the* life of this world, we shall surely have many a chance to make gentler some lives in this world. Maybe even beyond this world. After all, they might be the lives of angels.

When I was 5 years old, my mother always told me that happiness was the key to life. When I went to school, they asked me what I wanted to be when I grew up. I wrote down "happy." They told me I didn't understand the assignment, and I told them they didn't understand life. | John Lennon

To join the conversation on happiness education, please visit: educatingangels.co

EDUCATING ANGELS | NOTES

Chapter 1: AN EDUCATION WORTHY OF ANGELS

1. William James, *The Varieties of Religious Experience* (New York: The Modern Library, 1999), 90.
2. Daisaku Ikeda, *Soka Education: For the Happiness of the Individual* (Middleway Press, Kindle edition, 2010, acquired January 13, 2013, Amazon.com), location 1883.
3. John Dewey, *The School and Society* and *The Child and the Curriculum* (Seven Treasures Publications, Kindle edition, 2011, acquired January 19, 2013, Amazon.com), location 188.

Chapter 2: THE PURPOSE OF LIBERAL EDUCATION

1. John Adams, "Thoughts on Government" in *The Portable John Adams* (New York: Penguin Classics, 2004), 233.
2. Thomas Jefferson and Eric Petersen, *Light and Liberty: Reflections on the Pursuit of Happiness* (Modern Library, Kindle edition, 2004, acquired May 29, 2008, Amazon.com), location 232.
3. Aristotle, "Nicomachean Ethics" in Louis P. Pojman, ed., *Classics of Philosophy* (New York: Oxford University Press, 1998), 289, 292.
4. John Locke, "Letter Concerning Toleration" in Steven M. Cahn, *Classics of Modern Political Theory: Machiavelli to Mill* (New York: Oxford University Press, 1997), 302.
5. Immanuel Kant, adherents of various religious persuasions, existentialists, and ideological nationalists, or "speciesists," who see individuals as dispensable cells serving the larger cause of nation or species have argued thus. Morality as categorical imperative without regard to feeling, morality understood as the will of God and demanding sacrifice, and the survival and welfare of nation or species are among the primary ends they insist are more worthy than happiness.
6. Nel Noddings, *Happiness and Education* (Cambridge: Cambridge University Press, 2003), 2.
7. Martin Seligman, *Authentic Happiness* (The Free Press, Kindle edition, 2004, retrieved July 16, 2008, Amazon.com), location 851.
8. Immanuel Kant, "Foundation for the Metaphysic of Morals" in Pojman, *Classics of Philosophy*.
9. Jeremy Bentham, *An Introduction to the Principles of Morals and Legislation* (Evergreen Review, Kindle edition, 2007, acquired May 26, 2009, Amazon.com), location 87.
10. Kant, "Foundation for the Metaphysic of Morals" in Pojman, *Classics of Philosophy*, 829.
11. John Dewey, *Democracy and Education* (Teddington, U.K.: The Echo Library, 2007), 10.
12. Ibid.
13. John Stuart Mill, "On Liberty" in William Ebenstein, *Great Political Thinkers: Plato to the Present* (Hinsdale, Illinois: Dryden Press, 1969), 595.
14. This has long been the reality, but the case for the economic purpose of education was made perhaps most forcefully in linking the quality of education with international economic competitiveness in the alarmist governmental report that started the latest wave of educational reform, *America: A Nation at Risk*, the product of The National Commission on Excellence in Education (Washington, D.C.: U.S. Government Printing Office, 1983).
15. Robert Reich, *The Work of Nations* (New York: Vintage Books, 1992).
16. A sampling of the books that advocate focusing education on the acquisition of "21st century skills": Milton Chen, *Education Nation: Six Leading Edges of Innovation in Our Schools* (San Francisco: Jossey-Bass Teacher, 2010); Bernie Trilling and Charles Fadel, *21st Century Skills: Learning for Life in Our Times* (San Francisco: Jossey-Bass, 2009); Allan Collins and Richard Halverson, *Rethinking Education in the Age of Technology: The Digital Revolution and Schooling in America*

(New York: Teachers College Press, 2009).

17. In a major address on education reform, President Obama said "Now, I know some argue that during a recession, we should focus solely on economic issues … but education is an economic issue, if not the economic issue of our time." CNN.com, "Obama says education plan includes charter schools, teacher salaries," July 29, 2010, http://www.cnn.com/2010/POLITICS/07/29/education.speech/index.html.

18. Anyone who pays attention to public discussions about school reform should be quite familiar with the unquestioned assumption that the purpose of education and the measure of success in education are primarily economic. That is the underlying message of Bill Gates' engagement in educational reform: "When I compare our high schools to what I see when I'm traveling abroad, I am terrified for our work force of tomorrow." Quoted in Alicia Mundy, "Gates 'appalled' by high schools," *The Seattle Times*, February 27, 2005, http://seattletimes.nwsource.com/html/education/2002191433_gates27m.html. A business-led initiative in my state of Delaware called Vision 2015 stresses international economic competitiveness as its primary concern: http://www.vision2015delaware.org. Barack Obama echoes a dominant refrain in politics when he decries that "in a world where knowledge determines value in the job market, where a child in Los Angeles has to compete not just with a child in Boston but also with millions of children in Bangalore and Beijing, too many of America's schools are not holding up their end of the bargain" — *The Audacity of Hope* (New York: Three Rivers Press, 2006), 161. The reforms usually called for — smaller classes, better-qualified teachers, and accountability — would indeed serve the interests of students better than prevailing conditions, but the emphasis on work-related subjects and skills in both curricula and tests manifestly slight non-economic dimensions of empowerment.

19. Nic Marks, *The Happiness Manifesto*, Amazon Digital Services, acquired May 11, 2011, Amazon.com), location 161.

20. Primitive nationalist propaganda and brainwashing in schools, the suppression and distortion of scientific inquiry and findings, the violation of the civil rights of educators, and the diversion of resources to efforts of military interest were by no means limited to authoritarian states, especially in times of war.

21. "Public education's failings degrade national security" in the *The News Journal*, December 23, 2010, A12.

22. Daisaku Ikeda, *Soka Education*, location 296.

23. Parker J. Palmer, *Healing the Heart of Democracy: The Courage to Create a Politics Worthy of the Human Spirit* (Jossey-Bass, Kindle edition, 2011, acquired August 24, 2011, Amazon.com), location 409.

24. Philip H. Phenix, "Liberal learning and the Practice of Freedom" (originally published in 1967; retrieved May 26, 2009, http://www.religion-online.org/showarticle.asp?title=2533).

25. Robert S. Brumbaugh and Nathaniel M. Lawrence, *Philosophers on Education: Six Essays on the Foundations of Western Thought* (Boston: Houghton Mifflin, 1963), 181.

26. John Dewey, *Democracy and Education*, 166.

27. Sir Ken Robinson in a video of his speech at a TED (Technology, Entertainment, and Design) conference: http://www.ted.com/talks/ken_robinson_says_schools_kill_creativity.html.

28. Harry R. Lewis, *Excellence Without a Soul: How a Great University Forgot Education* (Public Affairs, Kindle edition, 2006, acquired June 8, 2008, Amazon.com), location 609.

29. Parker J. Palmer, *Healing the Heart of Democracy*, location 2795.

30. Matthew Lipman, *Thinking in Education* (Cambridge, U.K.: Cambridge University Press, 2003), 9.

31. John Stuart Mill, "On Liberty" in William Ebenstein, *Great Political Thinkers*, 596.

32. Parker J. Palmer, *The Courage to Teach: Exploring the Inner Landscape of a Teacher's Life* (Jossey-Bass, Kindle edition, 1997, acquired January 19, 2009, Amazon.com), location 291.

33. Diane Ravitch, *The Death and Life of the Great American School System: How Testing and Choice*

Are Undermining Education (Basic Books, Kindle edition, 2010, acquired July 29, 2010, from Amazon.com), location 4221.

Chapter 3: THE NATURE OF HAPPINESS

1. A response to Simon Critchley, "Happy Like God," *The New York Times*, May 25, 2009, http://opinionator.blogs.nytimes.com/2009/05/25/happy-like-god/?_r=0.
2. Martin Seligman, *Authentic Happiness*, locations 1233, 1244, 1251.
3. Jonathan Haidt, *The Happiness Hypothesis: Finding Modern Truth in Ancient Wisdom* (New York: Basic Books, 2006), 31.
4. Mihaly Csikszentmihalyi, *Flow: The Psychology of Optimal Experience* (HarperCollins, Kindle edition, 1991, acquired April 25, 2009, from Amazon.com), location 664.
5. Robert Holden, *Happiness Now! Timeless Wisdom for Feeling Good Fast* (Hay House, Kindle edition, 1998, acquired March 5, 2009, from Amazon.com), location 749.
6. Quoted in ibid.
7. Jill Bolte Taylor, *My Stroke of Insight* (Viking, Kindle edition, 2008, acquired March 28, 2009, Amazon.com), location 1960.
8. Eric Swanson and Yongey Mingyur Rinpoche, *The Joy of Living: Unlocking the Secret and Science of Happiness* (Harmony, Kindle edition, 2007, acquired March 5, 2009, from Amazon.com), location 658.
9. Jonathan Haidt, *The Happiness Hypothesis*, 125.
10. Jill Bolte Taylor, *My Stroke of Insight*, location 1863.
11. Eric Swanson and Yongey Mingyur Rinpoche, *The Joy of Living*, location 729.
12. Jonathan Haidt, *The Happiness Hypothesis*, 14.
13. Ibid., 17.
14. Ibid., 26.
15. Sonja Lyubomirsky, *The How of Happiness* (Penguin, Kindle edition, 2007, acquired March 5, 2009, from Amazon.com), location 464; and Jonathan Haidt, *The Happiness Hypothesis*, 33.
16. Robert Emmons argues his techniques can substantially increase one's set-point in *Thanks! How the New Science of Gratitude Can Make You Happier* (New York: Houghton Mifflin Harcourt, 2007). Sissela Bok cites the doubts in *Exploring Happiness* (Yale University Press, Kindle edition, 2010, acquired September 3, 2010, from Amazon.com), location 2517.
17. Sonja Lyubomirsky, *The How of Happiness*, location 292.
18. Lynne McTaggart, *The Intention Experiment: Using Your Thoughts to Change Your Life and the World* (Free Press, Kindle edition, 2007, acquired March 2, 2009, Amazon.com), location 1565.
19. Eric Swanson and Yongey Mingyur Rinpoche, *The Joy of Living*, location 1394.
20. Mihaly Csikszentmihalyi, *Flow*, location 292.
21. Ibid., location 617.
22. Abraham H. Maslow, "A Theory of Human Motivation" in Frank G. Goble and Abraham H. Maslow, *The Third Force: The Psychology of Abraham Maslow* (Maurice Bassett, Kindle edition, 2007, acquired January 11, 2009, from Amazon.com), location 2765-3150.
23. See www.businessballs.com/maslow.htm.
24. Darrin McMahon, *Happiness: A History* (New York: Atlantic Monthly Press, 2006), 57.
25. Martin Seligman, *Authentic Happiness*, location 1969.
26. Sri Nisargadatta Maharaj, *I Am That: Talks with Sri Nisargadatta Maharaj* (Wadala, Mumbai, India: Sundaram Art Printing Press, 1973), 7.
27. From the song "Our Deliverance"
28. Eric Swanson and Yongey Mingyur Rinpoche, *The Joy of Living*, location 2090.
29. Randall E. Osborne, *Self: An Eclectic Approach* (Boston: Allyn and Bacon, 1996), 16.
30. David Hume, "A Treatise of Human Nature" in *Works of David Hume* (Mobile Reference, Kindle

edition, 2008, acquired April 18, 2009, Amazon.com), location 10247.

31. Quoted in Darrin McMahon, *Happiness: A History*, 54.

32. Sonja Lyubomirsky, *The How of Happiness*, location 4377.

33. Wayne Davis, "Pleasure and Happiness" in Steven Cahn and Christine Vitrano, *Happiness: Classic and Contemporary Readings in Philosophy* (New York: Oxford University Press, 2008), 165.

34. Martin Seligman, *Authentic Happiness*, location 1921; Daniel Heybron, "Why Hedonism Is False" in Cahn and Vitrano, *Happiness*, 176; Jonathan Haidt, *The Happiness Hypothesis*, 96; and David Hume, "The Sceptic" in Cahn and Vitrano, *Happiness*, 91.

35. Martin Seligman, *Authentic Happiness*, location 2186.

36. Jonathan Haidt, *The Happiness Hypothesis*, 125.

37. Ibid., 125-6.

38. Paul Bloom, "The Long and Short of It" in *The New York Times*, September 15, 2009, http://opinionator.blogs.nytimes.com/2009/09/15/the-long-and-the-short-of-it.

39. Mihaly Csikszentmihalyi, *Flow*.

40. Ibid., location 1096.

41. Ibid.

42. Ibid., location 1314.

43. Ibid., locations 1408, 1424.

44. Ibid., location 1096.

45. Jean-Jacques Rousseau, *Reveries of the Solitary Walker* (New York: Penguin Classics, 2004), 88, 89.

46. Robert Solomon, *Spirituality for the Skeptic: The Thoughtful Love of Life* (Oxford University Press, Kindle edition, 2006, acquired June 3, 2009, Amazon.com), location 121.

47. Eric Swanson and Yongey Mingyur Rinpoche, *The Joy of Living*, location 3593.

48. Eckhart Tolle, *The Power of Now: A Guide to Spiritual Enlightenment* (Novato, California: New World Library, 1999), 24.

49. Jill Bolte Taylor, *My Stroke of Insight*, location 1799.

50. Jonathan Haidt, *The Happiness Hypothesis*, 124-127.

51. Abraham H. Maslow, *Toward a Psychology of Being* (New York: Van Nostrand Reinhold,1968), 42.

52. Frank G. Goble and Abraham H. Maslow, *The Third Force*, location 372.

53. Abraham H. Maslow, *Religions, Values, and Peak Experiences* (New York: Penguin Books, 1976), 59.

54. Aside from the "seeing God" assertions about LSD use, there are many recent studies involving the use of drugs to induce states similar, often descriptively identical, to the peak experiences described by James and Maslow. See, for example, Rick Strassman, *DMT: The Spirit Molecule: A Doctor's Revolutionary Research into the Biology of Near-Death and Mystical Experiences* (Rochester, Vermont: Park Street Press, 2000). Lynne McTaggart described earlier experiments that involved stimulating the right temporal lobe of the brain to produce altered states of mind in *The Intention Experiment*, location 2245.

55. William James, *The Varieties of Religious Experience*, 460.

56. Abraham H. Maslow, *Religions, Values, and Peak Experiences*, 75.

57. Ibid., xiv; Sophy Burnham, *The Ecstatic Journey* (New York: Ballantine Books, 1997), 80.

58. William James, *The Varieties of Religious Experience*, 423.

59. Jill Bolte Taylor, *My Stroke of Insight*, location 565.

60. Abraham H. Maslow, *Religions, Values, and Peak Experiences*, 62.

61. Ibid., 63.

62. Sophy Burnham, *The Ecstatic Journey*, 79.

63. Ibid., 80.

64. Jill Bolte Taylor, *My Stroke of Insight*, location 594.

65. Eckhart Tolle, *Stillness Speaks* (Novato, California: New World Library, 2003), 57.

66. William James, *The Varieties of Religious Experience*, 432

67. Abraham H. Maslow, *Religions, Values, and Peak Experiences*, 66.
68. Ibid., 65-66.
69. William James, *The Varieties of Religious Experience*, 423.

Chapter 4: THE SOURCES OF HAPPINESS

1. Aristotle, "Rhetoric" quoted in Darrin McMahon, *Happiness*, 46.
2. Gary Gutting, "Happiness, Philosophy and Science" in *The New York Times*, August 31, 2011, http://opinionator.blogs.nytimes.com/2011/08/31/happiness-philosophy-and-science.
3. Sonja Lyubomirsky, *The How of Happiness*, location 866.
4. Quoted in Arthur C. Brooks, *Gross National Happiness: Why Happiness Matters for America and How We Can Get More of It* (New York: Basic Books, 2008), 118.
5. David Leonhardt, "Maybe Money Does Buy Happiness After All," *The New York Times*, April 16, 2008, http://www.nytimes.com/2008/04/16/business/16leonhardt.html?
6. Arthur C. Brooks, *Gross National Happiness*, 111-127.
7. Ibid., 121.
8. Sonja Lyubomirsky, *The How of Happiness*, location 874.
9. Martin Seligman, *Authentic Happiness*, location 1079.
10. Ibid., location 2206.
11. Stefan Klein, *The Science of Happiness: How Our Brains Make Us Happy and What We Can Do to Get Happier* (New York: Marlow and Company, 2006), xvii.
12. Mihaly Csikszentmihalyi, *Flow*, location 426.
13. Jonathan Haidt, *The Happiness Hypothesis*, xii; Sonja Lyubomirsky, *The How of Happiness*, location 930; Arthur C. Brooks, *Gross National Happiness*, 118-119.
14. Sonja Lyubomirsky, *The How of Happiness*, location 995.
15. Mihaly Csikszentmihalyi, *Flow*, location 248.
16. Joshua Wolf Shenk, "What Makes Us Happy?" in *The Atlantic* Online, June 2009, www.theatlantic.com/doc/200906/happiness.
17. Jennifer Hecht, *The Happiness Myth*, 147-156.
18. Sonja Lyubomirsky, *The How of Happiness*, location 497.
19. Nel Noddings, *Happiness and Education*, 35.
20. Jonathan Haidt, *The Happiness Hypothesis*, 88
21. Martin Seligman, *Authentic Happiness*, location 3330.
22. Sonja Lyubomirsky, *The How of Happiness*, location 951.
23. Ibid., location 995.
24. Robert Holden, *Happiness Now!*, location 744.
25. See, for example, Arthur C. Brooks, *Gross National Happiness*, 83-90.
26. Ibid., 115-116.
27. See Stefan Klein, *The Science of Happiness*, xvii; and Greg Jaffe, "VA Study Finds More Veterans Are Committing Suicide," *The Washington Post*, February 1, 2013, http://articles.washingtonpost.com/2013-02-01/national/36669331_1_afghanistan-war-veterans-suicide-rate-suicide-risk.
28. Quoted in Darrin M. McMahon, *Happiness: A History*, 381.
29. Jonathan Haidt, *The Happiness Hypothesis*, 222.
30. Martin Seligman, *Authentic Happiness*, location 2952.
31. Frank G. Goble and Abraham H. Maslow, *The Third Force*, location 417.
32. Martin Seligman, *Authentic Happiness*, location 4453.
33. Mihaly Csikszentmihalyi, *Flow*, location 1169.
34. Ibid., location 207.
35. Eckhart Tolle, *The Power of Now*, 42.
36. Richard Taylor, "Virtue Ethics" in Cahn and Vitrano, *Happiness*, 233.

37. Ibid., 232.
38. Quoted in Darrin McMahon, *Happiness*, 328.
39. Jonathan Haidt, *The Happiness Hypothesis*, 223.
40. See, for example, Julia Annas, "Happiness as Achievement" in Cahn and Vitrano, *Happiness*, 238-244.
41. Robert Holden, *Happiness Now!*, location 731.
42. Ibid., 173; Martin Seligman, *Authentic Happiness*, location 254.
43. Jack Kornfield, *The Wise Heart: A Guide to the Universal Teachings of Buddhist Psychology*, (Bantam, Kindle edition, 2008, acquired March 5, 2009, Amazon.com), location 5145.
44. John Stuart Mill, *Utilitarianism* (Classics-Unbound, Kindle edition, 2008, acquired May 27, 2008, Amazon.com), location 612.
45. David Hume, "The Sceptic" in Cahn and Vitrano, *Happiness*, 91.
46. Frank G. Goble and Abraham H. Maslow, *The Third Force*, location 547.
47. Ibid., location 543.
48. Jonathan Haidt, *The Happiness Hypothesis*,171.
49. Jack Kornfield, *The Wise Heart*, location 5157.
50. Darrin McMahon, *Happiness*, 105-172.
51. Martin Seligman, *Authentic Happiness*, location 1159.
52. John Stuart Mill, *Autobiography*, (LeClue 22, Kindle Edition, 2008, acquired May 27, 2008, Amazon.com), location 3893.
53. Martin Seligman, *Authentic Happiness*, location 1244; David D. Burns, *Feeling Good: The New Mood Therapy* (New York: Harper, 1999), 12.
54. Stefan Klein, *The Science of Happiness*, xvi.
55. Ibid.
56. Mihaly Csikszentmihalyi, *Flow*, location 182.
57. Jill Bolte Taylor, *My Stroke of Insight*, location 1857.
58. Ibid., location 1944.
59. Stefan Klein, *The Science of Happiness*, xvii.
60. Eckhart Tolle, *The Power of Now*, 15.
61. Jill Bolte Taylor, *My Stroke of Insight*, location 1944.
62. Viktor Frankl, *Man's Search for Meaning*, location 502.
63. Quoted in Frank G. Goble and Abraham H. Maslow, *The Third Force*, location 411.
64. For instance, Jack Kornfield, *The Wise Heart*; Sonja Lyubomirsky, *The How of Happiness*; and Marci Shimoff, *Happy for No Reason: 7 Steps to Being Happy from the Inside Out* (New York: Free Press, 2008).
65. Mike Robbins, *Focus on the Good Stuff: The Power of Appreciation* (San Francisco: Jossey-Bass, 2007); Sonja Lyubomirsky, *The How of Happiness*; Robert Emmons, *Thanks! How the New Science of Gratitude Can Make You Happier*; Deborah Norville, *Thank You Power: Making the Science of Gratitude Work for You* (Nashville: Thomas Nelson, 2007); and Glenn R. Schiraldi, *The Self-Esteem Workbook* (Oakland, California: New Harbinger Publications, 2001).
66. Mihaly Csikszentmihalyi, *Flow*, location 471.
67. Chris Prentiss, *Zen and the Art of Happiness* (Power Pr, Kindle Edition, 2006, acquired March 5, 2009, Amazon.com), location 95.
68. Quoted by John Kekes, "Attitudinal and Episodic Happiness" in Cahn and Vitrano, *Happiness*, 183.
69. Mihaly Csikszentmihalyi, *Flow*, location 282.
70. Ibid., location 4347.
71. Ibid., location 4555.
72. Eckhart Tolle, *A New Earth*, 265.
73. Eric Swanson and Yongey Mingyur Rinpoche, *The Joy of Living*, location 999.

74. Lynne McTaggart, *The Intention Experiment*, location 1559.
75. Ibid., location 1578.
76. Eckhart Tolle, *The Power of Now*, 23-24.
77. Christopher Willard, *Child's Mind: Mindfulness Practices to Help Our children Be More Focused, Calm, and Relaxed* (Parallax Press, Kindle edition, 2010, acquired February 17, 2011, Amazon.com), location 173.
78. Steven C. Hayes, *Get Out of Your Mind and Into Your Life: The New Acceptance and Commitment Therapy* (Oakland, California: New Harbinger Publications, 2005), 2.
79. Eckhart Tolle, *The Power of Now*, 27.
80. Sri Nisargadatta Maharaj, *I Am That*, 18.
81. Friedrich Nietzsche, "On the Uses and Disadvantages of History for Life" in Cahn and Vitrano, *Happiness*, 154.
82. Christopher Willard, *Child's Mind*, location 128.
83. Steven C. Hayes, *Get Out of Your Mind and Into Your Life*, 6.
84. See, for example, Daniel J. Siegel, *The Mindful Brain: Reflection and Attunement in the Cultivation of Well-Being* (New York: W.W. Norton, 2007), and Mark Williams, John Teasdale, Zindel Segal, and Jon Kabat-Zinn, *The Mindful Way Through Depression: Freeing Yourself from Chronic Unhappiness* (New York: The Guilford Press, 2007). A less recent book is Ellen J. Langer, *Mindfulness* (Cambridge, Massachusetts: Da Capo Press, 1990).
85. Shauna L. Shapiro, Kirk Warren Brown, and John A. Astin, "Toward the Integration of Meditation into Higher Education: A Review of Research" (Center for Contemplative Mind in Society, 2008, acquired July 25, 2010, from www.contemplative mind.org/resources/publications.html).
86. Eric Swanson and Yongey Mingyur Rinpoche, *The Joy of Living*, location 1791.
87. Jack Kornfield, *The Wise Heart*, location 1521.
88. Ibid., location 1552.
89. Jill Bolte Taylor, *My Stroke of Insight*, location 2150.
90. Deborah Schoeberlein and Suki Sheth, *Mindful Teaching and Teaching Mindfulness* (Wisdom Publications, Kindle edition, 2009, acquired July 29, 2010, Amazon.com), location 171.
91. Ibid., location 223.
92. David Hume, "The Sceptic" in Cahn and Vitrano, *Happiness*, 91.
93. Martin Seligman, *Authentic Happiness*, location 1264.

Chapter 5: EMPOWERING THE PURSUIT OF HAPPINESS

1. Martin E.P. Seligman, Randal M. Ernst, Jane Gillham, Karen Reivich, and Mark Linkins, "Positive education: positive psychology and classroom interventions" in *Oxford Review of Education*, Vol. 35, No. 3, June 2009, 293.
2. See Part 2 of Nel Noddings, *Happiness and Education*.
3. Susan K. Greenland, *The Mindful Child* (Free Press, Kindle edition, 2010, acquired February 17, 2011, Amazon.com), location 364.
4. Barry Boyce, ed., *The Mindfulness Revolution: Leading Psychologists, Scientists, Artists, and Meditation Teachers on the Power of Mindfulness in Daily Life* (Boston: Shambhala, 2011).
5. Christopher Willard, *Child's Mind*, location 173.
6. Eric Swanson and Yongey Mingyur Rinpoche, *The Joy of Living*, location 739.
7. Linda Lantieri and Daniel Goleman, *Building Emotional Intelligence: Techniques to Cultivate Inner Strength in Children* (Sounds True, Kindle edition, 2008, acquired June 15, 2011, Amazon.com), location 349.
8. Ian Morris, *Teaching Happiness and Well-Being in Schools: Learning to Ride Elephants* (Network Continuum, Kindle edition, 2009, acquired November 18, 2012, Amazon.com), location 2785.

9. Deborah Schoeberlein and Suki Sheth, *Mindful Teaching and Teaching Mindfulness*, location 366.

10. Ibid., location 548.

11. Gareth Matthews argues that "Instead of viewing children as beings whose essential nature it is to lack knowledge and skills that adults normally have, we should think of them as having valuable abilities that adults lack, as well as lacking valuable abilities that adults normally have." Gareth B. Matthews, "Getting Beyond the Deficit Conception of Childhood: Thinking Philosophically with Children" in Michael Hand and Carrie Winstanley, eds., *Philosophy in Schools* (New York: Continuum, 2009), 40.

12. Deborah Schoeberlein and Suki Sheth, *Mindful Teaching and Teaching Mindfulness*, location 1107.

13. Maureen Healy, "Calming a Child's Mind" in *Tathaastu*, January-February, 2010, Vol. 4, No. 1, 26.

14. Ibid.

15. For a sampling of anecdotal evidence, see Linda Lantieri and Daniel Goleman, *Building Emotional Intelligence*, location 154; Patricia Leigh Brown, "In the Classroom, a New Focus on Quieting the Mind," *The New York Times*, June 16, 2007, http://www.nytimes.com/2007/06/16/us/16mindful.html; Patricia Jennings, "Mindful Education," Greater Good, May 13, 2010, http://greatergood.berkeley.edu/article/item/mindful_education; and Jill Suttie, "Mindful Kids, Peaceful Schools," Summer 2007, http://greatergood.berkeley.edu/article/item/mindful_kids_peaceful_schools.

16. Patricia Jennings, "Mindful Education," Greater Good.

17. Linda Lantieri and Daniel Goleman, *Building Emotional Intelligence*, location 166.

18. Matthew Lipman, *Thinking in Education*, 138.

19. Ian Morris, *Teaching Happiness and Well-Being in Schools*, locations 1157-1168.

20. Ibid.

21. Ingrid Wickelgren, "Schools Add Workouts for Attention, Grit and Emotional Control" in *Scientific American*, September 12, 2012, http://www.scientificamerican.com/article.cfm?id=schools-add-workouts-for-attention-grit-emotional-control.

22. Ibid.

23. Susan K. Greenland, *The Mindful Child*, location 280.

24. Linda Lantieri and Daniel Goleman, *Building Emotional Intelligence*, location 386.

25. Ian Morris, *Teaching Happiness and Well-Being in Schools*, location 1288.

26. Ibid., location 1288.

27. Lyobomirsky, for instance, was asked by school principals in Compton, California, to work on such a curriculum. See Jennifer Ruark, "An Intellectual Movement for the Masses," *The Chronicle Review*, August 3, 2009, http://chronicle.com/article/An-Intellectual-Movement-fo/47500.

28. Ian Morris, *Teaching Happiness and Well-Being in Schools*, location 2684.

29. Matthieu Ricard, *Happiness: A Guide to Developing Life's Most Important Skill* (Little, Brown and Company, Kindle edition, 2008, acquired June 3, 2009, Amazon.com), location 1071.

30. Ibid.

31. Ibid., location 1059.

32. Sonja Lyubomirsky, *The How of Happiness*, location 6814.

33. Ian Morris, *Teaching Happiness and Well-Being in Schools*, location 1982.

34. Susan K. Greenland, *The Mindful Child* (Free Press, Kindle edition, 2010, acquired February 17, 2011, Amazon.com), location 590.

35. Matthew McKay, Martha Davis, and Patrick Fanning, *Thoughts and Feelings: Taking Control of Your Moods and Your Life* (Oakland, California: New Harbinger, 2007); Martin E. P. Seligman, *Learned Optimism: How to Change Your Mind and Your Life* (New York: Vintage, 2006); and Stephen C. Hayes, *Get Out of Your Mind and Into Your Life*.

36. Martin E.P. Seligman et al, "Positive education: positive psychology and classroom interventions," *Oxford Review of Education*, 305; Ian Morris, *Teaching Happiness and Well-Being in Schools*, location 1506.

37. Ian Morris, *Teaching Happiness and Well-Being in Schools*, location 1537.

38. Chris Barker and Brian Martin, "Dilemmas in teaching happiness," *Journal of University Teaching and Learning Practice*, Vol. 6, Issue 2, Article 2, 2009, 6.

39. Ibid.

40. Ibid.

41. http://www.thepowerofforgiveness.com/about/index.html.

42. Chris Barker and Brian Martin, "Dilemmas in teaching happiness," *Journal of University Teaching and Learning Practice*, 7.

43. Martin E.P. Seligman et al, "Positive education: positive psychology and classroom interventions," *Oxford Review of Education*, 304.

44. Ian Morris, *Teaching Happiness and Well-Being in Schools*, location 2244.

45. Ibid., location 2105.

46. Martin E.P. Seligman et al, "Positive education: positive psychology and classroom interventions," 307.

47. Linda Lantieri and Daniel Goleman, *Building Emotional Intelligence*, location 450.

48. http://www.compassionandwisdom.org.

49. Jim Burke, *What's the Big Idea?* (Heineman, Kindle edition, 2010, acquired October 18, [year?], Amazon.com).

50. Ibid., location 340.

51. Linda Lantieri and Daniel Goleman, *Building Emotional Intelligence*, location 595.

52. Ibid., location 621.

53. Ibid., location 960.

54. Ibid.

55. Ibid., location 1467.

56. Jill Bolte Taylor, *My Stroke of Insight*, location 1944.

57. Patricia Leigh Brown, "In the Classroom, a New Focus on Quieting the Mind," *The New York Times*, June 16, 2007, http://www.nytimes.com/2007/06/16/us/16mindful.html?pagewanted=print&_r=0.

58. Patricia Jennings, "Mindful Education," Greater Good.

59. Ibid.

60. Shauna L. Shapiro et al., "Toward the Integration of Meditation into Higher Education: A Review of Research," Center for Contemplative Mind in Society, 5.

61. Quoted in Jill Suttie, "Mindful Kids, Peaceful Schools," Greater Good.

62. Ibid.

63. M. Napoli, P.R. Krech, and L.C. Holley, "Mindfulness training for elementary school students: The Attention Academy" in *Journal of Applied School Psychology*, Vol. 21, Issue 1, July 2005, 99-125; Ian Morris, *Teaching Happiness and Well-Being in Schools*, location 2760.

64. Jill Suttie, "Mindful Kids, Peaceful Schools," Greater Good.

65. Susan K. Greenland, *The Mindful Child*, location 454.

66. Daniel Goleman, "Introduction" in Lantieri and Goleman, *Building Emotional Intelligence*, location 87.

67. Ibid.

68. Martin E.P. Seligman et al, "Positive education: positive psychology and classroom interventions," *Oxford Review of Education*, 294.

69. Ibid., 302.

70. Ian Morris, *Teaching Happiness and Well-Being in Schools*, location 2961.

71. Martin Seligman, *Authentic Happiness*, location 823.

72. Sonja Lyubomirsky, *The How of Happiness*, location 4348.

73. Ibid., location 4387.

74. Ibid., locations 228, 4387; Martin Seligman, *Authentic Happiness*, location 810; and Stefan

Klein, *The Science of Happiness*, xviii.

75. Robert Holden, *Happiness Now!*, location 373.
76. Stefan Klein, *The Science of Happiness*, xvii, xviii.
77. Sonja Lyubomirsky, *The How of Happiness*, location 4348.
78. Ibid., location 228; Martin Seligman, *Authentic Happiness*, location 797.
79. Lynne McTaggart, *The Intention Experiment*, location 2851.
80. Sonja Lyubomirsky, *The How of Happiness*, location 4387; Stefan Klein, *The Science of Happiness*, lxviii; Jonathan Haidt, *The Happiness Hypothesis*, 175; Martin Seligman, *Authentic Happiness*, location 851.
81. Stefan Klein, *The Science of Happiness*, xviii.
82. Martin Seligman, *Authentic Happiness*, location 851.
83. Sonja Lyubomirsky, *The How of Happiness*, location 530.
84. Frank G. Goble and Abraham H. Maslow, *The Third Force*, location 522.
85. Robert Holden, *Happiness Now!*, location 371.
86. Ibid., location 771.
87. Ibid., location 376.
88. Jack Kornfield, *The Wise Heart*, location 160.
89. Terry Hyland, "Mindfulness and the Therapeutic Function in Education," *Journal of Philosophy of Education*, Vol. 43, No. 1, 2009, 129.
90. Jill Bolte Taylor, *My Stroke of Insight*, location 1807.
91. Lantieri and Goleman, *Building Emotional Intelligence*, location 2118.
92. Abraham H. Maslow, *The Farther Reaches of Human Nature* (New York: Viking Press, 1973), 195.

Chapter 6: TEACHING VALUES

1. Nel Noddings, *Philosophy of Education*, (Boulder, Colorado: Westview Press, 2007), 167-168.
2. An analysis of the *Interpersonal Reactivity Index* from 1979 to 2009 suggests a decline in empathy among college students. See Megan Gibson, "Who Cares? Not College Students: Study Finds Co-ed Empathy Decreasing" in *Time* Newsfeed, December 30, 2010, http://newsfeed.time.com/2010/12/30/who-cares-not-college-students-study-finds-co-ed-empathy-decreasing/.
3. David Aspin and Judith Chapman, eds., *Values Education and Lifelong Learning: Principles, Policies and Programmes* (Dordrecht, Germany: Springer, 2007), 5.
4. Jonathan Haidt, *The Happiness Hypothesis*, 165.
5. Louis Raths, Merrill Harmin, and Sidney B. Simon, *Values and Teaching: Working with Values in the Classroom* (Columbus, Ohio: Charles E. Merrill Publishing, 1966), 53.
6. John Taylor Gatto, *Dumbing Us Down: The Hidden Curriculum of Compulsory Schooling* (Gabriole Island, B.C., Canada: New Society Publishers, 1992), 69.
7. Martha C. Nussbaum, *Not for Profit: Why Democracy Needs Humanities* (Princeton University Press, Kindle edition, 2010, acquired September 25, 2010, Amazon.com), location 2180.
8. Robert C. Solomon, *A Passion for Justice, Emotions and the Origins of the Social Contract* (Lanham, Maryland: Rowman & Littlefield, 1995), 8.
9. Sura Hart and Victoria Kindle Hodson, *The Compassionate Classroom: Relationship Based Teaching and Learning* (Encinitas, California: PuddleDancer Press, 2004), 6.
10. See Ibid.
11. Ian Morris, *Teaching Happiness and Well-Being in Schools*, location 2161.
12. Martha C. Nussbaum, *Not for Profit*, location 663.
13. Chris Barker and Brian Martin, "Dilemmas in teaching happiness," *Journal of University Teaching and Learning Practice*, 6.
14. Susan K. Greenland, *The Mindful Child*, location 266.
15. Deborah Schoeberlein and Suki Sheth, *Mindful Teaching and Teaching Mindfulness*, location 1209.

16. Ibid., location 1270.
17. Ibid., location 1288.
18. Ibid., location 1319.
19. Parker J. Palmer, "Toward a Philosophy of Integrative Education" in Parker J. Palmer and Arthur Zajonc, *The Heart of Education: A Call to Renewal* (Jossey-Bass, Kindle edition, 2010, acquired July 29, 2010, Amazon.com), location 762.
20. Parker J. Palmer, *Healing the Heart of Democracy*, location 2544.

Chapter 7: PHILOSOPHY

1. Stanley N. Katz, "College students deserve more than they get" in *The News Journal*, May 12, 2003, A9.
2. Michael Hand and Carrie Winstanley, "Introduction" in Hand and Winstanley, eds., *Philosophy in Schools*, xii.
3. Carrie Winstanley, "Philosophy and the Development of Critical Thinking" in Ibid., 85-95.
4. Robert Fisher, "Philosophical Intelligence: Why Philosophical Dialogue is Important in Educating the Mind" in Ibid., 96-104.
5. A.C. Grayling, "Foreword" in Hand and Winstanley, eds., *Philosophy in Schools*, viii.
6. Ibid., ix.
7. Ibid.
8. Bertrand Russell, *The Problems of Philosophy* (Public Domain Books, Kindle edition, 2004, acquired August 1, 2009, Amazon.com), location 1580.
9. Robert C. Solomon, *The Passions: Emotions and the Meaning of Life* (Indianapolis, Indiana: Hacket Publishing, 1993), 4.
10. See, for example, Daniel T. Willingham, *Why Don't Students Like School?: A Cognitive Scientist Answers Questions About How the Mind Works and What It Means for the Classroom* (Wiley, Kindle edition, 2009, acquired January 30, 2009, Amazon.com).
11. See Alfie Kohn, *Punished by Rewards: The Trouble with Gold Stars, Incentive Plans, A's, Praise, and Other Bribes* (New York: Mariner Books, 1999).
12. I have a sizable collection of such books on political, social, and educational issues. I use books in the *Taking Sides* series from McGraw Hill in a number of my political science courses. An accessible book for children that provides different philosophical perspectives on major questions is Sharon Kaye and Paul Thomson, *Philosophy for Teens: Questioning Life's Big Ideas* (Austin, Texas: Prufrock Press, 2006).
13. Harry Brighouse, "The Role of Philosophical Thinking in Teaching Controversial Issues" in Hand and Winstanley, eds., *Philosophy in Schools*, 65-66.
14. Matthew Lipman, *Thinking in Education*, 20.
15. Robert Fisher, "Philosophical Intelligence: Why Philosophical Dialogue is Important in Educating the Mind" in Hand and Winstanley, eds., *Philosophy in Schools*, 102-103.
16. Matt Copeland, *Socratic Circles: Fostering Critical and Creative Thinking in Middle and High School* (Stenhouse Publishers, Kindle edition, 2005, acquired August 22, 2009, Amazon. com), location 582.
17. Gareth B. Matthews, "Getting beyond the Deficit Conception of Childhood: Thinking Philosophically with Children" in Hand and Winstanley, eds., *Philosophy in Schools*, 34.
18. Parker J. Palmer, "When Philosophy Is Put into Practice" in Palmer and Zajonc, *The Heart of Education*, location 973.
19. Laurie Goodstein, "Basic Religion Test Stumps Many Americans" in *The New York Times*, September 28, 2010, http://www.nytimes.com/2010/09/28/us/28religion.html?_r=1&src= me&ref=homepage.
20. Peter Steinfels, "Trend Gaining in Public Schools to Add Teaching About Religion" in *The New*

York Times, March 19, 1989, http://www.nytimes.com/1989/03/19/us/trend-gaining-in-public-schools-to-add-teaching-about-religion.html?pagewanted=all&src=pm.

21. Charles C. Haynes, "To advance religious freedom, teach it" in *The News Journal*, December 11, 2007, A11.

22. Michael J. Sandel, *Justice* (Farrar, Straus, and Giroux; Kindle edition, 2009, acquired November 26, 2009, Amazon.com), location 4922.

23. Harry Brighouse, *On Education* (Taylor & Francis, Kindle edition, 2007, acquired June 8, 2008, Amazon.com), location 410.

24. Parker J. Palmer, *Healing the Heart of Democracy*, location 410.

25. Bertrand Russell, *The Problems of Philosophy*, location 1604.

26. Nel Noddings, *Philosophy of Education*, 1205.

27. Zack Budryk, "Survey finds that business executives aren't focused on the majors of those they hire" *Inside Higher Education*, April 10, 2013, http://www.insidehighered.com/news/2013/04/10/survey-finds-business-executives-arent-focused-majors-those-they-hire.

28. Jim Burke, *What's the Big Idea?*

29. William Damon, *The Path to Purpose* (Free Press, Kindle edition, 2008, acquired October 19, 2010, Amazon.com).

30. Tony Judt, *Ill Fares the Land* (Penguin Press, Kindle edition, 2010, acquired September 25, 2010, Amazon.com), location 98.

31. William Damon, *The Path of Purpose*, location 92.

Chapter 8: HIGHER EDUCATION

1. Andrew Hacker and Claudia Dreifus, *Higher Education? How Colleges Are Wasting Our Money and Failing Our Kids — and What We Can Do About It* (Times Books, Kindle edition, 2010, acquired August 27, 2010, Amazon.com), location 270.

2. Michael Oakeshott, *The Voice of Liberal Learning* (Indianapolis: Liberty Fund, 2001), 106.

3. Stanley Fish, "The Last Professor" in *The New York Times*, January 18, 2009, http://fish.blogs.nytimes.com/2009/01/18/the-last-professor.

4. Harry R. Lewis, *Excellence Without a Soul*, location 295.

5. Andrew Hacker and Claudia Dreifus, *Higher Education?*, location 1596.

6. Mark C. Taylor, "End the University as We Know It" in *The New York Times*, April 27, 2009, http://www.nytimes.com/2009/04/27/opinion/27taylor.html.

7. Harry R. Lewis, *Excellence Without a Soul*, location 284.

8. Helen Vendler, "The Ocean, the Bird, and the Scholar: Centering Humanistic Study on the Arts," in *Liberal Education*, Vol. 96, No. 1, Winter 2010, 6-13.

9. Peter Conn, "We Need to Acknowledge the Realities of Employment in the Humanities" in *The Chronicle Review*, April 9, 2010, B9.

10. Carol Geary Schneider, "In Defense of a Liberal Education" in Forbes.com, August 10, 2009, acquired November 20, 2009, from http://www.forbes.com/2009/08/10/liberal-arts-education-curriculum-degree-opinions-colleges-geary-schneider.html.

11. Gerald Graff, "The Costs of Runaway Disconnection Have Come Home to Roost" in *Liberal Education*, Vol. 96, No. 1, Winter 2010, 27.

12. This is what Anthony Kronman contends in *Education's End: Why Our Colleges and Universities Have Given Up on the Meaning of Life* (Yale University Press, Kindle edition, 2007, acquired February 11, 2009, Amazon.com).

13. Quoted in Thomas S. Hibbs, "Stanley Cavell's Philosophical Improvisations," *The Chronicle of Higher Education: The Chronicle Review*, October 10, 2010, http://chronicle.com/article/Stanley-Cavells-Philosophical/124830/.

14. See Jeffrey Brainard, "Are the Humanities on the Ropes? Maybe Not" in *The Chronicle of Higher*

Education, Volume LVI, No. 25, March 5, 2010, A30; and Peter Conn, "We Need to Acknowledge the Realities of Employment in the Humanities," B6.

15. Lizette Alvarez, "To Steer Students Toward Jobs, Florida May Cut Tuition for Select Majors," *The New York Times*, December 9, 2012, http://www.nytimes.com/2012/12/10/education/florida-may-reduce-tuition-for-select-majors.html?pagewanted=all.

16. Martha C. Nussbaum, *Not for Profit*, location 169.

17. Anthony T. Kronman, *Education's End*, location 938.

18. David Tritelli, "From the Editor" in *Liberal Education*, Vol. 95, No. 1, Winter 2009, 4.

19. Quoted in David Glenn, "2 Colleges in Vermont, 2 Paths That Defy Tradition" in *The Chronicle of Higher Education*, Volume LVI, No. 25, March 5, 2010, A23.

20. Ibid., A24.

21. Quoted in Ibid., A23.

22. Ibid., location 2606.

23. Parker J. Palmer, "When Philosophy Is Put into Practice" in Palmer and Zajonc, *The Heart of Education*, location 1001.

24. Alexander W. Astin, Helen S. Astin, and Jennifer A. Lindholm, *Cultivating the Spirit: How College Can Enhance Students' Inner Lives* (San Francisco, California: Jossey-Bass, 2010), 2.

25. Parker J. Palmer, "Toward a Philosophy of Integrative Education in Palmer and Zajonc, *The Heart of Education*.

26. Louis Menand, *The Marketplace of Ideas: Reform and Resistance in the American University* (W.W. Norton and Company, Kindle edition, 2010, acquired September 25[, year?], Amazon.com), location 1236.

27. See Paul Hanstet, *General Education Essentials: A Guide for College Faculty* (San Francisco, California: Jossey-Bass, 2012).

28. Parker J. Palmer and Arthur Zajonc, "Introduction," *The Heart of Education: A Call to Renewal* (Jossey-Bass, Kindle edition, 2010, acquired July 29, 2010, Amazon.com), location 410.

29. The quoted phrase is from Ibid., location 467.

30. Gaye Tuchman, "The Future of Wannabe U," *The Chronicle of Higher Education: The Chronicle Review*, October 17, 2010, http://chronicle.com/article/The-Future-of-Wannabe-U/124917/.

31. See Peter Conn, "We Need to Acknowledge the Realities of Employment in the Humanities," *The Chronicle Review*.

32. Harry R. Lewis, *Excellence Without a Soul*, location 149.

33. Alfie Kohn presents a great deal of evidence in *Punished by Rewards*.

34. Quoted in Arthur Zajonc, "Experience, Contemplation, and Transformation" in Palmer and Zajonc, *The Heart of Education*, location 2039.

35. Ibid.

36. Louis Menand, *The Marketplace of Ideas*, location 195.

37. Chris Barker and Brian Martin, "Dilemmas in teaching happiness," *Journal of University Teaching and Learning Practice*, 3.

38. Ibid.

39. Arthur Zajonc, "Experience, Contemplation, and Transformation" in Palmer and Zajonc, *The Heart of Education*, location 2014.

Chapter 9: TRANSFORMATION

1. Martin E.P. Seligman et al, "Positive education: positive psychology and classroom interventions," *Oxford Review of Education*, 295.

2. Lantieri and Goleman, *Building Emotional Intelligence*, location 68.

3. http://www.projecthappiness.org

4. Jennifer Ruark, "An Intellectual Movement for the Masses" in *The Chronicle Review*, August 3,

2009, http://chronicle.com/article/An-Intellectual-Movement-fo/47500.

5. Dahlia Colman, "Teaching Happiness: The Prime Minister of Bhutan Takes on Education," *Solutions Journal*, May 2011, http://www.thesolutionsjournal.com/node/934.

6. NAIS News, "Educating for sustainable happiness," Fall 2012, http://www.nais.org.

7. http://www.wellingtoncollege.org.uk/2288/school-life/well-being.

8. Stephanie Northen, "Schools strive for pupils' happiness," *The Guardian*, January 16, 2012, http://www.guardian.co.uk/education/2012/jan/16/children-wellbeing-schools-ofsted.

9. Ibid.

10. Maggi Evans, "Teaching happiness — A brave new world?" *The Psychologist*, Vol. 24, No. 5, May 2011, 344.

11. http://www.actionforhappiness.org/about-us/happiness-in-schools.

12. William Stewart, "Progressives take up cudgels against Tory proponents of 'back to basics,'" *TES Newspaper*, May 28, 2010, http://www.tes.co.uk/article.aspx?storycode=6045167.

13. Anne Soutter, Billy O'Steen, and Alison Gilmore, "Wellbeing in the New Zealand Curriculum" *Journal of Curriculum Studies*, Vol. 44, Issue 1, February 2012, 111; "Scoping study into approaches to student wellbeing" Australian Government: Department of Education, Employment and Workplace Relations, http://deewr.gov.au/scoping-study-approaches-student-wellbeing.

14. http://www.positiveschools.com.au/

15. Stephanie Northen, "Schools strive for pupils' happiness," *The Guardian*.

16. Patricia Jennings, "Mindful Education"; Megan Cowan, "Tips for Teaching Mindfulness to Kids," Greater Good, May 13, 2010, http://greatergood.berkeley.edu/article/item/tips_for_teaching_mindfulness_to_kids/; Jill Suttie, "Mindful Kids, Peaceful Schools" Greater Good; and M. Napoli, P.R. Krech, and L.C. Holley, "Mindfulness training for elementary schools students: The Attention Academy," *Journal of Applied School Psychology*.

17. http://contemplativemind.org.

18. http://compasionandwisdom.org.

19. http://loveandforgive.org.

20. http://kindcampaign.com.

21. Nikhil Goyal, "GOOD Education: The Rise of Democratic Schools and 'Solutionaries': Why Adults Need to Get Out of the Way" *Cooperative Catalyst*, November 19, 2012. http://coop-catalyst.wordpress.com/2012/11/19/good-education-the-rise-of-democratic-schools-and-solutionaries.

22. Stephanie Northen, "Schools strive for pupils' happiness," *The Guardian*.

23. Ibid.

24. Quoted in Martin Stewart, "Progressives take up cudgels against Tory proponents of 'back to basics,'" TES Newspaper, May 28, 2010, http://tes.co.uk/article.aspx?storycode=6045167.

25. Terry Hyland, "Mindfulness and the Therapeutic Function of Education," *Journal of Philosophy of Education*, 128.

26. Ibid.

27. Martin E.P. Seligman et al, "Positive education: positive psychology and classroom interventions," *Oxford Review of Education*, 295.

28. Quoted in Peter Wood, "What Were They Thinking?" *The Chronicle of Higher Education*, July 6, 2012. http://chronicle.com/blogs/innovations/what-were-they-thinking/33367.

29. Sidney Callahan, "Happiness Examined: What can the social sciences tell us about the good life?" *America*, February 23, 2009, 22.

30. Ibid.

31. Anthony Seldon and Frank Furedi, "Can we teach people to be happy?" *The Guardian*, February 18, 2008. http://guardian.co.uk/education/2008/feb/19/highereducation.uk1.

32. Ibid.

33. Alex C. Michalos, "Education, Happiness and Wellbeing," a paper prepared for the International Conference on "Is happiness measurable and what do those measures mean for public policy?" at Rome, 2-3 April 2007. Retrieved from www.oecd.org/dataoecd/22/25/ 38303200.pdf on September 21, 2009.

34. David Sosa, "The Spoils of Happiness" *The New York Times*: Opinionator, October 6, 2010. http://opinionator.blogs.nytimes.com/2010/10/06/the-spoils-of-happiness/.

35. Rick Ackerly, "Our Socratic Oath" *independent School*, Vol. 70, Issue 3, Spring 2011, 58.

36. See Terry Hyland, "Mindfulness and the Therapeutic Function of Education," *Journal of Philosophy of Education*, 122.

37. Anthony Seldon and Frank Furedi, "Can we teach people to be happy?" *The Guardian*.

38. Diane Ravitch, *The Death and Life of the Great American School System*, location 337.

39. Pasi Sahlberg, *Finnish Lessons: What Can the World Learn from Educational Change in Finland?* (New York, NY: Teachers College Press, 2011).

40. Ibid.

41. Stephanie Northen, "Schools strive for pupils' happiness," *The Guardian*; Julian Fraillon, "Measuring Student Well-Being in the Context of Australian Schooling: Discussion Paper," *Ministerial Council on Education, Employment, Training and Youth Affairs*, December 2004; Anne Soutter, Billy O'Steen, and Alison Gilmore, "Wellbeing in the New Zealand Curriculum," *Journal of Curriculum Studies*; and Anne Konu, "School well-being in Grades 4-12," *Health Education Research*, Vol. 21, Issue 5, October 2006.

42. http://www10.edu.fi/hyvinvointiprofiili/info-eng.html.

43. "Ofsted — Measuring Happiness," *Education Journal*, Issue 135, July 20, 2012.

44. Chris Barker and Brian Martin, "Dilemmas in teaching happiness," *Journal of University Teaching and Learning Practice*, 8.

45. Ibid., 11.

46. Ian Morris, *Teaching Happiness and Well-Being in Schools*, location 192.

47. Ibid., location 187.

48. For example, Teachers College, which was founded in 1889 and incorporated into Columbia University a decade later, is credited with promoting progressive education throughout the United States. See E.D. Hirsch, Jr., *The Making of Americans: Democracy and Our Schools* (Yale University Press, Kindle edition, 2009, acquired January 26, 2010, Amazon.com), location 394.

49. Deborah Schoeberlein and Suki Sheth, *Mindful Teaching and Teaching Mindfulness*, location 297.

50. Susan K. Greenland, *The Mindful Child*, location 3247.

51. Jill Suttie, "Mindful Kids, Peaceful Schools," Greater Good.

52. Parker J. Palmer, *The Courage to Teach*, location 2143.

53. Ibid., location 2152.

54. Ibid., location 2267.

55. Ibid., location 2268.

56. http://actionforhappiness.org/about-us/happiness-in-schools.

57. Daisaku Ikeda, *Soka Education*, location 78.

58. Parker J. Palmer, "A Conversational Strategy of Change" in Palmer and Zajonc, *The Heart of Education*, location 2158.